LIVERPOOL
MATCHES
OF MY LIFE

LIVERPOOL
MATCHES
OF MY LIFE

From Second Division
to World Champions

IVAN BUTLER

First published by Pitch Publishing, 2020

Pitch Publishing
A2 Yeoman Gate
Yeoman Way
Worthing
Sussex
BN13 3QZ
www.pitchpublishing.co.uk
info@pitchpublishing.co.uk

A CIP catalogue record is available for this book
from the British Library.

ISBN 978 1 78531 671 5

Typesetting and origination by Pitch Publishing
Printed and bound in the UK by TJ International Ltd.

Contents

For my dad who, sadly, died while
I was writing this book, and others
who are suffering from dementia and
Alzheimer's. May books like this
help to keep memories alive.

Acknowledgements

I WOULD like to thank Jane Camillin at Pitch Publishing for taking a chance on me as a new author and for everyone at Pitch for their help in producing this book. Also, thanks to Dean Rockett for giving me my first proofreading role at Pitch, which has led, through reading several similar books over the last three years, to my gaining the confidence to write one myself.

When I started out on this book, I was very grateful for the advice provided by Matt Anson, who has written a similar book on Sheffield United that I proofread. Since then, Graham Hales has provided help and advice on how best to present the book, for which I'm also grateful.

While I've used various sources to research information for this book, particular thanks should go to those who maintain lfchistory. net, which provides a host of information on matches, players and managers that has proved to be incredibly valuable to me.

Finally, thanks to my wife, Gwen, for her patience, support and encouragement while I've been writing this book and for not complaining when I want to watch football on the TV and more often than not end up shouting just a bit too loud.

Introduction

I'VE WORKED as a freelance proofreader for Pitch Publishing for the last three years and have the great pleasure of reading about sport as part of my job. My particular passion is football, although I must admit I'm purely an armchair supporter. You try to get tickets to watch Liverpool these days. I was recently online for over three hours in a queue of over 70,000 trying, and failing, to get tickets, and a friend of my wife finally got a season ticket after 20 years on the waiting list.

Pitch has previously published a series of books on various clubs' greatest matches, so I was amazed to find that no one had written one of these for Liverpool FC. I've never attempted to write a book before, but the events of 2018/19 triggered something that persuaded me to give it a go.

My immediate problem was how to select 50 great Liverpool matches, given their massive success over the years. I decided to put a slight twist on the idea and have chosen matches played during my lifetime, which is why this book only covers the last 60 years. This still made the choices very difficult, and it's been so tempting to delay the book for a few months to see how 2019/20 pans out and whether Liverpool can finally win the Premier League in my 60th year.

I realise that some of you will disagree with the match choices, although I'm sure several would be in most people's selections. You will all have your particular favourites for a variety of reasons. The ones I've chosen include many of the trophy-winning matches but there wasn't room for all of them, as I wanted to include matches that meant something to me in particular.

You will also notice that there are perhaps a disproportionate number of matches from the Jürgen Klopp era, but I think that what is happening at Liverpool now is significant. For me, these matches are iconic as they are laying a great foundation of what the team is now about. They show the style, flair and new-found doggedness that I'm sure will bring Liverpool even more success in the coming years.

It's also obvious that some of the matches included weren't necessarily great to watch, but they were iconic in that they meant something special at the time. To be honest, the recent Champions League victory over Spurs wasn't a great spectacle, but how could I not include it?

As Liverpool FC existed and had success way before I was born, I've started with a brief history to provide details of events pre-1960. As I was born in May 1960, the matches start from the 1960/61 season, and the book is written in chronological order rather than in order of how iconic the matches are. That would have been another impossible job.

Each chapter provides a brief update on the intervening period between my chosen matches, some periods longer than others, particularly in recent less successful years. Each chapter then provides a brief report on the match itself and, in most cases, I've also included a brief profile of a key player, to bring a bit of a personal touch to them.

Finally, I conclude with a tongue-in-cheek assessment of whether Liverpool are the greatest English team during my lifetime. Of course, you know how that's going to turn out, otherwise I would have just left it in the spreadsheet.

So, sit back, relax, and I hope you enjoy the matches of my life.

Liverpool FC to May 1960

LIVERPOOL FC was formed in August 1892, ironically born out of Everton FC, which is the only nice thing you will find in this book about Everton, by the way. Everton's president, John Houlding, owned the Anfield Road stadium, where the team originally played. Everton and Houlding fell out, so Everton decided to move across Stanley Park to their current ground. Houlding, meanwhile, decided to set up a new club, Liverpool Football Club, which was to play in the Lancashire League.

Their first match was against Higher Walton in the 1892/93 season, which resulted in a resounding 8-0 win at Anfield, under manager William Barclay. Amazingly, the Liverpool team for that match included ten Scottish-born players.

Their successful first season saw them playing in the Second Division in 1893/94, playing their first Football League match against the wonderfully named Middlesbrough Ironopolis, at the equally wonderfully named Paradise Field, winning 2-0. At this time there were only two divisions in the Football League, and it was the old two points for a win system.

They won the Second Division but, in those days, they had to play off, in something called a Test Match, against the bottom team of the First Division to see who would play in the top league the next season. Interestingly, their opponents were Newton Heath, who they beat 2-0. Newton Heath were later to become Manchester

United, so this was Liverpool's first great success against their future arch-rivals.

Unfortunately, their stay in the top league was all too brief, as they were relegated in their first season, after losing a Test Match against Bury. Yes, that's the same Bury that while I was writing this book were expelled from the English Football League. They were once in the First Division.

Liverpool bounced straight back by winning the Second Division in 1895/96 and coming through the Test Match ordeal at the end of the season. Then only five years later, in 1900/01, they were crowned First Division champions for the first time. Now managed by Tom Watson, they pipped Sunderland by only two points after defeating West Brom in the final match of the season.

An awful 1903/04 saw Liverpool relegated but, once again, they bounced straight back the following season as Second Division champions, then claimed their second First Division title the following season, despite losing their first three matches and conceding 11 goals in the process.

During these early years there hadn't been an inkling of any cup success, the closest being FA Cup semi-final defeats in 1897 and 1899, but eventually their chance came when they reached the final of 1913/14, played at Crystal Palace. In front of nearly 73,000 people, they faced mid-table Burnley, who had finished only one point above them in the league that season. Surely this was their chance!

Although it was a close-fought encounter, it wasn't to be, as Burnley scored the only goal of the match. This was the first FA Cup Final played in front of royalty, with King George VI presenting the cup to the Burnley captain.

After a break during the First World War, the Football League resumed in 1919/20, and in 1921/22 Liverpool secured their third league title, with the next not far away, as they won back-to-back titles for what wouldn't be the last time.

Was this a sign of things to come, a dominant Liverpool team winning endless league titles? Not yet anyway, as their fifth title didn't come until 1947, a 24-year gap, and there was no cup success during this period either.

The 1946/47 league championship win went down to the last matches of the season. Wolves were top of the league by one point going into their final match, crucially against Liverpool at Molineux. The Reds pulled off a 2-1 win to pip Wolves by one point, but then had to wait to claim the title, as Stoke City still had a match in hand and could pip Liverpool on goal average. However, the Potters were held to a draw by Sheffield United, so Liverpool were crowned champions. Unfortunately, they were beaten in an FA Cup semi-final replay by Burnley, to spoil their chances of a first league and cup double.

Despite their league championship successes, cup silverware continued to elude them, and they were once again beaten FA Cup finalists in 1950, 36 years after their first appearance in the final. This time it was Arsenal who lifted the cup after a 2-0 victory at Wembley, and it would be another 15 years before the Reds got their chance of FA Cup glory.

Following Liverpool's 1946/47 title success, it was mid-table mediocrity, until things got even worse. They finished rock bottom in 1953/54 and were relegated after 50 years in the First Division. Worse still, Everton replaced them in the top tier after finishing runners-up in the Second Division.

This time there was no immediate bouncing back for Liverpool. In successive seasons, 1955/56 and 1956/57, they came agonisingly close, finishing third, at a time when only the top two teams were promoted. This was followed by two fourth-place finishes and another third place, so they were always there or thereabouts in the late 50s.

Surely the top flight beckoned. Perhaps all they needed was something or someone special just to give them that final push. Manager Phil Taylor had consistently achieved good finishes in the

Second Division, but the club yearned for First Division football and, with Liverpool sitting 11th in the table, Taylor resigned in November 1959.

So, enter Shanks. Bill Shankly was appointed just a couple of weeks later, and despite losing his first match 4-0, he guided Liverpool up the table. However, they once again finished third in 1959/60, so even Shanks couldn't provide miracles – not immediately anyway.

So, we now arrive at May 1960, the year I was born. Apparently, I was born at home, and while my mum was upstairs in labour, the doctor and my dad were downstairs watching sport on TV. I guess that's where my love of sport emanates from.

I can't remember exactly when I got into football, but it must have been at around the age of seven or eight. Unfortunately, I was only six when England won the World Cup, and while I was aware that 'something special' had happened, I didn't know what. That's surprising really as my dad was a West Ham fan and a huge admirer of Bobby Moore, so I'm sure he must have been watching it that day and would have been shouting at the TV.

As I was born in Wisbech, Cambridgeshire, there was no big local team to support. The closest I had was Peterborough United, who had just come up from non-league to win the Fourth Division, but I wanted to support a First Division team.

It's confession time ... my name is Ivan Butler, and I once supported Leeds United. There, it's out now. I'm hoping that diehard Liverpool fans don't stop reading at this point – we all make mistakes. Leeds were the top team of the day in 1969 and if you don't have a local team to follow, you tend to go for the top team. Just look at how many new Manchester City supporters there are nowadays, and it was the same in the heyday of Arsenal, Chelsea and Manchester United.

However, it didn't take me long to see why Leeds had the nickname 'Dirty Leeds', and I actually hated their captain, Billy

Bremner, so how could I carry on supporting them? I wanted to support a clean-cut team with some flair, and anyway, their white kit was boring, and I'm sure my mum hated having to try to keep my football shirt gleaming white.

Every other week, I used to watch Wisbech Town play in the Eastern Counties League. They played in all red, so there was I with my red scarf (possibly a home-knitted one) and my red rosette (definitely home-made by my mum), cheering on the Fenmen. So, who else could I support now that my fickle ways had deserted Dirty Leeds?

It was obvious. Why buy another scarf and rosette when I could support another team in all red? So, Liverpool it was from 1970, which means I've no personal memories of some of the early matches in this book, but that doesn't make them any less iconic to me.

When I was born, Liverpool were a Second Division club that had been on the cusp of promotion for the previous six years. Bill Shankly had been in the hot seat for only a few months but was to go on to manage the team for over 600 matches. During the early years of my life, Shanks would win the First Division title three times, the FA Cup twice and the UEFA Cup. It seems that I was born at exactly the right time to witness the great days ahead for this wonderful club.

1

Return to the Top Flight

Liverpool 2 Southampton 0

Second Division
21 April 1962
Anfield
Attendance: 40,410

Liverpool	Southampton
Furnell	Godfrey
Byrne	Patrick
Moran	Traynor
Milne	Wimshurst
Yeats	Knapp
Leishman	Huxford
Callaghan	Paine
Hunt	Clifton
Lewis	Reeves
Melia	Mulgrew
A'Court	Penk
Manager: Bill Shankly	*Manager:* Ted Bates

BILL SHANKLY was considered to be a whole-hearted player during his time at Carlisle United and Preston North End. We would come to see this same whole-hearted attitude applied to his management style. He'd even made one appearance for Liverpool during the time that the Football League was suspended during the Second World War. Liverpool beat Everton 4-1 at Anfield. It probably didn't mean that much to him at the time, but I would like to bet he reminded a few Blues about this years later.

After the war, he returned to Preston, then eventually went back to Carlisle as their manager. Following this he managed Grimsby Town, Workington and Huddersfield Town, where he gave a debut to a 16-year-old Denis Law, so he obviously had an eye for spotting young talent.

Immediately on his arrival at Liverpool he set about improving facilities at the club and bringing in some fresh faces to the playing squad. Two early signings were Ron Yeats and Ian St John, who would go on to play a significant role in Liverpool's emergence from the doldrums, but most of his early signings were low-key ones, such as Kevin Lewis from Sheffield United.

During his first full season in charge, 1960/61, Liverpool again finished third in the Second Division. This was becoming an annoying habit, but was one that was soon to be broken, as 1961/62 got off to a blistering start with ten wins and a draw in the first 11 matches.

Liverpool led the league after three matches, following a 5-0 thumping of Leeds United, and that's where they stayed for the rest of the season. They were a free-scoring team, netting 99 league goals, 68 of those at Anfield, where they remained unbeaten in league and cup all season. As well as thrashing Leeds, they had big wins against Bury (5-0), Walsall (6-1), Swansea (5-0) and Middlesbrough (5-1). A taste of the style to come.

The Reds reached the fifth round of the FA Cup but lost after a second replay to Shankly's old club Preston at the neutral venue of Old Trafford. The only goal of the match was scored by Peter Thompson, who was later to become a Liverpool legend.

By April, however, the league was almost won with matches to spare. On 21 April Liverpool faced sixth-placed Southampton, knowing that a win would seal the championship and the long-awaited return to the First Division.

※ ※ ※

Southampton were one of the few teams that had beaten the Reds during the season, when they triumphed 2-0 at The Dell, so it wasn't a forgone conclusion that Liverpool would romp to the league title. However, given that they had a further five matches to play after this one, they could be forgiven for feeling pretty confident going into the match, particularly at fortress Anfield.

Liverpool's regular striker Ian St John was suspended for this one, so Kevin Lewis was brought in up front. The young striker was to brighten up a damp Anfield with the only two goals of the match within the first half hour. Lewis joined Liverpool from Sheffield United for £13,000, scoring on his debut in August 1960, aged just 19. During his three-year stay at Liverpool, he would go on to play 82 matches, scoring 44 times, not a bad return for such a young striker. He was a winger, rather than an out-and-out striker, and faced stiff competition from Ian Callaghan for a spot in the team. Having lost his place to Callaghan, his recall for the Southampton match came after four months out of the team, and back then there was no substitutes' bench for him to warm.

The Reds started the match against Southampton well and had already hit the post early on through A'Court before Lewis scrambled in his first goal on 19 minutes. Moran took a free kick that Hunt helped forward. The ball bounced off a Southampton defender, Knapp, falling to Lewis, who was facing away from the goal. He turned and shot but the ball cannoned off Knapp again and back to Lewis. Second time around he made no mistake, although he needed the help of the woodwork.

Liverpool were ahead and on their way back to the First Division, and the all-important win was confirmed just ten minutes later. Liverpool scrambled the ball away from their own penalty area and quickly found Callaghan on the right wing. He crossed to the far post, where Hunt headed the ball back across. Although the

20

Southampton goalkeeper knocked the ball away, it went straight to Lewis, who headed in his and Liverpool's second goal.

The Reds continued to push forward throughout the match, creating more chances to put Southampton to rest. Hunt and Byrne went close, and Lewis nearly claimed his hat-trick, but there was to be no addition to the scoreline. At the final whistle, there were celebrations all round and the players returned to the pitch for a lap of honour. They were enveloped by fans, who had swarmed on to the pitch to congratulate their heroes.

※ ※ ※

Finally, Liverpool had won promotion back to the top flight, and Bill Shankly was just beginning what would become a trophy-laden managerial career with his beloved club.

For Kevin Lewis, this was to be the highlight of his Liverpool career. He did get a place in the team, although he had to switch wings to the left. However, once Peter Thompson was signed from Preston in the summer of 1963, Lewis's opportunities were again looking few and far between, so he moved on to Huddersfield for two years, before moving to South Africa to play for Port Elizabeth. He spent three years there before a serious knee injury forced him into premature retirement at the age of 28.

However, even though in years to come there would be many famous names to grace the Anfield hall of fame, Kevin Lewis's name should be fondly remembered as the man who scored the goals that took Liverpool back to the First Division, where they have been ever since.

The following season was to be one of consolidation for Liverpool, as they finished a creditable eighth in the First Division, which was won by the arch-enemy Everton.

The First Division table from that year includes some interesting names, such as Blackpool and Leyton Orient, teams which many people today wouldn't believe were once in the top flight. In fact, what had been fortress Anfield the previous season was immediately breached by Blackpool, who won 2-1 there in the season's opener. This was one of five matches lost at Anfield in the league that season.

There were some highlights though, including a 4-1 victory over Manchester City, a 5-0 drubbing of bottom club Leyton Orient and a 5-1 win over Birmingham. But the most spectacular matches were against Spurs at home and away. Spurs were the current league champions and were to finish runners-up behind Everton this season. However, Liverpool thrashed them 5-2 at Anfield in April 1963, only to lose 7-2 at White Hart Lane two weeks later. Spurs were undoubtedly the team of the early 60s, which is probably why my older brother supports them and why I enjoy Liverpool beating them so much.

The highlight of Liverpool's season, though, was an FA Cup run to the semi-final stage. The Reds were still seeking their first FA Cup success and again came close. Victories over Wrexham, Burnley, Arsenal and West Ham took them into a semi-final against Leicester at Hillsborough. Leicester won 1-0 thanks to an 18th-minute goal, but Bill Shankly described this as the most one-sided match he'd ever seen, as Liverpool had 80 per cent of the possession but couldn't find a way past the brilliant Gordon Banks in the Leicester goal. So once again the chance of cup success had gone.

2

Back on Top

Liverpool 5 Arsenal 0

First Division
18 April 1964
Anfield
Attendance: 48,623

Liverpool	Arsenal
Lawrence	Furnell
Byrne	Magill
Moran	McCulloch
Milne	Neill
Yeats	Ure
Stevenson	Snedden
Callaghan	Skirton
Hunt	Strong
St John	Baker
Arrowsmith	Eastham
Thompson	Armstrong
Manager: Bill Shankly	*Manager:* Billy Wright

SILVERWARE WASN'T long in arriving back at Anfield, as Liverpool swept to their sixth league title in 1963/64. To make matters even better, Everton were second and Manchester United third, so they had pipped their two north-west rivals to top spot.

They hadn't had a great start to the season, losing three and drawing one of their first seven matches. Again, Anfield wasn't the bastion that Shankly predicted it would be, as they had lost at home to Nottingham Forest, Blackpool (again) and West Ham, but they were unbeaten away from home. However, normal Anfield service was resumed with a 6-0 mauling of Wolves, which kick-started a good run of form that eventually saw them hitting top spot in November after a 1-0 win against Manchester United at Old Trafford.

Some big Anfield wins followed: 5-2 against Aston Villa, 6-1 against Stoke, 5-0 against Derby, 6-1 against Sheffield United and 6-0 against Ipswich. By the time Liverpool faced Arsenal at Anfield on 18 April 1964, they led Manchester United by three points and had two matches in hand. United only had two matches left to play, so the title was there for the taking with victory over the Gunners, who were sitting seventh in the table.

※ ※ ※

The crowds flocked in early for the match, hoping to see Liverpool crowned champions with three matches left to play. Arsenal's captain was Jim Furnell, who had left Liverpool for the Gunners the previous September after only 18 months with the Reds. He won the toss, asking Liverpool to attack the Kop in the first half, presumably well aware of the Kop effect in the second half of matches. If this was his plan it failed, however, as Liverpool were two up by half-time and the match was effectively over.

Liverpool struck early to settle any nerves when St John slid the ball in after good work by Hunt and Arrowsmith. They then had a slightly shaky spell (some things never change), but were still very dangerous at the other end, with Callaghan and Arrowsmith coming close to doubling the score, while Furnell was playing well against his old club.

Things looked to be going pear-shaped for Liverpool though, when Arsenal were awarded a penalty on 29 minutes. Up stepped Eastham but Lawrence in the Liverpool goal brought off a magnificent save that had the crowd and players in raptures, believing that this might just be their day.

Arsenal were to pay dearly for that miss, as Liverpool finally doubled their lead just nine minutes after the penalty incident. The mercurial Thompson weaved through the Arsenal defence and crossed, where St John met the ball with what was actually a poor header. However, it found Arrowsmith waiting to head it firmly past Furnell to give the Reds a 2-0 half-time lead.

This was to be a great match for Peter Thompson, who created this goal and later scored two himself. He'd arrived from Preston at the start of the 1963/64 season, having been a schoolboy sensation and much in demand by several top clubs. He was to remain at Liverpool for ten years, winning two league titles and an FA Cup, playing over 400 matches and scoring 54 goals. However, he was a creator rather than a goalscorer.

We've already seen how he scored the winner for Preston against Liverpool in the FA Cup of 1961/62, where he turned in a great performance that undoubtedly remained in the memory of Bill Shankly. The right-winger loved to torment the opposition, often choosing to beat the full-back more than once before providing what was often a pinpoint cross. However, this desire to outwit the full-back more than once could often be frustrating for the forwards waiting for his cross.

On this day, the arch-provider was to turn goalscorer seven minutes after the break. He drove in from the wing, before slotting the ball firmly past Furnell into the corner of the net. Then only five minutes later he was at it again, this time scoring from long range to make it 4-0.

Liverpool were rampant now, knowing that they had all but won the championship. On 60 minutes Hunt got in on the scoring, with Thompson again involved in the build-up. Then four minutes later Arrowsmith scored again, only for the referee to disallow the goal because he'd awarded Liverpool a penalty.

If I'd been in the crowd, I would have been yelling for Thompson to step up to take the penalty to claim his hat-trick, but it was

Callaghan who stepped up, only for his kick to be saved by Furnell. You should have taken it, Peter.

Never mind; the Reds saw out the rest of the match, and the referee's final whistle brought jubilation on and off the pitch. The team left the pitch to rapturous applause but soon returned for the obligatory lap of honour. Not only had Bill Shankly got Liverpool back into the top flight, but only two years later he'd won the First Division title for his first, and the team's sixth, time.

%% %% %%

For Peter Thompson, this was the start of a great career at Liverpool. He was also to go on to win 16 international caps under Alf Ramsey, but the England manager wasn't a fan of wingers, and unfortunately Thompson wasn't included in either the 1966 or 1970 World Cup squads. He really should have won many more caps.

His long Liverpool career also ended unfortunately, as he suffered a series of injuries that curtailed his appearances in the last two years at the club. Bill Shankly is well known for not having any time for injured players, despite the fact that they may have provided great service over the years. He's said to have even ignored players completely, refusing to speak to them if they were injured.

For Thompson, at 30 years old, this meant his Liverpool career was over in 1973. For Liverpool, a young Steve Heighway was making a great impression on the wing and was also to go on to have a glittering career with the Reds.

As far as Liverpool were concerned, they were now to play in European competition for the first time the following season. The European Cup had been introduced in 1955, being dominated by the magnificent Real Madrid for the first five competitions, before two victories for Benfica and one for each of the Milan teams. Now Liverpool were entering the fray to compete against the giants of Europe. How could anyone know just how wonderful an adventure that would turn out to be over the ensuing 50-plus years?

Although they won their first match of their title defence in 1964/65 by beating Arsenal 3-2, overall the season started poorly for the Reds, as they lost four of their first seven matches, before being thrashed 4-0 by Everton at Anfield. Not a great start to the defence of their league title by any means, as they were second from bottom, with only Wolves below them. By the end of October, following a 2-0 home defeat by Manchester United, Liverpool were still down at the bottom end of the table, sitting 19th, as United led the way.

Fortunately, their form improved, leading to a 14-match unbeaten run that moved them up to sixth by February. However, inconsistent league form from February onwards brought about a seventh-place finish, as Manchester United pipped Leeds on goal average, 17 points ahead of Liverpool.

But 1964/65 was to be a big year for Liverpool, as they finally buried that hoodoo of never having won the FA Cup.

3

Ee Aye Addio, We Won the Cup

Liverpool 2 Leeds United 1 (aet)

FA Cup Final
1 May 1965
Wembley
Attendance: 100,000

Liverpool	Leeds United
Lawrence	Sprake
Byrne	Reaney
Moran	Bell
Milne	Bremner
Yeats	Charlton
Stevenson	Hunter
Callaghan	Giles
Hunt	Storrie
St John	Peacock
Arrowsmith	Collins
Thompson	Johanneson
Manager: Bill Shankly	*Manager:* Don Revie

LIVERPOOL STARTED their 1964/65 attempt on the elusive FA Cup with an away tie at The Hawthorns against a high-flying West Brom. This tie came during a resurgence in Liverpool's league form, so perhaps their 2-1 victory was less of a surprise than it would

28

have been earlier in the season. Goals from Hunt and St John put the Reds 2-0 up before Astle pulled one back late on for the Baggies.

There was a particularly strange incident during this match when Ron Yeats, Liverpool's captain colossus, picked the ball up in his own penalty area. Liverpool were comfortably 2-0 up and there were only 13 minutes to go, when big Ron was fouled by two West Brom players. He later said that he heard a whistle and knew he'd been fouled, so he picked the ball up to place it for a free kick.

Both the linesman and Tommy Lawrence agreed with Yeats, but the referee confirmed that he'd not blown for a foul as Liverpool had the advantage. Surely the sensible thing to do now would be for the referee to award the free kick, as Liverpool didn't have the advantage and others had heard the 'false' whistle, but oh no, he gave the penalty.

In these days of 'over-sportsmanship' where players stop the match if someone from the opposition has broken a fingernail, or a team even lets another score if they know there has been some injustice in a goal that they have scored themselves, I'm sure West Brom would just take the penalty and kick it out for a goal kick. But such sportsmanship didn't exist in those days of course. Cram stepped up to take the penalty, having a 100 per cent record so far that season from the spot, only to put the ball yards wide of the goal. Perhaps this was a sporting gesture after all.

Next was a home tie against Fourth Division Stockport County, a team that was to finish rock bottom of the Football League at the end of the season. However, this wasn't an era when teams rested players in the FA Cup when facing lower league opposition. The Liverpool team for this match was their strongest but they still only managed a 1-1 draw. Just a few days later, Liverpool did finally overcome Stockport in the replay, but a 2-0 win was hardly convincing, as a Hunt brace sealed the victory and a fifth-round match away to Bolton Wanderers, who were doing well in the Second Division.

This match, at Burnden Park, was another tight affair, and Liverpool were looking far from being a team that would lift the cup at the end of the season. Despite a lot of pressure and several attempts on goal either saved or blocked, it took until the 85th minute for Callaghan to score the winner. In their excitement, Liverpool fans fell through the railings behind the goal, but fortunately no one was seriously hurt.

In the sixth round, the Reds now had a tricky away tie at Filbert Street against Leicester City, who had Gordon Banks in goal. Leicester were, and would go on to be, a bogey team for Liverpool. They had won six of the last seven meetings coming into the FA Cup tie, so it was always going to be a tough one.

The match ended goalless, as Liverpool defended stoutly and never really threatened to score. For their part, Leicester missed a golden opportunity on 48 minutes when Lawrence was caught in no-man's land outside his penalty area and Stringfellow only had to lob the ball accurately to score. However, fortunately for Lawrence and Liverpool, he shot wide and the match went to a replay at Anfield four days later.

The replay was again a tight match and was clearly only ever going to be decided by one goal. It took a while to arrive, but finally it was Hunt who broke the deadlock in the 72nd minute with his 32nd goal of the season. This was Liverpool's first goal against Leicester at Anfield since their promotion back in 1961/62, and how important it was. There was no further score, and Liverpool were through to the semi-final, where they would face Chelsea at Villa Park.

At that stage of the season, Chelsea were top of the First Division and were going for a domestic treble. They had a young team of top players, including Peter Bonetti, John Hollins, Ron (Chopper) Harris, George Graham and Terry Venables. They were a team of flair, apart from maybe Chopper Harris (I love that nickname, which he lived up to), and were managed by Tommy Docherty.

Chelsea were clear favourites as, only three days before, Liverpool had been involved in a European Cup quarter-final in Rotterdam and had played extra time, so tiredness must play a part against such a young Chelsea team. In fact, Liverpool had unsuccessfully tried to get the FA Cup semi-final put back a few days, but the FA wouldn't hear of it. Apparently, Chelsea were so confident that they had prepared a cup final brochure in advance – or was that just a Shankly ruse to tell his players so that they were wound up and more determined?

At Villa Park, 68,000 fans watched a close-fought contest. The first half was goalless but was being played at a fast pace. St John had the best chance of the half but shot wide after Bonetti had spilled Callaghan's shot. As the hour mark passed, it would take a piece of individual brilliance to open the scoring, Thompson cutting in from the left wing to shoot past Bonetti. Just 16 minutes later, St John, perhaps lucky to still be on the pitch after punching Harris (who had chopped him of course), was brought down in the penalty area. The usual penalty taker, Milne, didn't fancy it, so up stepped Stevenson to score, albeit with a mishit shot. But who cares? The Reds were now in the final, where they would face the might of Leeds United, who themselves were looking for a league and cup double but would ultimately be pipped on both fronts.

For Liverpool, the run-up to the cup final wasn't a promising one. They lost Milne to injury, won only three of their final ten league matches and were thrashed 4-0 by a vengeful Chelsea.

Meanwhile, Leeds had lost out only on goal average to Manchester United in the league title race and were 17 points ahead of the Reds, so they were clear favourites going into the final at Wembley, but May Day 1965 has gone down in the history of Liverpool FC as a particularly special day, as the club finally won its first FA Cup trophy in its third final. As for Leeds, they had never won the FA Cup either, but would go on to greater things as they ruled the roost for a few years in the late 60s and early 70s.

※ ※ ※

As is the case in many cup finals, the 1965 FA Cup Final wasn't a classic match by any means, not helped when the rain started to fall. For Liverpool, it got off to a bad start when Byrne was seriously injured in a clash with Collins but, as there were no substitutes in those days, he returned to the action after lengthy treatment. Subsequently, it was found that he had a broken collar bone. They made them tough in those days.

Liverpool were the better team in a match where defences were well on top, and 20-year-old Gary Sprake in the Leeds goal was the busier of the two keepers, but Liverpool could find no way through. The match ended goalless, the first time in the FA Cup Final for nearly 20 years.

Extra time got underway, and things rapidly changed as Liverpool continued to attack. Only three minutes had elapsed when Liverpool took the lead through Hunt. The move was started by Stevenson, who passed to Byrne on the left. His low cross was met by Hunt's stooping header, and at last the Reds had the breakthrough their play deserved.

However, Leeds were always fighters (quite literally on many occasions) and weren't done yet. Just ten minutes later, Charlton knocked the ball down to Bremner, who lashed in the equaliser. Leeds had scored with a rare foray forward, just as it seemed that Liverpool may have the match won.

Liverpool didn't lose heart though, and their patient play finally paid off with just nine minutes of extra time remaining. Callaghan, as so often the case, was the orchestrator of the winning goal. His cross from the right wing was met by a difficult diving header by St John that flew past Sprake to give the Reds what would be a 2-1 victory and their first FA Cup. At last Liverpool had the opportunity to climb those famous Wembley steps where the Queen was waiting in the Royal Box to present the FA Cup to captain Ron Yeats.

%. %. %.

It's great to hear the commentary on this match, where St John is referred to as 'Sinjun' throughout and, of course, in those days all commentators spoke with a very posh voice. The feisty Scottish international had won the FA Cup for Liverpool four years after joining the club as a Shankly signing. He went on to play for the club for a further six years and, overall, played over 400 matches and scored over 100 goals, but perhaps none as important as this one.

Interestingly, St John very nearly ended up managing Leeds a few years later. When Don Revie left Leeds to manage England, St John looked set to be appointed in his place, but a sudden change of plan saw Brian Clough chosen for what was to become a very famous short stint.

Despite winning league championships in the past, this was the trophy that the Liverpool team, manager and supporters craved, and there was a huge crowd to welcome the team back to Liverpool the day after their cup final victory, with an estimated quarter of a million people turning out on the streets for the parade, then to watch the cup being held aloft at the town hall. This was something the people of Liverpool, well the red side anyway, would get used to over the years.

4

First Great European Night

Liverpool 3 Inter Milan 1
European Cup Semi-Final First Leg
4 May 1965
Anfield
Attendance: 54,082

Liverpool	Inter Milan
Lawrence	Sarti
Lawler	Burgnich
Moran	Facchetti
Strong	Tagnin
Yeats	Guarneri
Stevenson	Picchi
Callaghan	da Costa
Hunt	Mazzola
St John	Peiró
Smith	Suárez
Thompson	Corso
Manager: Bill Shankly	*Manager:* Helenio Herrera

LIVERPOOL'S LEAGUE championship win in 1963/64 meant that for the first time they were to enter the European Cup in 1964/65, which at the time was for national champions only.

It's quite ironic really that it's now called the Champions League when it can actually be won by a team finishing fourth in the

34

Premier League in the previous season, but obviously Liverpool can't complain about that little anomaly.

The Reds first had to go through a preliminary round, and this is where it becomes a real test of my spelling, even as a proofreader. Liverpool were matched with Knattspyrnufélag Reykjavíkur of Iceland (who from now on I will simply call Reykjavik), playing the first leg away in August 1964, before the league season had commenced.

Only two days previously, Liverpool had played West Ham in the Charity Shield, drawing 2-2, before flying off to Iceland into what was for them the unknown. Not only was this a long and adventurous trip via London and Prestwick, including flying over an erupting volcano, it was the first match in what was to become a long and adventurous European adventure.

Over 10,000 people turned up to watch a match that started well for the Reds, as Wallace put them ahead after only three minutes, after being set up by Hunt. Although Liverpool dominated the first half, they failed to add to the scoreline, but took total control in the second half and ran out comfortable 5-0 winners, with two goals from Hunt, one from Chisnall and another for Wallace.

Liverpool's first venture into European competition had been a resounding success, and they were to follow this up with another emphatic win over the Icelanders in the home leg four weeks later. Reykjavik were given a huge ovation by the Anfield crowd of over 32,000, who even jokingly booed their own players when they committed a foul. In fact, perhaps the biggest cheer of the night was when Reykjavik scored through Felixson after 36 minutes. However, Liverpool were already two goals to the good by this time, through Byrne and St John, so the Kop could afford to be light-hearted about a goal conceded.

After the break Liverpool finished the job, goals from Hunt, Graham, Stevenson and St John giving them a 6-1 victory on the night, 11-1 on aggregate for a place in the first round proper, a victory that must have caught the attention of the rest of Europe, despite the lowly opposition.

Liverpool's first-round opponents were a strong Anderlecht team that included several Belgian internationals, including the great Paul van Himst, so the first leg at Anfield was a must-win match to give Liverpool a good lead to take over to Belgium. This match was the first in which Liverpool wore an all-red kit, apparently another tactical ploy of Bill Shankly. He claimed that the all-red strip gave Liverpool a psychological advantage over their opponents, as it made their players look taller and more menacing. I think Ron Yeats was probably menacing enough! It must have worked, as did most of Shankly's tactical ploys, as goals from Hunt, St John and Yeats meant that Liverpool ran out comfortable 3-0 winners against the Belgian champions.

The away tie at the Heysel Stadium saw the Belgians attack more as Liverpool sat back and let them, but they still failed to score. There were a few anxious moments, but the defence and Lawrence stood firm. Meanwhile, Hunt was playing more or less as a lone frontman for the entire match, and in the last minute he got the reward for his tireless work when he beat the Belgian team's offside trap to give Liverpool a 1-0 victory on the night and an emphatic 4-0 victory overall.

The European Cup, unlike the Champions League now, was actually quite a short competition, and Liverpool were already into the quarter-final after playing only two rounds. They drew Cologne, thankfully avoiding Real Madrid, Benfica and Inter Milan, but this quarter-final was to be a marathon that was decided in very unusual circumstances.

Cologne had some top players, including the two Wolfgangs, Weber and Overath, but were held 0-0 in the first leg in freezing conditions at the Müngersdorf Stadion. It wasn't a great match, but this was a great result for the Reds, as two-leg tie tactics were very different in those days. Playing at home, a team was usually happy to win 2-0, as long as they didn't concede, as they hoped to go away and only lose 1-0 maybe, or steal an away goal, as the home team had to attack. The team playing away in the first leg rarely went all out for the away goal but were always happy to come away at 0-0, or even with a 1-0 defeat.

After the away draw against Cologne, the second leg also finished goalless, in what was a rearranged match after the first attempt was snowed off at the last minute. In those days, there was no extra time and penalties in the second leg to decide the tie. Instead, a decider was played in neutral Rotterdam a week later.

Liverpool looked to be well on their way to the semi-final when they led 2-0 after goals by St John and Hunt. However, the marathon was to continue, as Cologne fought back, scoring either side of half-time to earn a 2-2 draw. This time there was extra time, but there was no further score. So, after five hours of football, the teams could still not be separated.

I know we all say we hate penalty shoot-outs and that they are a cruel way to lose a match, but could it be crueller than to lose on the toss of a coin? Well, this is how they decided it in those days. Apparently, the first toss of the coin by the referee ended up with the coin on its edge in the mud, so he tried again. This time it was successful for the referee … and for Liverpool, who had gone through, and I suppose we should all feel sorry for the Germans. Maybe not.

In the semi-final, the Reds were to face the might of Inter Milan. Inter were the current European champions, following their defeat of Barcelona in the 1963/64 final, and Italian football was all-powerful in Europe, as AC Milan had won the cup the previous year, shaking off the hold that Spain and Portugal had over the competition.

※ ※ ※

The semi-final first leg at Anfield came just three days after the FA Cup Final against Leeds that had gone to extra time. The team would have been on a high, no doubt, but just how much had that match taken out of them, given the effort they had put into that cup win?

Before the semi-final first leg at Anfield, Gordon Milne and Gerry Byrne, who weren't in the Liverpool team on the night, paraded the FA Cup before the adulating fans. Was this yet another Shankly masterstroke to unsettle the Italians, showing that Liverpool were winners and stoking up the atmosphere even higher than it must already have been?

The gates at Anfield had opened at 3pm for this match, even though it was a 7.30pm kick-off, and if the crowd was fired up by the parading of the FA Cup before the match, it got even better after only four minutes of the start as Hunt scored with a brilliant volley from a Callaghan cross to test the nerves of the Italian team.

However, Inter were clearly made of stern stuff, and so they should have been as European champions, and with such players as Giacinto Facchetti and Alessandro Mazzola in their line-up. It was Mazzola who struck next, taking advantage of a Yeats mistake, to get an all-important away goal.

Liverpool weren't daunted though, and local hero Callaghan shot them back in front on 34 minutes and gave the Reds a 2-1 half-time advantage. The goal came from a brilliantly worked free kick about 30 yards out, which Callaghan dummied to take but he ran over the ball, which was played into the penalty area for Hunt. He chipped the ball on to the still-running Callaghan, who slotted the ball past the keeper as the defenders stood watching, and of course vainly claiming for offside, as all Italian defenders do.

Callaghan, who was born in Toxteth, signed for Liverpool aged 15, making his debut a week after his 18th birthday. He would go on to spend 18 years at the club, winning an array of trophies: five First Division titles, two FA Cups and two European Cups, and was the Football Writers' Association (FWA) Player of the Year in 1974. He played over 850 matches for the Reds, a club record, scoring 68 goals, but he, like Peter Thompson, was a great provider of goals for the likes of Hunt and St John.

It was St John who gave Liverpool real hope of making their first European Cup Final when he gave them a two-goal advantage in the 75th minute. A move starting deep in Liverpool's own half found its way out to Smith marauding forward on the right wing. His cross was met by Hunt, whose shot was parried by the keeper, but straight to St John, who knocked it in.

The crowd sang loudly, 'Go back to Italy', as Liverpool kept going forward but there were no further goals, and the match ended 3-1. Would that away goal come back to haunt the Reds in Milan?

This was the first truly great European night at Anfield, full of passion, atmosphere and a raucous crowd urging the Reds to a great victory over European football royalty. Of course, there would be many more, as you will read later, but first would come one of Liverpool's most notorious European nights in the return leg a week later.

※ ※ ※

All Liverpool's great work at Anfield was to be undone by a Spanish referee (you know who you are, Señor Ortiz de Mendibil), who wilted in a hostile atmosphere at the San Siro. In fact, the atmosphere the night before was also pretty hostile, as Liverpool's players were kept awake by chanting Inter fans, and church bells nearby.

Inter applied early pressure and were awarded a spurious free kick by the referee. However, he appeared to indicate that it was indirect, so imagine Liverpool's horror when Corso put the ball into the net without it touching another player, and the referee allowed the goal to stand. Only eight minutes had passed, and the Italians were right back in it.

Worse was to come one minute later. In those days, goalkeepers could bounce the ball around in the penalty area as they prepared to launch a kick upfield. However, as Lawrence did this, Peiró challenged him and kicked the ball into the unattended net.

Liverpool players furiously chased and surrounded the referee to complain about the challenge but to no avail. So now the tie was level, following two goals that should have been disallowed. Could Liverpool regain their composure, given that only nine minutes had elapsed and there was plenty of time for them to recover?

Well, unfortunately not, despite a brave performance in trying circumstances. The referee continued to make decisions that seemed to favour Inter, penalising Liverpool players' challenges at every opportunity. Apparently Inter were awarded 20 free kicks to only three for Liverpool, which seems highly dubious when we all know what Italian teams' tackling was like in those days!

Bill Shankly would later describe this match as a disgrace, but there was no getting away from the quality of Inter's third goal, scored by Facchetti, which sealed the tie and Inter's place in the final. Just to add further fuel to the flames, the referee allegedly took a bow at the end of the match!

Seven Up

Liverpool 2 Chelsea 1

First Division
30 April 1966
Anfield
Attendance: 53,754

Liverpool	Chelsea
Lawrence	Dunn
Lawler	Kirkup
Byrne	Harris
Milne	Hollins
Yeats	Hinton
Stevenson	Boyle
Callaghan	Houseman
Hunt	Tambling
St John	Osgood
Smith	Murray
Thompson	Robson
Manager: Bill Shankly	*Manager:* Tommy Docherty

DESPITE THE disappointment of the previous season's European Cup semi-final defeat in controversial circumstances, 1965/66 was to be a great season for Liverpool in the league and very nearly in the European Cup Winners' Cup. And, of course, it was to turn out to be a great season for English football, as England won the World Cup at Wembley.

As far as I was concerned, I'd not yet discovered football. I was five years old and about to start school in the September, and it would take me another couple of years after that to start taking an interest. In fact, so I'm told, it wasn't until I discovered football, and was able to play before going into school lessons each day, that I stopped running away from school, as I hated it so much. So perhaps I've football to thank for not getting into trouble for truancy and having my parents dragged before the school inspector, Mr Baker!

Liverpool's early-season form didn't really reflect what was to come for the team, as they won only one of their first four matches, although that was away to bogey team Leicester, 3-1. However, a good run followed, including a 5-1 victory at West Ham, who had three players who would become World Cup heroes – Bobby Moore, Martin Peters and Geoff Hurst – in their ranks. Roger Hunt was Liverpool's own hat-trick hero in this one though.

There was also an Anfield thrashing of Everton, 5-0, which saw Liverpool move into sixth place in the league by the time the Cup Winners' Cup got under way, where they faced Italian opposition again, in the form of Juventus. I'm sure there was some trepidation over what sort of reception and refereeing performance they would get in Italy this time.

They did go down to defeat in Stadio Communale, Turin, but the 1-0 deficit wasn't the end of the world. In fact, Liverpool were unlucky to lose at all, as they stifled Juventus and looked to be on their way to a goalless draw. However, in the 81st minute, Leoncini hit a long-range shot that flew into the top-right corner of Lawrence's net to claim victory. Bill Shankly believed that 1-0 wouldn't be enough for the Italians, despite them having the best defence in Europe, and he was proved right, as Liverpool won the home leg 2-0, with goals from defenders Lawler and Strong. They were through to face Standard Liège of Belgium in the second round.

Meanwhile, league form was good, apart from a 3-0 defeat to West Brom. Six victories between the Cup Winners' Cup rounds saw Liverpool leading the table by two points from Burnley, who they beat 2-1 in the match before the first leg against Standard Liège. There were a couple of big wins too, over the two teams who would be relegated that season, Northampton Town (5-0) and Blackburn Rovers (5-2).

Confidence going into the Liège match was high, and the Reds took the first leg 3-1 at Anfield, although the Belgians' away goal could have proved to be important. Things did look a bit tricky when Liège took the lead on 43 minutes in the second leg, but any jitters were soon settled when Hunt and St John, those reliable goalscorers, scored in quick succession to see Liverpool comfortably through 5-2 on aggregate.

The next round of European competition was now three months away, so it was all-out assault on the league title, especially once Liverpool lost to Chelsea in the FA Cup in the first match of their defence of the trophy that had taken them so long to win. Crucial league victories over rivals Leeds and Manchester United helped their league title tilt. The Reds were also in good goalscoring form, scoring four in three consecutive matches, against Blackburn (4-1), Sunderland (4-0) and Blackpool (4-1).

Despite a surprise 2-0 setback against Fulham, who were bottom of the league at the time, the Reds still sat on top of the pile by the time the Cup Winners' Cup came around again. The first leg of the quarter-final saw them taking a trip to Hungary to face Honvéd, the Hungarian Army team. As was normal for Liverpool, they defended stoutly in the away leg, which finished goalless. Lawrence performed brilliantly in goal, as did Yeats and Smith in defence.

A week later the job was completed when Liverpool won 2-0 at Anfield, with goals from Lawler and St John. It was a more comfortable win than the scoreline suggests, and Liverpool fans were jubilant, hoping that the first FA Cup victory would now be followed by their first European trophy, as the Reds moved into the semi-final to face a tough tie against Celtic.

Before that, Liverpool faced six more league matches, in which they remained unbeaten, although three draws meant that the league title was still very much up for grabs. Once again, just before the Cup Winners' Cup first leg, Liverpool's league form deserted them, with draws away at struggling Sunderland and Northampton, teams they had beaten easily at home earlier in the season.

The Reds still led the league by seven points from Burnley, who mathematically couldn't catch them, but Leeds and Chelsea, both with matches in hand, could equal Liverpool's points haul, although only Leeds stood any chance of pipping them on goal average.

The first leg of the Cup Winners' Cup semi-final was at Celtic Park against a team that the following season would go on to win the European Cup. This was a seriously good Scottish team that included such players as Tommy Gemmell, Bobby Murdoch, Billy McNeill, Jimmy Johnstone and Bobby Lennox. Celtic really should have had the match won in the first leg but missed chances meant that they had to settle for the solitary goal scored by Johnstone. Once again, Bill Shankly claimed that Celtic's one-goal lead wouldn't be enough for them to triumph at Anfield and reach the final. And, once again, Shanks was spot on.

The second leg at Anfield was watched by over 54,000 in a raucous atmosphere. After a goalless first half, Liverpool took control with two goals in six minutes, by Smith and Strong, to give them a 2-1 advantage overall. However, Celtic didn't roll over, and looked to have scored the all-important away goal in the dying minutes, only for it to be ruled offside. Celtic fans invaded the pitch in protest and caused a hold-up in proceedings and the police were on guard for the final few minutes of the match. However, Liverpool held on and were now in their second cup final in two years, but there was still the league to focus on.

In their next league match, Liverpool lost away at second-placed Burnley, so Leeds were still in the hunt for the title. In their penultimate match, Liverpool faced fourth-placed Chelsea, knowing that a single point would give them their seventh First Division title.

※ ※ ※

The Reds could have hoped for easier opposition in this crucial match, as Chelsea had challenged for the title for most of the season and reached the semi-final of the FA Cup. However, at home, the Reds were expected to seal the title with a match to spare. Chelsea must also have expected this, as they formed a guard of honour for them as they ran on to the pitch.

It was Liverpool who got off to the better start, applying early pressure in search of the goal that would settle everyone's nerves. St John, as ever, was busy up front, but Chelsea were also dangerous, with Osgood and Houseman always a threat.

The closest to a goal in the first half was a Hunt shot that hit the inside of the post and, luckily for Chelsea, bounced straight into their keeper's arms to leave the score 0-0 at half-time and the Liverpool fans still on tenterhooks.

They didn't have to wait long after the break though, as Hunt got the all-important breakthrough on 48 minutes. These days, it would be one for the 'dubious goals panel' to decide whether it was Hunt's goal or an own goal by Chelsea keeper Dunn. Either way, Liverpool were ahead. Byrne released Hunt on the left, who got to the byline and pulled it back, only for the keeper, diving out to prevent the cross, to somehow punch it into his own goal. Not much doubt that it was an own goal really, but who cares?

The league title was heading back to Liverpool, and no one in the crowd really cared who had scored, although I'm sure a goalscorer like Roger Hunt would gladly claim it. The England international played for Liverpool for ten years after signing from non-league football, scoring 285 goals in 492 matches – a fantastic goals per match ratio. So, of course, he was going to claim the goal.

He was the club's top scorer eight years in a row and their record goalscorer until a certain Ian Rush came on the scene, although

Hunt still holds the record for the most league goals with 245. And, of course, he was only three months away from being one of the immortal players who played in and won the World Cup for England in the 4-2 defeat of West Germany.

After Hunt's (or Dunn's) goal, Liverpool kept the pressure on Chelsea, but Dunn kept them at bay, before Chelsea pounced at the other end on 62 minutes to put the Anfield party on hold. Yeats had been causing Chelsea's defence some problems in the air but then he was caught out by a quick piece of passing and the pace of Murray. Yeats couldn't attempt to tackle Murray, as it would have led to a certain penalty, and the Chelsea player coolly slid the ball past Lawrence for an excellent equaliser.

However, Hunt was soon at it again. Just seven minutes later he weaved his way through on the left and shot from a narrow angle across Dunn, who could only half stop it, and in it went. This time it was definitely Hunt's goal, and the Anfield crowd erupted once more, as Dunn sat forlornly watching the Liverpool players celebrate. Not his best day.

St John went close again, but there were no further goals, and the 2-1 scoreline meant that the Reds had sealed their seventh league title and could now look forward to the European Cup Winners' Cup Final against Borussia Dortmund, and a potential double success.

※ ※ ※

Liverpool faced Dortmund at Hampden Park just five days after the Chelsea match but unfortunately it wasn't to end in triumph. The opposition, with five German internationals, took the lead on 61 minutes but Hunt equalised seven minutes later. He then had a chance to seal the win in the final minute, having a one on one with Dortmund's keeper, but he hit a tame shot that Tilkowski easily saved.

The match went into extra time and luck was to go against the Reds in the 107th minute. After Lawrence saved at the feet of Held, Libuda lobbed the loose ball towards the goal. It hit the post, bounced back, and struck the covering Yeats, who couldn't prevent it going into the goal to give the Germans what would turn out to be a fortunate 2-1 victory. Liverpool had failed to win their first European trophy, but they wouldn't have to wait long for another tilt.

6

First European Trophy

Liverpool 3 Borussia Mönchengladbach 0
UEFA Cup Final First Leg
10 May 1973
Anfield
Attendance: 41,169

Liverpool	Borussia Mönchengladbach
Clemence	Kleff
Lawler	Netzer
Lindsay	Vogts
Smith	Bonhof
Lloyd	Michallik
Hughes	Danner
Keegan	Wimmer
Cormack	Kulik
Toshack	Jensen
Heighway (Hall 83)	Rupp (Simonsen 82)
Callaghan	Heynckes
Manager: Bill Shankly	*Manager:* Johannes Weisweiler

AFTER A great start to the 1960s, where Liverpool got back into the First Division, won it twice, claimed their first FA Cup, reached the semi-final of the European Cup and finished runners-up in the European Cup Winners' Cup, they entered a period in the doldrums.

It wasn't exactly a complete fall from grace, but there were no further trophies for six years. Their best league finish was as runners-up to Leeds in 1968/69, but they were never out of the top five come the end of the season, as the league title was shared around six different teams.

They reached the FA Cup Final of 1970/71, which is the first really big Liverpool match I can remember watching on TV. This was at the time when the FA Cup experience on TV started on the Saturday morning and the entertainment went on right up until kick-off at 3pm. It was earlier that season that I'd finally decided that Liverpool were my team, and I watched their progress excitedly in the cup as they beat Everton in the semi-final and faced league champions Arsenal at Wembley. That excitement turned to despair as Arsenal won the double, after it looked as if Heighway's goal in extra time may be enough for the Reds. Lucky Arsenal went on to win the match though, after a fortunate scrambled Kelly goal, and a super strike by Charlie George, for which I hated him for the rest of his career.

However, 1972/73 was to be a great year for Liverpool as they bounced back to the top of the table and won a double of their own with what was, by now, a much-changed team. In had come the likes of Ray Clemence, Emlyn Hughes, Kevin Keegan and John Toshack, who were all to play key roles for the Reds over the coming years.

The league campaign got off to a great start with two home wins over the two Manchester teams, and by the time of their UEFA Cup first-round match against Eintracht Frankfurt, they were sitting handily placed in fourth.

Their European campaign also started well when they defeated the Germans in the first leg at Anfield 2-0, with goals from Keegan and Hughes. Two weeks later, a goalless draw at the Waldstadion was enough to see Liverpool comfortably through.

In the second round they faced AEK Athens. Again, the first leg, at Anfield, more or less decided the tie, as goals from Boersma, Cormack and Smith saw them to a 3-0 victory, making the second leg a mere formality. The Reds then won 3-1 in Athens, thanks to two goals from Hughes and the third from Boersma, for a comfortable 6-1 aggregate victory.

Although a decent unbeaten league run came to an end in their next league match, 2-0 away to Manchester United, victories over Newcastle, Leeds and Spurs saw the Reds still leading the table, with Leeds in close attendance. Meanwhile, in the UEFA Cup third round, Liverpool were away in the first leg against Dynamo Berlin. A goalless draw was far from conclusive, but surely the Anfield roar would help to take Liverpool through to the quarter-final.

League form was a little patchy before the second-leg match, but Liverpool retained their top position, with both Arsenal and Leeds now in contention for the title. However, normal Anfield service in Europe continued against Dynamo in December. The Reds got off to a brilliant start when Boersma scored in the first minute, but hearts were in mouths when Netz equalised just seven minutes later, to give the East Germans the away goal. With a name like Netz, he must have been a pun-making sportswriter's dream every time he scored. Goals from Heighway and Toshack sealed a 3-1 aggregate victory.

The quarter-final, against another Dynamo from East Germany, this time Dresden, was three months away, so it was time to concentrate on the league for a while. The Reds suffered just two league defeats in this time, the second of which was at home to Arsenal and saw the Gunners leapfrog Liverpool to top the league by one point, although the Reds had a crucial match in hand.

As Arsenal slipped up, Liverpool had returned to the top of the league by the time of the UEFA Cup quarter-final at Anfield against the East German league leaders. The Reds came away with a 2-0 victory, Hall and Boersma the goalscorers, which looked like being enough to seal a place in the semi-final. They then had two more league victories before the second leg in Dresden. At this stage of the season, matches were stacking up, and the Reds seemed to be playing every three or four days. They were two points clear of Arsenal, having now played their match in hand, but Leeds were lurking in third place, six points behind, but with three matches in hand.

March was turning out to be a great month for the Reds, with four league wins and one draw, and the UEFA Cup quarter-final first leg victory. It got even better when they went to Dresden and came away with a 1-0 win, courtesy of a Keegan goal, to progress 3-0 on aggregate.

However, April started poorly when Liverpool lost to Birmingham City. Fortunately, Leeds had slipped up in one of their matches in hand, but now Arsenal were only one point behind the Reds. It looked as if the title race would go down to the wire.

Up next was an all-English UEFA Cup semi-final tie against Spurs, with the first leg at Anfield. Spurs had already beaten Liverpool 3-1 at White Hart Lane and had gained a 1-1 draw at Anfield only 11 days previously, so this was likely to be a real challenge … and so it proved.

For once, Liverpool didn't have the tie more or less won after the first leg. A rare Lindsay goal meant that they came away with a 1-0 victory, but crucially they hadn't conceded an away goal. Despite dominating the match, the Reds couldn't get the all-important second goal, as Spurs' keeper Jennings kept them at bay.

Two days before the second leg, Liverpool had what would turn out to be a crucial victory over Leeds, which put the Yorkshire team out of the title race. Arsenal could catch the Reds on points, but their vastly inferior goal average meant that Liverpool were virtually guaranteed the title.

Attention was now fixed on the UEFA Cup semi-final second leg at White Hart Lane. In what turned out to be a great match, given that both teams had endured a long season, Liverpool were on top in the first half, which finished goalless. All the good work was soon undone in the second half though, as Spurs took the lead through skipper Peters to level the tie at 1-1. Liverpool fought back immediately and were soon rewarded when Keegan set up Heighway to give Liverpool that all-important away goal. Back came Spurs but they now needed to score two goals in the remaining 35 minutes. They managed one, again through Peters, but were unable to breach the Liverpool defence a third time. Spurs won the match 2-1, but the Reds won on away goals and were into the UEFA Cup Final.

Before their tilt at a European trophy, Liverpool just needed a point at home to Leicester City to take their eighth league title, and that's just what they got. An uninspiring 0-0 draw meant that they had won the title for the eighth time. The result was hardly surprising, given that this was their fourth match in eight days, but they now had a two-week break before the first leg of the UEFA Cup Final at home to Borussia Mönchengladbach.

※ ※ ※

The first leg was due to be played on 9 May but had to be abandoned after 30 minutes due to a deluge of rain making play impossible. The match was hastily rearranged for the following evening. This delay gave Bill Shankly the opportunity to take advantage of a weakness he'd spotted in the German defence in the abandoned match. He brought in lanky John Toshack in place of the diminutive Brian Hall, which proved to be yet another Shankly masterstroke.

Borussia were one of the best teams in Europe, as can be seen by their line-up, which included Günter Netzer, (Dirty) Berti Vogts, Rainer Bonhof and Jupp Heynckes. However, Tosh caused all sorts of problems for their defenders, creating two goals for Keegan in the first half. The first goal came after 21 minutes when Toshack nodded a Lawler cross back across towards the penalty spot for a diving header scored by Kevin Keegan. How often were we to see this combination in the coming years? This goal was simple but brilliant and gets regular replays on TV, as it was just typical of the great understanding these two had.

Liverpool should have doubled their lead just two minutes later when a penalty was awarded for handball. However, Keegan's earlier joy was replaced with despair as Kleff saved his weakly hit penalty.

Kev wasn't to be denied though, and only ten minutes later the Toshack-Keegan combination was at it again, the big man's nod-down this time met with Keegan's boot for a 2-0 lead, which Liverpool held until half-time. Toshack was causing absolute havoc in the Borussia defence, and they just couldn't handle him at all, as Shankly's hunch paid off.

In the second half it was another big man in red who was to give Liverpool a 3-0 lead, as a completely unmarked Larry Lloyd leapt to head in from a Keegan corner.

The important thing now was to make sure they kept a clean sheet, and not allow the German team any encouragement with an away goal. This looked a forlorn hope though, when only two minutes after Lloyd's goal, Borussia were awarded a penalty of their own. Heighway was adjudged to have fouled Jensen, although he clearly played the ball before the Borussia player fell to the ground. However, this time it was Clemence's turn to produce the heroics as he dived to save Heynckes's spot kick. The Liverpool players ran to congratulate Clemence, as they realised the importance of this save in the context of the away goals rule.

Earlier in the season, Clemence had made his England debut, and was to go on to win 61 caps in all. He would have had many more if it hadn't been for England managers being unable to decide between him and Peter Shilton. For me, Ray was by far the best keeper in England at the time and should have had the number of caps that Shilton achieved … but then I'm slightly biased.

For Liverpool he was setting records for the least number of goals conceded in a season, and his penalty save in this match meant that Liverpool were able to take a 3-0 lead to Germany, which surely enough to bring them their first European trophy.

※ ※ ※

Clemence's penalty save was to be crucial in Liverpool picking up their first of many European trophies. In the away leg two weeks later, Borussia tore into Liverpool from the start, and looked likely winners when they raced into a 2-0 first-half lead with two Heynckes goals, the second a brilliantly curled shot into the top-left corner of Clemence's goal.

With Liverpool now 3-2 up on aggregate, the German team would surely at least take the final to extra time. However, they were to rue their poor first-leg performance and that missed penalty, as Liverpool gamely held on. Borussia eventually ran out of steam after their big effort of the first half and couldn't add to their goal tally. The referee's whistle blew, and finally Liverpool had their hands on a European trophy, winning 3-2 on aggregate in a fiercely fought encounter. Having won the league, however, this meant that they wouldn't defend the UEFA Cup but would play in the European Cup once again.

Their penalty-saving hero Ray Clemence would go on to play for the club for a further eight years, totalling over 460 appearances and winning a hatful of trophies at the club: five league championships, one FA Cup, one League Cup, two UEFA Cups and three European Cups. Only Ian Callaghan and Jamie Carragher have more Liverpool appearances. After Bruce Grobbelaar took his place, Ray had a new lease of life at Spurs, and ended up with over 1,000 appearances overall in his career. Not bad for a lad from sunny Skeggy who apparently wasn't as good as Peter Shilton!

7

Keegan's Cup Final

Liverpool 3 Newcastle United 0
FA Cup Final
4 May 1974
Wembley
Attendance: 100,000

Liverpool	Newcastle United
Clemence	McFaul
Smith	Clark
Lindsay	Kennedy
Thompson	McDermott
Cormack	Howard
Hughes	Moncur
Keegan	Smith (Gibb 76)
Hall	Cassidy
Heighway	Macdonald
Toshack	Tudor
Callaghan	Hibbitt
Manager: Bill Shankly	*Manager:* Joe Harvey

BILL SHANKLY'S dream of winning the European Cup in 1973/74 wasn't to be. It would be left to others to bring that magnificent trophy to the city. After coming through the first round against opponents from Luxembourg, the Reds were beaten home and away by Red Star Belgrade, so they would have to concentrate on the domestic scene from November onwards.

The league season hadn't started too well either, with only four victories in their first nine matches, so a league title defence wasn't looking too likely at this stage, as Leeds set the early pace. In fact, after losing away to Leeds in October, the Reds were down in eighth, already eight points behind Leeds, who were unbeaten in their first 12 league matches.

After the European Cup exit, however, things improved for Liverpool, and after a Merseyside derby victory in December, they were up to second in the table. They were now only six points behind Leeds, who were remarkably still unbeaten after 19 matches, but had drawn six times, so weren't really breaking away from the chasing pack.

In the FA Cup, what should have been an easy third round tie against Doncaster Rovers, a team that was struggling in the Fourth Division, was nearly very embarrassing. Liverpool trailed 2-1 at Anfield to the Yorkshire team after only 18 minutes, and only a Keegan goal in the second half saved them from an ignominious exit, as they scraped a 2-2 draw, with Doncaster hitting the woodwork in the closing minutes. Thankfully, three days later, Heighway and Cormack ensured that Liverpool weren't knocked out at their first hurdle, to keep cup dreams alive for the Reds.

Maybe this 'near disaster' sparked something in the team, as they went on an unbeaten run in the league and FA Cup of 16 matches, winning 12. By the time they eventually lost in April at Bramall Lane against Sheffield United, Liverpool were second in the league table, four points behind Leeds but with three matches in hand.

The Reds had also progressed well in the FA Cup during this great spell. They again needed a replay in the fourth round after a goalless home draw with Carlisle United, who were going well in the Second Division and would be promoted at the end of the season. Goals from Boersma and Toshack were enough for victory at Brunton Park in the replay.

The fifth round was a bit easier, and this time the Reds managed to win at Anfield at the first time of asking, beating high-flying Ipswich 2-0. Hall and Keegan scored the goals that took Liverpool into the latter stages of the cup and must have raised hopes of a league and cup double to make up for the disappointment of the failure in Europe this season.

The FA Cup semi-final was against Leicester at Old Trafford, ending goalless. Liverpool should have won it, with Keegan having two shots cleared off the line then hitting the woodwork in the closing minutes, but it wasn't to be. In those days it meant having a replay, which took place four days later at Villa Park.

This time Liverpool made no mistake in despatching their opponents. After a goalless first half, which must have had the crowd wondering whether anyone was ever going to score in this semi-final, it all sparked off in the 46th minute when Hall gave the Reds the lead with a lucky goal. Then Leicester woke up and equalised only two minutes later to restore the stalemate. After nearly going behind, Liverpool finally took control, and it was Keegan who did the damage, clipping the ball over Shilton to restore Liverpool's lead. Then, as the clock ticked down, it was his strike partner Toshack who scored to seal the victory and send Liverpool to Wembley.

The Reds now had a month to concentrate on winning the league, but alas it wasn't to be. After the Sheffield United setback, they only lost one more match, at home to Arsenal, but a series of disappointing draws was to cost them. They won only one league match in the run-in, and Leeds ended up winning the title comfortably by five points.

At least the Reds had Wembley, and a certain Malcolm Macdonald and Newcastle United to look forward to. 'Supermac' was a great striker, and a Toon hero. He played 187 times for Newcastle, scoring 95 goals, and had an even better strike rate for his previous club, Luton Town. He was never short of confidence and went into the cup final telling the media what he was going to do to Liverpool, after scoring twice in the semi-final against Burnley. Many were labelling this one as Keegan versus Macdonald.

% % %

Newcastle were unbeaten in their previous five Wembley finals and, as well as Macdonald, their line-up for the 1974 FA Cup Final included two faces that were to become legends for Liverpool in the near future, Terry McDermott and a 19-year-old Alan Kennedy.

Supermac was made to eat his words as Liverpool dominated proceedings and Newcastle hardly got a look-in. He was a mere bystander as Keegan stole the show, with a superb two-goal performance.

Keegan had joined Liverpool from Scunthorpe United three years earlier, scoring on his debut against Nottingham Forest and immediately becoming a hero to fans. He became a poster boy for Liverpool, England and for football in general while at the Reds, and during the rest of his long and illustrious career. What I remember about him most is his sheer effort and work rate, as I didn't think he was the most skilful of players, but he made the most of what he had, that's for sure.

As a Liverpool fan, this cup final was as near to perfection as you could hope for, except perhaps that the Reds should have scored more goals. Newcastle were a decent team and Macdonald was a great striker, but they didn't have a chance against a superb Liverpool performance throughout the team, and the result was never in doubt. It's not often these days that I can relax when watching Liverpool – maybe when they are four goals up – but this was as comfortable as it gets.

The first half was one of few clear-cut chances but was completely within Liverpool's control as they dominated the play, and McFaul in the Newcastle goal was kept busy. The second half, however, was something else entirely. Liverpool again had Newcastle on the ropes, as Keegan lashed a shot wide when he should perhaps have done better.

The Reds should then have been ahead through an excellent Lindsay goal. He won the ball in his own half with a strong tackle, surged forward, played an attempted one-two with Keegan, although Keegan dummied the ball, and it bounced back to Lindsay off the defender. Lindsay lashed the ball past the keeper from an acute angle with his left foot. It was a fantastic finish and the players celebrated for what seemed like ages before they were called back for a linesman's offside flag. Replays show that the linesman got this one wrong. Maybe one day they will invent something to replay such decisions during the match, and perhaps call it something like video assistant referee. Just an idea, but it will never catch on I expect.

However, just a few minutes later the Reds were deservedly ahead when Keegan smashed home a Smith cross on 57 minutes. Further chances came and went, and Liverpool's midfield was controlling the match, with Hughes coming closest with a rasping shot just over the bar.

Clemence was enjoying a quiet afternoon, but it was his long kick on 75 minutes that was headed on by Toshack for Heighway to slot home. Then with only two minutes remaining Liverpool were stroking the ball around, with Newcastle unable to get a touch. Smith played a one-two down the right and crossed low for Keegan to stretch his leg out and score his second.

At the referee's final whistle, the players and fans celebrated Liverpool's second FA Cup success and Emlyn Hughes collected the cup from Princess Anne. Meanwhile, Bill Shankly left them to enjoy the occasion. I wonder what was going through his mind?

※ ※ ※

Kevin Keegan went on to play over 300 matches for Liverpool and scored 100 goals. He won three league titles, one FA Cup, one European Cup, two UEFA Cups, as well as being the FWA Footballer of the Year in 1976. He shocked Liverpool and their fans in 1976 by announcing that he was going to play for Hamburg SV, at a time when an English player playing abroad was a rarity. I thought it was the end of the world. How would we survive without my hero Kevin Keegan?

He won the European Footballer of the Year award two years in a row while in Germany, and earned 63 England caps, scoring 21 goals for his country. He also had an interesting management career, some of which we will come across later in this book, taking the helm at Newcastle (twice), Fulham and Manchester City, as well as a short and unsuccessful stint as England boss.

However, his departure from Liverpool was still a few years away, but for now there was a bigger shock in store for the club. Just two months after this cup final victory, Bill Shankly announced that he was retiring as manager. After almost 15 years and nearly 800 matches in charge of the club, the great man, the messiah, was going. Fans were stunned, as was I, and nobody really wanted to believe it was happening. He'd won so much at the club but never managed to win the elusive European Cup. He was almost immediately replaced by his assistant, Bob Paisley. I must admit that I knew nothing about the new boss at the time, but everyone was soon to find out about the man who was to become Liverpool's most successful manager ... so far!

8

Record European Win

Liverpool 11 Strømgodset 0
European Cup Winners' Cup First Round First Leg
17 September 1974
Anfield
Attendance: 24,743

Liverpool	Strømgodset
Clemence	Thun
Smith	Wølner
Lindsay	Karslen
Thompson	Alsaker-Nøstdahl
Cormack	Pedersen
Hughes	Amundsen (F. Olsen 75)
Boersma	E. Olsen
Hall	Henriksen
Heighway	Halvorsen
Kennedy	Pettersen
Callaghan	T. Olsen (Wibe 69)
Manager: Bob Paisley	*Manager:* Erik Eriksen

THE FOLLOWING season, 1974/75, saw a new era commencing for Liverpool with Bob Paisley at the helm, although it wasn't a drastic change and was typical of the way the Reds were to appoint from within the famous Boot Room. However, Uncle Bob didn't set the world alight in his first season, which ended with no trophies and no decent cup runs. Derby County were the surprise package in the league, pipping Liverpool by two points, so it wasn't a complete flop for the Reds.

They had also gone into the season with high hopes of winning the European Cup Winners' Cup now that they had had a taste of European glory from 1972/73. I've always been interested in world geography from when I was a kid, and I'm pretty good at knowing where countries and cities are on a map, but as a 14-year-old, Strømgodset was a new one on me. I soon discovered that they were a Norwegian team but, on this night, it was perhaps the Norwegians who wished they had never heard of or come to play in Liverpool.

The Reds were red-hot favourites to progress to the second round, as Strømgodset were amateurs, and only a reasonably successful team in their own country. Some of their players were more famous for playing bandy, a winter version of football. However, they were the current Norwegian cup holders and at Anfield to attempt a giant-killing.

※ ※ ※

It was to be a record-breaking night at Anfield, the Reds going one better than a 10-0 victory over Irish team Dundalk five years previously, and it's one that has never since been bettered. Bob Paisley was taking no chances, selecting a strong team, and what surprises me is that despite being 5-0 up at half-time, and 8-0 up with 15 minutes to go, all of Liverpool's substitutes remained on the bench. There was no resting of players or giving players a run from the bench in those days. Fortunately for the commentators, Strømgodset did make some substitutions, making sure that there were only two Olsens on the pitch at any one time to make life easier.

Any hope that the Norwegians had of an upset took an early blow, as they conceded a penalty after only three minutes. Lindsay slotted the kick home to start the ball rolling, and what a snowball it turned out to be. Boersma added the second on 13 minutes, before defender Thompson ventured forward to score a good goal on the half-hour mark. It was turning out to be a comfortable night for the Reds, but they weren't about to ease off. Before half-time, Boersma had hit his second, and Heighway got in on the act to make it 5-0 at the break.

It's quite a surprise that, despite scoring 11 in this match, not one player scored a hat-trick, but this Liverpool team had goals in it from any position and didn't rely just on their forward line. Nine different players got on the scoresheet on this night. Boersma had started the season in good goalscoring form, and his two in this match made it eight so far in the season, and it was still only mid-September.

In the second half, things got off to a slow start for Liverpool, who failed to score for 20 minutes, until Cormack made it six. No doubt the amateurs had come out with a second wind after half-time, but Liverpool's superior fitness was soon to tell against them. Thompson scored his second after 74 minutes, Hughes added the eighth only two minutes later, before Smith, Callaghan and Kennedy rounded off the rout with three more in the final five minutes.

※ ※ ※

After this emphatic win in the first leg, it was surprising that Bob Paisley didn't give a few reserves a run-out in the second leg, but he again put out a strong line-up. The second surprise was that the Reds only won 1-0, with Kennedy scoring in the 17th minute. This time, the avalanche didn't follow. And that was as good as it got for the Cup Winners' Cup, as the Reds provided a third surprise when they were knocked out on away goals by Ferencváros of Hungary.

As far as Phil Thompson was concerned, he was, to be fair, not in the team to score goals, but to prevent them at the other end, so his double in the first leg against Strømgodset was a bit of a rarity. In fact, he only scored 13 goals for the club in over 470 appearances, but the local lad was to become a legend at the club for many reasons other than goalscoring. His honours list alone is worth reading:

seven league titles, one FA Cup, two League Cups, two European Cups and two UEFA Cups – not a bad haul.

Although he was a defender, he wasn't in the mould of Ron Yeats, and was a good passer of the ball, which was recognised nationally, as he received 41 international caps for England. He was also made Liverpool captain in 1979, such were his leadership qualities, and these qualities also shone through after his retirement as a player, as he first took on coaching responsibilities, then later was assistant manager to Gérard Houllier. He even had a short spell in the top job when he stood in for Houllier while he recovered from a heart attack.

You can now see him on Sky Sports, still as animated as ever about the game of football, and still a Red through and through, but completely unbiased of course!

Despite Bob Paisley not having won anything in his first year in charge, it wouldn't take long for him to make his mark and break his trophy duck. In fact, he did better than that and marked 1975/76 with two trophies. Little did we know then that Paisley would go on to manage the team for nine years, winning a huge array of trophies, but first let's concentrate on his very first trophy in the UEFA Cup of 1975/76.

Paisley Starts His Trophy Haul

Liverpool 3 Club Brugge 2
UEFA Cup Final First Leg
28 April 1976
Anfield
Attendance: 49,981

Liverpool	Club Brugge
Clemence	Jensen
Neal	Bastijns
Smith	Krieger
Thompson	Leekens
Kennedy	Volders
Hughes	Cools
Keegan	Vandereycken
Fairclough	de Cubber
Heighway	van Gool
Toshack (Case 46)	Lambert
Callaghan	Lefèvre
Manager: Bob Paisley	*Manager:* Ernst Happel

LIVERPOOL'S FIRST tie in the 1975/76 UEFA Cup pitched them against Scottish opposition in Hibernian, in a match-up that the Reds were expected to win comfortably. However, Hibs surprisingly got the better of the first leg at Easter Road, winning

1-0, but it was only thanks to Clemence and a penalty save that the scoreline wasn't made more difficult for the second leg. Liverpool were poor on the night, but they were still favourites to progress, with home advantage to come and just a one-goal deficit.

The Reds weren't setting the league table alight either, as by the time of the second leg, they were sitting down in eighth and looking a long way from being champions. Against Hibs, however, it was Anfield European form as usual, although the night didn't go entirely without a fright. John Toshack, though, would prove to be the hero of the night, scoring a hat-trick to ensure progress to the second round. His first came on 21 minutes, but the scare came when Hibs equalised before half-time, and led on away goals at the break. However, any hopes they had of an upset were put to bed when Tosh scored twice in the second half to seal a comfortable win for the Reds.

Liverpool were drawn against Spanish opposition in Real Sociedad in the second round. What appeared to be a tough assignment on paper, with the away leg first, became a stroll in the park, as the Reds secured a comfortable away-leg win, 3-1, with goals from Heighway, Callaghan and Thompson, only slightly spoiled by a late consolation for the Spanish team.

The second leg showed Liverpool's true class and European credentials. Although their line-up hardly changed from week to week, for this match they had a 19-year-old debutant in Brian Kettle at full-back, who was replaced two minutes from time by another 19-year-old, Max Thompson, but not before Kettle had set up two goals with some great overlapping full-back play. Liverpool also brought on an 18-year-old David Fairclough for his debut in place of the injured Callaghan early in the second half. We will hear much more about Fairclough later in the book, but he was to score on his debut to start his European escapade.

In fact, the Reds again showed their versatility and the ability to score goals from any position, as the 6-0 win featured five different scorers – Toshack, Kennedy, Fairclough, Heighway and Neal, with only Kennedy getting two. The magnificent 9-1 aggregate win must have had the rest of the UEFA Cup teams hoping not to draw them in the next round.

The third round found the Reds travelling to Poland to play Slask Wroclaw in the first leg, on an icy pitch that proved to be a difficult surface. It was, however, a fruitful journey, as they came away with a crucial 2-1 victory that set them in good stead for the second leg at Anfield. The two away goals from Kennedy and Toshack were perhaps more than they expected in such tough conditions, but the tie was now theirs to lose, despite the Polish team clawing one back before the end of the match.

Liverpool's progress to the quarter-final was ensured in the home leg by a comfortable 3-0 victory, with a Case hat-trick in just 24 minutes. He'd only been drafted in when Heighway went down with tonsillitis but then kept his place for the next match, a 4-0 league victory over Spurs at White Hart Lane, where he scored again.

It seemed that Liverpool's UEFA Cup travels were having some impact on league performances as, for the second time, they surprisingly lost their league match in the week of their UEFA Cup tie. Teams played with pretty small squads in those days, rarely making sweeping changes to save players' legs, so these European trips were bound to have some effect.

In the UEFA Cup quarter-final they were off to East Germany for the first leg against Dynamo Dresden. This tie was to be a much tighter affair than the previous rounds. The Reds ground out a tactical goalless draw in the away leg, with Clemence yet again coming to the rescue with a penalty save on 51 minutes. This was becoming a bit of a habit, and this one was reported to be one of the greatest penalty saves of his career so far.

The home leg was equally as tight, although Liverpool at one stage looked like they were comfortable after Case and Keegan had given them a two-goal cushion by the time 47 minutes were on the clock. However, the East German team had not given up, and pulled one back just after the hour to make it a tense final 30 minutes. Liverpool were in control though, seeing the match out to progress 2-1 on aggregate and to next face the might of Barcelona in the semi-final.

The first leg took place at the famous Camp Nou, definitely the most impressive stadium I've visited. The Barcelona team included Johan Neeskens and Johan Cruyff, who were part of the brilliant Dutch national team of the time that really should have won the 1974 World Cup.

What transpired was a football lesson, not from the Dutch masters for the Spanish club, but from Liverpool, who outplayed their opponents and largely dominated the match. Barcelona hardly created a chance, as Toshack sealed a 1-0 victory with a goal on 13 minutes after being set up by strike partner Keegan.

With five minutes to go, Barcelona fans started to leave the stadium but, before they departed, they threw cushions on to the pitch in frustration at their team's inept performance. The referee had to halt the match to clear the pitch, but this was about as uncomfortable as it got for Liverpool on the night. The only danger for the return leg was that Barcelona couldn't possibly be as poor again, and Liverpool couldn't afford to be complacent.

It's as well that Liverpool didn't take their foot off the gas in the second leg, thinking they were as good as through, as they were made to fight for a place in the final, as you would expect from a Barça team. The Reds couldn't dominate as they had in the Camp Nou, and a first half of few clear-cut chances ended goalless. In fact, all the goal action took place within a five-minute spell shortly after the restart. Liverpool drew first blood, as Thompson scored from a well-worked free kick on 50 minutes. Then back came Barcelona, now needing two goals, equalising just two minutes later to leave the tie on a knife-edge. Just one more goal for Barça and they would be through on away goals.

However, it was Liverpool who continued to push forward, looking for the next goal that may prove crucial, but they failed to find it. So did Barça, as Cruyff had another very quiet night and failed to make an impact. No further goals meant that the Reds were into the two-legged final to face Belgian team Club Brugge (Bruges to you and me) after this 2-1 aggregate victory against one of the giants of Spain.

%% %% %%

It may seem strange that I've chosen the first leg of the final as an iconic match, given that the result was very much in the balance by the end of it and the Belgian team, with two away goals, must have been favourites to lift the trophy at the midway stage. However, the circumstances of the match will not be too unfamiliar to those of you who have watched the Reds over the years, in that they rarely seem to do things the easy way, but also never know when they are beaten.

Mind you, the same could be said about Club Brugge, who had overcome a 3-0 first leg deficit in the second round to get past Ipswich. They had then beaten Roma, AC Milan and Hamburg to reach the final, so they were certainly going to be tough opponents. I can't say that I'd heard of any of the Brugge players other than Raoul Lambert, who had featured for Belgium in the 1970 World Cup, the first one I can remember, and the European Championships of 1972.

Lambert was soon to make his mark in this first leg match at Anfield, scoring after only five minutes to shock the Reds and the crowd of nearly 50,000. The goal came from a mistake by the usually reliable Neal, who didn't get enough on a back-header to Clemence, leaving Lambert free to lob the ball in over the keeper.

Although Keegan forced a great save from the Brugge keeper, Jensen, things got worse for Liverpool's cup hopes on 15 minutes, as Cools finished off some excellent approach play to smash the ball in to double the lead for what looked like a certain Brugge victory on the night, with their home leg to come.

The only good thing Liverpool could take from this was that they still had 75 minutes to play, so plenty of time in which to salvage a result of some kind to give themselves some hope in the return leg, and their away form in the previous rounds had been impressive. However, nothing materialised in the first half, despite Smith going close, and at the break Bob Paisley decided to replace Toshack with Case.

Jimmy Case was a local lad and had been at Liverpool for nearly three years, becoming a regular in the team in the previous 12 months. He was a tough-tackling midfielder with a ferocious shot, scoring many a spectacular long-range goal in his time with the Reds. He'd already shown his goalscoring ability during this season, and his appearance in the second half was to prove pivotal in Liverpool's change of fortunes, although not in his usual rocket shot style.

It didn't start well for Case though, as he missed a golden opportunity to pull one back and slashed his shot well wide. Then on 59 minutes, Heighway set up Kennedy, another player with a powerful shot on him, to smash one into the roof of the net to give Liverpool's supporters some hope of a comeback. Kennedy was then in on the act again only two minutes later as his shot hit the post and rebounded to Case, who bundled the ball over the line for the equaliser. Not a typical Case goal, but it was now game on.

Liverpool had made a great comeback, but it was still advantage Brugge with those two away goals, so there was no point in the Reds being happy with salvaging a draw. Of course, they didn't, as they surged forward again and capped a magnificent five-minute spell when they were awarded a penalty after Heighway was felled in the area. Up stepped Keegan to send the keeper the wrong way and give the Reds the lead with nearly half an hour to play.

Both teams could have added to their tally in the remaining period, but the scoreline remained 3-2 to the Reds, who had a narrow lead to take to Belgium for the second leg but would surely need to score at least once to bring away the trophy.

%, %, %,

Three weeks later Bob Paisley took his team to Bruges with a slender lead, but the Belgians were possibly slight favourites in most people's books, given their two away goals at Anfield.

At the Olympic Stadium it was that man Lambert again who was an early thorn in Liverpool's side as he put his team ahead after only 11 minutes from a penalty after Smith had handled in the area. This levelled the tie but gave the Belgians the edge on away goals.

This advantage didn't last long though, as Keegan's goal just four minutes later put Liverpool back in the driving seat but still with three quarters of the match remaining. Given that seven goals had been scored in the final so far, it looked unlikely to finish 1-1 on the night. But that's just what happened. There were chances at both ends but no further goals, so Emlyn Hughes lifted the UEFA Cup, Bob Paisley's first trophy as manager … and promptly dropped it!

10

European and Domestic Double

Wolverhampton Wanderers 1 Liverpool 3

First Division
4 May 1976
Molineux
Attendance: 49,981

Wolverhampton Wanderers	Liverpool
Pierce	Clemence
Sunderland	Smith
Palmer	Neal
Daley	Thompson
Bailey	Kennedy
Parkin	Hughes
Hibbitt	Keegan
Carr	Case (Fairclough 60)
Kindon	Heighway
Richards	Toshack
Kelly	Callaghan
Manager: Bill McGarry	*Manager:* Bob Paisley

LIVERPOOL'S 1975/76 league campaign got off to a bad start when they lost their first match away at eventual surprise runners-up QPR, who had some cracking players that season in Phil Parkes, Frank McLintock, Dave Webb, John Hollins, Gerry Francis and

72

Stan Bowles. I'm not sure why it was such a surprise that they nearly won the league with players of that calibre in their team.

A decent run for the Reds then followed, with victories over Spurs, Leeds (3-0 at Elland Road) and Sheffield United, before their second league defeat came at Portman Road against Ipswich. This defeat again led to Liverpool finding their form and they went on another decent league run of five wins and three draws, which included a 3-1 victory over title rivals Manchester United. This run put them up to third, before a shock 3-1 defeat at Anfield by Norwich dropped them down to sixth, as champions Derby topped the table from QPR at the end of November.

Perhaps the shock defeat at home to Norwich could be put down to the fact that Liverpool had played their UEFA Cup third round first leg away to Slask Wroclaw only three days before they met the Canaries. A midweek trip to Poland wasn't ideal preparation for a weekend league match, but to also play on an icy pitch must have sapped some energy.

Once again, a league defeat spurred the Reds on to an impressive unbeaten run, this time of 12 matches, including a 4-0 victory over West Ham and, more crucially, points gained from their title-chasing rivals. Anfield victories over QPR and Leeds, both 2-0, as well as an away goalless draw at Old Trafford against Manchester United would prove crucial come the end of the season.

By the time they played Middlesbrough at Anfield in early March, Liverpool were top of the table, but another home defeat to a mid-table team cost them top spot, as QPR took their place to lead by two points, with Manchester United and Derby in very close attendance.

Four days after a trip to Spain in the UEFA Cup, Liverpool faced the prospect of a Merseyside derby at Anfield. Everton were having a poor season though, sitting in the bottom half at this stage, although they did recover to ninth by the end of the season. It had looked like another disappointing post-UEFA Cup trip result until 'supersub' Fairclough, on for Toshack just 12 minutes earlier, pounced on an Everton defensive blunder to set off on a mazy run. He avoided several tackles, before striking the ball past Welsh keeper Dai Davies for the winner on 88 minutes. This was another crucial victory – despite Phil Neal, unusually for him, missing a last-minute penalty – that kept Liverpool just two points behind QPR with a match in hand, although Manchester United and Derby were still very close behind the Reds.

The gap to QPR was soon closed to just one point, but Liverpool had played their match in hand, so the ball was in QPR's court. The Reds had slipped up away to lowly Aston Villa in their match four days before facing Barcelona in the second leg of the UEFA Cup semi-final, but perhaps they can be forgiven for having their minds elsewhere.

Despite making it to the UEFA Cup Final, there was no time to relax, as Liverpool had the small matter of the First Division title to think about, with two matches within five days of the Barcelona triumph to get through. No problem though, as they won an exciting home match against Stoke City 5-3, followed by a 3-0 victory away at Manchester City. The victory at Maine Road was impressive, given the fixture backlog, as the Reds beat the team sitting seventh in the league comfortably.

Between the two legs of the UEFA Cup Final, Liverpool played their final league match of the season. Unlike now, when the entire Premier League programme on the final day of the season sees all matches kick off at the same time, in the First Division in those days it wasn't the case. Given Liverpool's involvement in Europe, closest challengers QPR had finished their league campaign and were top of the table by just one point from the Reds.

Liverpool's goal difference (which had now replaced goal average) was better than QPR's so a draw against third-from-bottom Wolves at Molineux would be enough to seal a ninth league title.

‰ ‰ ‰

For some reason, I've always quite liked Wolves, but I'm not sure why. I remember watching them in the all-English European Fairs Cup Final of 1972 against Spurs. It was one of the first European finals I can remember seeing on TV and as my brother supports Spurs, of course I wanted Wolves to win, just to annoy him, as younger brothers are supposed to. I also liked their gold-coloured shirts, in an era when most teams seemed to wear red, blue or white. There was also a claim to fame of my hometown, Wisbech, as the Wolves captain, Mike Bailey, was born there. However, I obviously wasn't backing them on this night.

Football on the TV was also not like it is now, and this critical league match wasn't being shown live. My memory of the match is that I was actually watching Wisbech Town on this Tuesday evening. I've no idea who they were playing or what the scoreline was, as all I was bothered about was getting out of the ground as soon as possible, back to my brother's car to find out how the other team in red had got on. If my memory serves me correctly, the scores were level when I started listening, so it was a nervous wait to see whether the Reds could hang on.

Although Wolves had struggled against relegation all season, they got off to a great start in their final match and must have had QPR fans going wild when they deservedly opened the scoring after only 13 minutes through Kindon, who outpaced Thompson to latch on to a through ball and strike it cleanly past Clemence.

Liverpool appeared to be nursing some kind of hangover from their UEFA Cup Final first leg only six days previously, as they simply didn't get going in the first half of a match that they were clear favourites to win. However, after this match they had a nice two-week break until the second leg, so there was no reason to save their energy.

For the first half hour of the match the Reds were second best and simply hanging in there, until Heighway sparked them into life with a run and cross that Toshack nearly equalised from. This seemed to settle their nerves, and for the remainder of the first half they were at least equal to Wolves and tested their keeper on more than one occasion. However, it remained 1-0 to Wolves at the break.

Liverpool's performance in the second half was more like it, and they put together a series of flowing moves. Toshack, Keegan and Kennedy all went close but still they couldn't find that all-important equaliser that would give them the league title. Ray Kennedy was pulling most of the strings and having a magnificent match in Liverpool's midfield. He'd joined Liverpool from Arsenal just under two years previously as one of Bill Shankly's final acts as manager, and his performances for the Reds had earned him an international call-up only a few weeks before this match.

For the Gunners he'd played primarily as a striker, but his tough tackling made him an ideal cog in Liverpool's midfield, and he contributed plenty of goals too. I can't remember who said it, but when asked about the toughest tackler they had ever played against, they said Ray Kennedy, and I'm not surprised.

As Liverpool couldn't find the net, supersub Fairclough entered the fray on the hour. Could he do it again? Well not this time, although he did cause some havoc in the Wolves defence, such was his speed and skill, which was to prove important as it freed up the other strikers.

Just when it seemed as if they would never score, Smith crossed, and it was the old one-two, a Toshack flick-on for a Keegan goal, and the Reds were level at last with only 14 minutes remaining to hold on. Liverpool fans invaded the pitch, which led to a short hold-up thankfully, so when Wisbech's match ended, Liverpool were still playing.

This was when I found the match on the car radio, with only five minutes remaining. I wasn't aware of what had gone before, and that Liverpool were now dominant. All I could think of was that if Wolves scored, the league title would be lost in the last five minutes of the season. Surely that couldn't possibly happen, could it?

Not this season, as no sooner had I put my seatbelt on (actually, perhaps I didn't wear one back then) than Kennedy headed the ball in the direction of Toshack, who twisted and turned before sliding the ball past the Wolves keeper. For some reason the linesman was flagging, but fortunately the referee ignored him.

Liverpool fans invaded the pitch again, and I probably went wild myself in the car. Thankfully my brother hadn't had time to drive off yet, so no accidents were caused. And Liverpool weren't done yet, as they came forward again, with the excellent Kennedy getting a deserved goal, as he side-stepped a defender before smashing the ball in from a tight angle in the 89th minute to seal a great win and take the league title back to Liverpool yet again.

Meanwhile, we made it safely back home without me causing my brother to steer the car off the road.

※ ※ ※

Bob Paisley was Manager of the Year, Kevin Keegan was voted Player of the Year, and the Reds had two more trophies in the cabinet, so a successful year all round. There were many heroes during the season, including the double act of Keegan and Toshack, and those vital penalty saves by Clemence, but it was the two hard men in midfield, Case and Kennedy, who featured largely in the two iconic matches.

Case went on to play for the Reds for six years before moving to Brighton & Hove Albion. As many others featured in this book, he won a huge array of awards with Liverpool: four league titles, one League Cup, three European Cups and, of course, one UEFA Cup. In 269 matches for the Reds, he scored 43 goals. I wonder how many of those were from outside the penalty area?

Kennedy also stayed at Liverpool for six years before becoming one of the ex-Liverpool players to grace Swansea City in the early 80s. In nearly 400 matches for Liverpool he scored 72 goals and had an identical trophy haul to Case, apart from winning one more league title after Jimmy had left for the south coast.

After such a successful season, I wonder whether Bob Paisley went to bed and dreamed about winning the European Cup, the trophy that had eluded his predecessor.

11

Supersub

Liverpool 3 Saint-Etienne 1
European Cup Quarter-Final Second Leg
16 March 1977
Anfield
Attendance: 55,043

Liverpool	Saint-Etienne
Clemence	Curkovic
Neal	Lopez
Jones	Janvion
Smith	Merchadier (H. Revelli 75)
Kennedy	Farison
Hughes	Bathenay
Keegan	Larqué
Case	Synaegel
Heighway	Rocheteau
Toshack (Fairclough 74)	Santini
Callaghan	P. Revelli
Manager: Bob Paisley	*Manager:* Robert Herbin

WHAT A season 1976/77 was to be, as Liverpool managed to exceed the previous season's success. Not since the Busby Babes of Manchester United in 1967/68 had an English team lifted the European Cup. Leeds had come close in 1974/75 against Bayern Munich, in a match where I for once wanted the Germans to win, but could this be the year that the recent Dutch and German stranglehold was to be broken? First it was a month of league action before Liverpool were to start their assault on Europe. A decent start saw the Reds win four and lose one of their opening matches in defence of their league title. It was nothing spectacular, but after a good win away at Derby, they were top of the table.

Liverpool were already out of the League Cup, but the European Cup was the main event, as they took on Northern Ireland's minnows, Crusaders, in the first round. However, the Irish team put up a gallant defensive performance in the first leg at Anfield, parking the bus to restrict the Reds to a 2-0 win, courtesy of Neal and Toshack, when everyone was expecting an avalanche of goals.

One win and one defeat in the league later, Liverpool still sat top, before the return match with Crusaders at Seaview. Again, it was quiet for half an hour, until Keegan broke the deadlock. Although Liverpool were never in any danger, it wasn't until the closing ten minutes that their superiority showed, as Johnson (2), McDermott and Heighway gave the scoreline some respectability. It was a 7-0 aggregate score that perhaps didn't do the Crusaders defensive display justice.

Middlesbrough had been matching Liverpool in the league, sitting second on goal difference, and they were at Anfield to face the Reds four days after the Crusaders match. A goalless draw didn't do either team any favours, as the two Manchester teams leapfrogged them, although all four teams had 11 points, with Everton and Arsenal just one point behind.

It was the Toffees who were next up for Liverpool at Anfield, and a crucial 3-1 win put the Reds back on top of the league prior to their return to European action, this time against Trabzonspor of Turkey. It was to be a rocky trip in more ways than one. The pitch was in an appalling condition, covered in rocks, the hospitality left something to be desired and, to cap it all, the referee gave the Turkish team a debateable penalty, which was converted to give them a surprise 1-0 win. Could Liverpool's dream be about to founder on the rocks?

Their league title bid didn't look to be in too much danger, as an away draw at Leeds was followed by victories over Leicester and Aston Villa, leaving Liverpool top, with a three-point lead over five chasing teams.

The focus now was on overcoming the one-goal deficit against Trabzonspor in the return at Anfield. The Turkish team were certainly not taking any prisoners though, as their fierce tackling infuriated the Liverpool players. However, the Reds blitzed them in the first 19 minutes, with goals from Heighway, Johnson and Keegan, before the Turkish tackling went over the top, resulting in a sending off late on. The Reds had negotiated a potentially tricky tie, and were through to the quarter-finals, which were four months away.

In the interim, it was league action aplenty for the Reds, although with mixed outcomes. Of the 16 matches played, Liverpool won only eight, drawing four, and losing four. There were some high points, notably a 5-1 drubbing of Leicester, a 4-0 victory over Stoke, 4-1 against Birmingham and two useful away draws at both title rivals from Manchester.

However, one match that sticks in my mind is a 5-1 hammering by Aston Villa. I couldn't remember my team ever being beaten by such a scoreline and I was distraught. It was usually Liverpool handing out such beatings but, on this night, they were 5-1 down at half-time to fifth-placed Villa, so it could have been much worse. It was their biggest defeat for ten years, so no wonder I'd not come across it before.

However, form was restored, and by the time of the European Cup quarter-final first leg away to much-fancied Saint-Etienne of France, Liverpool led the league table but only by two points from Ipswich, who had three matches in hand, with Manchester City a further point behind but with two matches in hand over the Reds.

The title defence was looking tough, but Liverpool were starting to consider a treble, as they had progressed through to the quarter-final of the FA Cup, with victories over Crystal Palace, Carlisle United and Oldham Athletic. But for now it was a trip across the Channel to continue their European Cup bid.

There was a great atmosphere in the Stade Geoffry-Guichard. Liverpool, without their injured talisman Kevin Keegan, put up a great display in France that looked like earning them a goalless draw to take back to Anfield. That's until a complete miskick at an attempted shot turned it into a cross that was converted to give the French team a narrow advantage in the tie. It was the only chance that Saint-Etienne created and was cruel on the Reds. However, they must have been confident that they could overcome this deficit in the second leg, although the French team had only conceded one goal in their previous nine away European matches, so it was never going to be easy.

%% %% %%

The second leg at Anfield will go down as the first big European comeback night at Anfield and a match that will make David Fairclough a name to remember in Liverpool annals for all time. He'd already started to earn a reputation for coming on as a substitute to clinch a vital win, but this match was to leave him with the 'supersub' nickname for the rest of his life.

Liverpool-born Fairclough had not long turned 20 and was battling for a first-team place, but was up against Keegan and Toshack, who had formed a deadly partnership, so he was mainly used as an impact substitute after making his debut in November 1975. Despite limited starts, he'd made a huge impact in helping the Reds to the title in 1975/76, scoring seven goals in only two starts and six substitute appearances, often scoring crucial goals. However, despite Keegan's absence through injury in the first leg in France, Bob Paisley's more conservative line-up meant Fairclough was on the bench again, where he stayed the whole match.

The atmosphere for the second leg was electric, including a large contingent over from France, and several fans were locked out, such was the size of the turnout. In fact, many who did manage to get in were delayed in getting to their seats and missed the first goal of the night.

Keegan was back from injury, and what an immediate impact he had, as Liverpool were fast out of the blocks in an attempt to overturn the 1-0 deficit from the first leg. They had a corner within the first two minutes, which Heighway played short to Keegan. He took the ball on a couple of yards before curling a beauty into the top corner of the goal, with the keeper flailing. We'll never know (or care for that matter) whether it was a shot or a cross.

It was just the start the Reds needed but they were then frustrated by the Saint-Etienne offside trap several times for the remainder of the first half and couldn't make the most of their excellent start. Meanwhile, the French team threatened at the other end, with Rocheteau having a goal disallowed for offside and Clemence called into action on more than one occasion. For the Reds, Toshack missed a headed chance and Case had a goal disallowed for a foul on Janvion, so it remained 1-0 at the break.

Liverpool had the opportunity to double their lead at the start of the second half, as Curkovic in the Saint-Etienne goal came racing out to clear with his head but didn't make good contact. Case tried to lob the ball in from distance but put it wide. The French team were then thwarted by Clemence, who saved well from Rocheteau, but they were rewarded for their positive approach on 51 minutes when Bathenay took advantage of Heighway losing possession to hit a 30-yard swerving shot past Clemence to silence the home crowd. The French fans, in green and white, went wild as their team now led the tie 2-1 on aggregate and Liverpool needed to score twice to progress to the semi-finals.

David Fairclough was warming up on the touchline already, but his introduction was delayed when Kennedy struck back just eight minutes later to give Liverpool hope. Callaghan's cross was challenged for by John Toshack, and the ball fell invitingly for Kennedy on the edge of the penalty area to smash home. One more goal needed. The atmosphere was rising inside Anfield. Many players have since commented on how they could hear it ... feel it ... sense the occasion. But Liverpool were getting caught offside as the French team frustrated them again and again.

Cometh the hour, cometh the man, as the saying goes. On 74 minutes, Fairclough entered the fray. Just 17 minutes to save the day, but before he could do this, Saint-Etienne very nearly had a chance to seal the win, when Clemence appeared to bring down Rocheteau in the box. Luckily, the referee saw it differently, to the relief of most people in the stadium.

Then came Fairclough's moment. With just six minutes left to play, Kennedy lobbed the ball over the French defenders and there was the red-headed supersub running on to it towards goal. For such a young player, he was remarkably cool in front of goal, but this was such a crucial situation for a young head. Never mind nerves, he nodded the bouncing ball into his path and held off a challenging defender, then simply slid the ball past the keeper, and Anfield erupted in joy.

Liverpool held on for a memorable 3-1 win and were now in the semi-final. It was a night that fans and players have never forgotten, and that David Fairclough has never been allowed to forget, but then why would he want to?

※ ※ ※

Unfortunately, Fairclough never really fulfilled his potential for the Reds, although with the quality of players ahead of him it was always going to be difficult, and he suffered some injury problems in the following seasons that didn't help. This is borne out by the fact that in seven and a half seasons at the club he played in only 154 matches, but scored 55 goals, so not a bad return. Despite this, he still managed to win three league championship medals, one League Cup, two European Cups and one UEFA Cup.

He's still a recognisable face around Liverpool, although not by me evidently. I was staying with my wife in the Shankly Hotel in Liverpool for my birthday, and as we came out, a group of people were in front of us. My wife, Gwen, nudged me hard and pointed out one of them: 'It's David Fairclough. Didn't you spot him?' Sorry, David, my powers of observation are pretty poor but at least Gwen recognised you immediately!

12

Champions of Europe

Liverpool 3 Borussia Mönchengladbach 1
European Cup Final
25 May 1977
Stadio Olimpico, Rome
Attendance: 56,000

Liverpool	**Borussia Mönchengladbach**
Clemence	Kneib
Neal	Vogts
Jones	Wittkamp
Smith	Schäffer
Kennedy	Klinkhammer
Hughes	Bonhof
Keegan	Wohlers (Hannes 79)
Case	Stielike
Heighway	Wimmer (Kulik 24)
Callaghan	Simonsen
McDermott	Heynckes
Manager: Bob Paisley	*Manager:* Udo Lattek

WITH THE European Cup semi-final first leg away to FC Zürich three weeks away, Liverpool had a league and FA Cup double to think about.

First up was the FA Cup quarter-final, which saw Fairclough have a rare start for the Reds, and he didn't waste it as he scored the first of Liverpool's goals in a 2-0 victory over Middlesbrough to take them into a semi-final clash with Merseyside rivals Everton.

In the league, things were still very tight at the top of the table, with any one of four teams in with a shout of the title, as Newcastle in fourth were only four points adrift of Liverpool, and Manchester City and Ipswich were hot on their heels.

The European Cup semi-final against the Swiss outfit was to prove a much easier affair than the Saint-Etienne tie. Although Zürich took an early lead, scoring after only six minutes through a controversial penalty given against Smith, a place in the final was all but sealed by two goals by Neal, sandwiching a Heighway goal, to give the Reds an excellent 3-1 lead to take back to Anfield. Surely Rome was beckoning.

Liverpool then had three league matches to play before the second leg, crucially beating Manchester City 2-1 at Anfield to put a dent in City's title hopes, before a goalless draw at Stoke and a 2-0 home win over Arsenal. Newcastle had slipped back, so now it looked like it was down to three for the title, but it was Liverpool's to lose.

Back at Anfield for the return leg against FC Zürich, the Reds booked a nice trip to Rome in the spring thanks to two goals from Case and a third by Keegan that gave them a comfortable 3-0 victory to seal a 6-1 aggregate scoreline and a place in their first European Cup Final, where they would face the old foe of Borussia Mönchengladbach, who they had beaten in the UEFA Cup Final four years previously.

The treble was still on for the Reds but first they had to get past arch-rivals Everton in the FA Cup semi-final at Maine Road. It was an eventful match, with both teams desperate to reach the Wembley final, but they would have to replay, the match ending 2-2 after a late Everton equaliser. This meant that Liverpool's fixture list got even more congested, as the two teams were scheduled to meet again just four days later at the same venue.

This time Liverpool made no mistake, winning 3-0 to book a trip to Wembley.

Next up was a crucial league match against second-placed Ipswich Town at Anfield, and it was the Reds who came out on top in their third match of the week. A 2-1 victory for Liverpool saw Ipswich slip down to third and seemingly only Manchester City now stood in the way of their tenth league title. The Reds then faced sixth-placed Manchester United, who they were also to face in the FA Cup Final less than three weeks later. A Keegan goal on 15 minutes sealed a 1-0 victory and Liverpool were now four points clear of Manchester City with only four matches left to play. However, they didn't make it easy for themselves, drawing their next two matches away at QPR and Coventry but City's form also deserted them, as they took only four points from their next three matches.

All this left Liverpool only needing a draw with West Ham at Anfield to seal the title with one match to spare. Although it was a match that sealed their tenth title, it's not included as an iconic match, as a dull goalless draw was enough to do the job, and Liverpool were crowned league champions. One down, two to go.

As a Liverpool fan, it will not surprise you to hear that I hate Manchester United. Not as much as I hate Everton, but I still hate them with a passion. I did actually cheer them on when they beat Bayern Munich to win the Champions League (which any United fan would never do for Liverpool), because they had an exciting team then and they deserved to be European champions. However, their team of 1976/77 was a dour and dull pack that had finished sixth in the league, ten points behind Liverpool. But of course, as United do, they spoiled the treble party and beat us in the FA Cup Final, albeit with a lucky deflected goal.

Everything happened in a four-minute spell early in the second half. Pearson raced through to score on 51 minutes. One minute later Case hit one of his specials, controlling, turning and shooting from the edge of the penalty area to equalise. Then came the moment and the goal I hate watching, as Macari's mishit shot, which was going wide, deflected off Greenhoff's leg and went over Clemence for what was to prove to be the winner.

Of course, I'm in no way bitter. Anyway, Liverpool had bigger fish to fry only four days later when they faced Borussia Mönchengladbach in the final of the European Cup in Rome.

*** *** ***

It was now that I finally got my life's priorities right. Previously my teenage years had been about my girlfriend, football and music, but it was on this night that I realised that football had leapfrogged to number one when I missed meeting my girlfriend as I had to see this match. (I did meet up with her afterwards though!)

Over 24,000 Liverpool fans were in the stadium on a warm evening to watch as their team dominated the first half. Kennedy had a good effort saved early on, but it was the German team that nearly took an undeserved lead on 22 minutes when Bonhof beat Clemence with a low long-range shot that rebounded off the post and fortunately fell straight to Hughes to clear the danger.

However, only five minutes later, Callaghan won possession from Bonhof in midfield, passed to Heighway on the right wing, and he placed a perfectly weighted pass for McDermott's well-timed run. He calmly slotted home to give the Reds a fully deserved lead.

It all looked too easy for Liverpool in the first half, but they were made to rue not adding to their goal tally early in the second half when the Dane, Allan Simonsen, took advantage of a misplaced Case pass to send a crashing shot past Clemence on 51 minutes. The goal seemed to give Borussia confidence and they dominated for a period, while Liverpool looked to be hanging on and maybe paying for having played in the FA Cup Final only a few days before. Twice the Germans nearly added to their tally, with Stielike and Simonsen missing chances to put their team ahead.

However, the defensive weaknesses that Borussia showed against Liverpool four years previously in the UEFA Cup Final hadn't been solved. Keegan, playing his final match for the Reds before departing for Hamburg, was giving Dirty Berti Vogts the runaround and was regularly being fouled by the slow German defender, who also appeared to bring him down in the penalty area on the hour, but the referee waved Liverpool's protests away.

Then came a magic moment. Liverpool-born Tommy Smith, having been at the club for 17 years, was Liverpool through and through. He'd even worked at the club as a groundsman and according to Bill Shankly 'wasn't born, he was quarried'. He was certainly a tough customer, but he could play as well and should have won far more than just a solitary England cap.

Tommy scored 48 goals in his Liverpool career but tonight, his 600th match for the Reds, was surely the pinnacle. He was in for the injured Phil Thompson, who had replaced him in the team during this season, but no one could have predicted that he would score a crucial goal to give Liverpool the lead. In fact, it took me and the commentator a while to realise just who had scored.

Liverpool won a corner on their left on 64 minutes, which Heighway swung over. Someone, it turns out it was Tommy Smith, rose above the defence to send a powerful header past the Borussia keeper. What a way to bring your long career to a close – the stuff dreams are made of.

From then on it was only going to be Liverpool's cup and Keegan finally got his penalty when Vogts brought him down in the area to halt his brilliant surging run. Neal, as reliable as ever, side-footed the penalty home to give the Reds a 3-1 lead with only eight minutes remaining. These were eight minutes of rejoicing, not worrying about a comeback, as Borussia were broken.

It was a fitting way for Smith and Keegan to bow out, as Emlyn Hughes raised the trophy for a unique double of league championship and European Cup. It was Liverpool's first European Cup, and as we all know, it wasn't to be their last.

※ ※ ※

Unfortunately, Tommy Smith died a few months before I started writing this book. What a fantastic and loyal servant he was for Liverpool. He played 638 matches for the Reds, winning four league championships, two FA Cups, one European Cup and two UEFA Cups.

He'd seen the writing on the wall at Liverpool with the emergence of younger defenders in Phil Neal, Joey Jones and Phil Thompson, so had announced that 1976/77 would be his last season at the club, and his testimonial was held at Anfield only two days after the European Cup Final, where the trophy was paraded around the stadium.

He did actually give it one more season before moving for a short spell at the Liverpool retirement home, Swansea City, under manager John Toshack. But he will always be remembered for that goal in Rome. RIP Tommy, and thank you for that wonderful memory.

13

Kevin Who?

Liverpool 6 Hamburg SV 0

European Super Cup Second Leg
6 December 1977
Anfield
Attendance: 34,931

Liverpool	Hamburg SV
Clemence	Kargus
Neal	Ripp
Smith	Kaltz
Thompson	Nogly
Kennedy	Hidien
Hughes	Zaczyk (Eigl 69)
Dalglish	Bertl
McDermott	Magath
Heighway (Johnson 46)	Keegan
Fairclough	Keller (Steffenhagen 69)
Case	Volkert
Manager: Bob Paisley	*Manager:* Özcan Arkoç

LIVERPOOL KICKED off 1977/78 as European champions, but it was a new era for the club as their talisman, Kevin Keegan, had left for Hamburg.

We all wondered whether things would ever be the same without him and I didn't know too much about his replacement, Kenny Dalglish, apart from the fact that he played for Celtic and Scotland,

and I'd watched him in the Home Internationals held at the end of each season.

In fact, Dalglish wasn't in my good books after his Scotland team had beaten England at Wembley in the deciding match of the British Championship earlier that year, which led to a massive pitch invasion. Dalglish had taken a blatant dive in the penalty area early on when challenged by Mick Mills, which thankfully was ignored by the referee, but he'd later scored Scotland's second and decisive goal … and then I'm expected to cheer him on for Liverpool?

The club had kept his signing under wraps, with Bob Paisley personally involved by visiting Dalglish in Glasgow, booking into a hotel under an assumed name, and working hard to persuade Jock Stein, the Celtic manager, to part with his prized striker. Bob got his way, and the rest is, of course, history.

Dalglish's Liverpool debut meant a return visit to Wembley for him as the league champions took on FA Cup winners Manchester United in the Charity Shield, which ended goalless. But it didn't take long for Dalglish to score his first goal for the Reds as he notched after only seven minutes in Liverpool's opening league match, a 1-1 draw at Middlesbrough. So, okay, I was already warming to him.

In fact, Liverpool's start to the league season was good, with only one defeat in their first 12 matches, that defeat being at Old Trafford. However, Nottingham Forest, under Brian Clough, a team that had only been promoted from the Second Division the season before, were setting the early pace.

When Liverpool returned to Manchester at the end of October 1977, just prior to a European Cup visit to Dresden, they suffered their second league defeat, this time to the blue half of the city, 3-1. The poor run of league form continued, as they lost their next two matches to drop to sixth in the table and were never able to get back on terms with Forest, who were to be surprise winners of the league and also defeated the Reds in the League Cup Final later in the season. In fact, for a spell they were to become Liverpool's bogey team.

For some reason, back then, the European Cup winners faced the European Cup Winners' Cup winners to decide the best team on the continent. Not sure why, as surely the European Cup is far more important, but anyway Liverpool had to play these extra two matches for the European Super Cup. Coincidentally, they were to play Kevin Keegan's new club Hamburg SV, the German team having beaten Anderlecht 2-0 to lift the 'inferior' European trophy.

The first leg in Hamburg ended 1-1, with that man Fairclough equalising Keller's goal to give Liverpool the advantage ahead of the return. So, it was welcome back to Anfield for Kevin Keegan for the second leg, and what a welcome it would be.

*% *% *%

Probably the best summary of this match was provided by the *Daily Mirror*, which suggested that Liverpool made 'mincemeat of Hamburg'; a bit corny perhaps but you have to love some of the puns these newspapers come up with.

It was another trophy for the cabinet, and showed Keegan just what he was missing, as the Reds ran riot to secure a 7-1 aggregate victory. His successor, Kenny Dalglish, did get on the scoresheet but not until the 88th minute, but local lad Terry McDermott, moved to a more central role, did all the damage with a hat-trick in a 16-minute spell either side of half-time.

Keegan received a good reception from the fans despite many, including myself, thinking he'd deserted our team, but he never got a look-in as Liverpool outclassed Hamburg and showed just who was the best team in Europe. Of course, the crowd had to ask, 'Keegan, Keegan, what's the score?' just to rub it in.

It took a while for Liverpool to hit their full stride, but on 21 minutes, Heighway's corner was challenged for by Thompson. He didn't get a clear header in but was alert enough to react first to hook home the loose ball.

Kargus in the Hamburg goal had already denied McDermott with a good save but was unable to do anything about Liverpool's second goal of the night. McDermott scored his first when Kennedy, as he had in the European Cup Final, played a through ball into space and Terry Mac ran on to it, chested it down, and hit it firmly past Kargus.

Heighway was causing the Hamburg defence all kinds of problems with mazy runs on both wings, and fired a dangerous cross in just before half-time, but nobody could get the vital touch, so it was 2-0 at the break, with Liverpool firmly in control.

This match, though, far from being a triumphant return for Keegan, was to be a personal triumph for McDermott. The local lad had signed for Liverpool six months after the Reds had despatched his previous team, Newcastle United, in the FA Cup Final. His energy and goals from midfield were to form part of what I think was the best Liverpool team of all time a few years later. He was to show all his dynamic qualities in this match.

Before he could do that though, Liverpool nearly scored a superb third early in the second half and it was very nearly another cup final goal for Tommy Smith, still running like a teenager. The ball was played up to Dalglish, who was on his own, and he held it up before playing a pass to a marauding Smith, who played the ball straight back to him. Dalglish then played it back to Smith, in a great move of one-touch football, but Tommy's shot went just the wrong side of the post.

It was then back over to McDermott. He completed his hat-trick with two goals in the space of a minute. First, he intercepted a stray pass, ran on unchallenged, and hit a 20-yard strike past Kargus into the top corner. It was then the Kennedy-McDermott show again, as Ray slid in another great pass for Terry Mac to slot in his third with his left foot to make it 4-0.

Then Smith was at it again, or very nearly, as he got forward to meet a McDermott cross with his head, but it went just wide, when he really should have scored. Dalglish then had a rasping shot beaten out by the keeper as Liverpool threatened again and again. McDermott should have had his fourth but missed an absolute sitter when Kennedy's powerful shot was parried straight into his path by the keeper, but he hit it wide when it would have been easier to score.

The fifth goal finally came when McDermott and Case played a one-two, and Case put in a perfect cross for Fairclough to head home on 86 minutes. Then just two minutes later, it was the 'new man' Dalglish who finished things off when he reacted first in the box to slot home after the keeper had saved a Fairclough shot.

After the referee blew the final whistle the Liverpool fans not only cheered their team after a magnificent display, but they chanted the name of their former hero Kevin Keegan, who had given them so much pleasure over the years.

※ ※ ※

Hat-trick hero Terry McDermott was to spend eight years at Liverpool, making over 300 appearances and scoring 81 goals from midfield. As well as 25 international caps for England, he won a whole host of honours with the Reds, including four league championships, two League Cups, three European Cups, one UEFA Cup, and he was voted the Player of the Year in 1980 by both the PFA (Professional Footballers' Association) and the FWA.

He returned to Newcastle in 1982 and also had spells as assistant manager there, including under Kevin Keegan, Kenny Dalglish and Graeme Souness, so he was to return to Anfield for some more classic matches, as you will read later.

14

Enter King Kenny

Liverpool 1 Club Brugge 0
European Cup Final
10 May 1978
Wembley
Attendance: 92,500

Liverpool	Club Brugge
Clemence	Jensen
Neal	Bastijns
Thompson	Krieger
Hansen	Leekens
Kennedy	Maes (Volders 71)
Hughes	Cools
Dalglish	de Cubber
Case (Heighway 64)	Kü (Sanders 60)
Fairclough	Vandereycken
McDermott	Sørenson
Souness	Simoen
Manager: Bob Paisley	*Manager:* Ernst Happel

IN 1977/78, as well as attempting to defend their league title, Liverpool were also defending the European Cup, and the first round pitched them against the East Germans of Dynamo Dresden, with the first leg at Anfield. The Reds made no mistake at home, racking up a decisive 5-1 win, with goals from Hansen, Case (2), Neal and Kennedy. Although the Reds went down to defeat in the return leg at Dresden, the 2-1 setback wasn't important, as they went through 6-3 on aggregate.

In the midst of some patchy league form, the Reds then faced Benfica in the quarter-final.

Benfica, as previous European Cup winners, were expected to be tough opposition but Liverpool's away performance in Portugal set them in good stead to move into the semi-final stage. Although they fell behind on 13 minutes on a rainy Lisbon night, they showed great character to fight back with goals from Case and Hughes for a vital 2-1 advantage at the halfway stage in the tie.

Two weeks later the job was completed in fine style at Anfield, where the damage was done early, with two goals (Callaghan and Dalglish) in the first 17 minutes giving them a 4-1 aggregate lead. Benfica did manage to pull one back on the half-hour mark, but Liverpool were coasting through and could have scored several more goals. Instead they had to settle for just two more, courtesy of McDermott and Neal, for a 6-2 aggregate victory, a scoreline that was indicative of Liverpool's dominance over the Portuguese champions.

Next up, guess who? Borussia Mönchengladbach, yet again. They must have been sick of meeting Liverpool, but at least they had the satisfaction of beating the Reds in the first leg in Germany, as they took the advantage of a 2-1 lead to Anfield. Ian Callaghan was playing a record 857th match for the Reds, and it was to be his last, so not the best way to go out, although they did have an all-important away goal, scored by Johnson, for their efforts.

If Liverpool fans had any nerves about the return leg at Anfield, they were soon dispelled when Kennedy levelled the aggregate score after only six minutes. Then on 35 minutes it was Dalglish's turn when he scored to give the Reds a 2-0 lead on the night and a 3-2 aggregate lead, although just one goal from Borussia would level things up overall. However, Liverpool didn't sit on this lead, as they surged forward looking for a third, which would all but seal victory.

That vital goal eventually came just before the hour, courtesy of Case with a powerful shot off the underside of the bar. That was enough to see Liverpool through 4-2 on aggregate and a date at Wembley in the European Cup Final, again against familiar opposition in Club Brugge of Belgium.

%%% %%% %%%

Wembley was a sea of red in May 1978 as Liverpool fans made up the vast majority within the stadium, but this match was by no means a classic, as the Belgian champions attempted to stifle Liverpool throughout with their offside trap.

Brugge were without Lambert, the player who had proved to be a thorn in Liverpool's side previously, while the Reds were without the injured Tommy Smith, who had apparently come off second best in an argument with a pickaxe. However, his replacement was a young Alan Hansen, who wasn't to have too busy a night, as Brugge weren't keen on venturing forward. However, Liverpool were forced to remain patient throughout, continuing to play their football despite the frustration of not being able to get the all-important early breakthrough that would have drawn Brugge out and perhaps opened them up to the counter-attack.

It was all Liverpool in the first half, although it took a while for the teams to settle, but the passing game of the Reds soon started to flow, with Case prominent and Souness spraying the passes. Clear chances were limited by the staunch Brugge defending, although one break after a Brugge corner left them short at the back, as Dalglish sent Fairclough away down the left flank, but his low cross was cleared as Case closed in for the kill.

Some of the Brugge defending began to get a little desperate, resulting in a yellow card for Vandereycken following a lunging foul on the marauding McDermott. Case thundered the free kick past the defensive wall, but Jensen saved well.

The keeper was soon in action again, racing out of his area to clear as Fairclough for once beat the offside trap. The ball found its way to Souness, who hit a rasping, dipping shot just over the bar. Then McDermott brilliantly sent Fairclough through, but again Jensen raced out to block his shot. Minutes later Jensen was the Belgian team's saviour again, tipping over a Hansen header.

Although Fairclough's speed was causing the Brugge defenders all sorts of problems, it remained goalless at half-time, but it seemed only a matter of time before Liverpool would score, as their pressure must tell eventually.

The breakthrough nearly came very early in the second half when Fairclough shrugged off a Brugge defender wide on the left before stroking a low cross into the goal area. Unfortunately, Dalglish was inches away from scoring, and the ball was put out for a corner as Case closed in on the loose ball.

Any time Brugge half-threatened the Reds defence, a cool and collected Hansen thwarted them as he was to do to many teams in his long career. Then at the other end, Liverpool seemed to have got the idea of how to breach the offside trap when Dalglish played a short inside pass for the onrushing McDermott, who timed his run from deep to race through on goal. However, Jensen came to the rescue once again, injuring himself in the process.

Dalglish was beginning to influence the match, dropping deep to collect the ball and set up attacking opportunities. Still Liverpool surged forward, but still the Brugge defence held firm. However, every time they cleared the ball it came straight back at them in a red swarm.

Heighway was sent on for Case, who was having a quiet second half, to give Liverpool more width and an additional attacking player. Just one minute later the goal finally came. Neal got forward from full-back and chipped the ball into the right-hand corner near to the touchline for McDermott, who lofted the ball into the penalty area to Dalglish. Although a defender cleared his cross, it only went as far as Souness, who timed his through ball to Dalglish to perfection to avoid the offside trap. Kenny did the rest, clipping the ball over the diving Jensen to give Liverpool the lead on 65 minutes, for his 30th goal of the season.

There was still plenty of time to go, but Brugge never really threatened to get back into the match, which was completely under Liverpool's control, as the chants of 'Dalglish' and a rendition of 'You'll Never Walk Alone' rang around Wembley.

Liverpool didn't sit on their lead and continued to throw everything at Brugge, Fairclough only inches away from scoring with a diving header as he tried to meet a driven Kennedy cross. Then Heighway jinked past a defender and sent a pass in for Dalglish, who hit his shot well over.

Brugge had created very little all night but 12 minutes from time Hansen had a lapse of concentration, playing a back pass too short for Clemence. Sørenson nipped in but Clemence managed to get to the ball first; however, it fell to Simoen, whose shot was cleared off the line by Thompson to the relief of all those in red.

It would have been cruel on Liverpool and thoroughly undeserved by Brugge, but the Reds knew they needed to stay alert, as the Belgian team finally started to seek the equaliser. However, the final ten minutes of the match led to no more chances at either end as play became a bit scrappy and Liverpool still kept falling foul of the Brugge offside trap, while Thompson was like a rock at the other end.

At the final whistle, the Wembley crowd, or 90 per cent of it, was ecstatic as Emlyn Hughes climbed the 39 steps through a throng of celebrating fans to collect the European Cup from the Royal Box. Liverpool had made history in becoming the first British team to win the European Cup twice, and Kenny Dalglish had well and truly replaced Kevin Keegan as the King of the Kop.

※ ※ ※

What can I say about Kenny Dalglish? The Glaswegian played for the Reds for almost 13 years, racking up a huge list of honours: six league championships, one FA Cup, four League Cups, three

European Cups, two FWA Footballer of the Year awards and a PFA Player of the Year award.

Kenny played over 500 matches for the Reds, scoring 172 goals, as well as representing his country over 100 times in a stellar career. But he wasn't finished there, of course, as he became Liverpool manager in the 1985/86 season, winning three league championships, two FA Cups, one League Cup and three Manager of the Year awards. He must have some trophy cabinet at home! Surely Liverpool's best-ever player. How could I ever have doubted him as a replacement for Kevin Keegan?

15

Seventh Heaven

Liverpool 7 Tottenham Hotspur 0

First Division
2 September 1978
Anfield
Attendance: 50,705

Liverpool	Tottenham Hotspur
Clemence	Daines
Neal	McAllister
A. Kennedy	Naylor
Thompson	Hoddle
R. Kennedy	Lacy
Hughes (Johnson 25)	Perryman
Dalglish	Villa
Case	Ardiles
Heighway	Taylor
McDermott	Duncan
Souness	McNab
Manager: Bob Paisley	*Manager:* Keith Burkenshaw

HAVING LOST their league title to Nottingham Forest the previous season, Liverpool kicked off 1978/79 determined to regain their crown. Before the visit of Spurs to Anfield in early September, the Reds had won their first three league matches, including impressive wins against FA Cup holders Ipswich (3-0) and at Maine Road against Manchester City (4-1).

Surprisingly, they had then been knocked out of the League Cup in the second round by Second Division Sheffield United, despite fielding a full-strength team, so maybe they were feeling a little angry by the time Spurs came to visit five days later.

We had just witnessed a fascinating World Cup in Argentina, which England had failed to qualify for, and Scotland probably wished they hadn't bothered making the journey to, after being beaten by Peru and scraping a miserable draw with Iran. It was very unusual for me to be supporting Argentina, given their history of violence against England in the 1966 World Cup, but this team had several players with great attacking style and flair, such as Mario Kempes, Leopoldo Luque, Oscar Ortiz, Osvaldo Ardiles and Ricardo Villa. They emerged as World Cup champions as Kempes inspired them to a 3-1 victory over the Netherlands.

Spurs then sent shockwaves through the First Division by signing Ardiles and Villa at a time when it was rare for overseas players to play in the English league. It was a major coup, especially as Spurs had just been promoted back to the First Division after spending a season in the second tier.

Perhaps too much was expected too soon of these two great players, and they certainly delivered in the longer term, but joining a Spurs midfield that also included Glenn Hoddle certainly gave the Lilywhites a bit of a superstar look, at least in some areas of the pitch.

My abiding memory of this match is getting back to my brother's car after we had finished playing in our local league match and turning on the radio for the football results. Given that Spurs had these two players who I'd admired so much during the World Cup, I was a little concerned that they would turn on the style and I would have to suffer the ignominy of having to put up with my brother's crowing all the way home.

Imagine my joy, and my brother's shock, when we heard the 7-0 scoreline. Of course, I didn't gloat at all and I've never mentioned it since ... as if.

※ ※ ※

Perhaps Spurs should have been warned by the fact that Liverpool had scored nine goals in their first three matches but, even then, they couldn't have expected this onslaught. However, it was Spurs who posed the first danger, as Villa glided through Liverpool's midfield before releasing a good through ball to Duncan, who attempted but failed to take it past Clemence. If Duncan had succeeded, he had two Spurs players waiting in the goal area for a simple tap-in and this match could have been a whole lot different.

Soon after this, Dalglish blazed over when a long ball over the top caught out Perryman in the Spurs defence, but Kenny soon made amends. Case surged forward before mishitting the ball, which fortunately went straight to Dalglish in the penalty area. He did one of his trademark turns and shot low past Daines to give the Reds the lead after only eight minutes.

Steve Heighway was then sent through on goal but was cynically brought down by Perryman, for what would these days be a straight red card, but he escaped punishment. Heighway hit a bending shot around the wall from the free kick, but Daines was able to gather at the second attempt.

Although he was not to score in this match, Heighway was to play a significant role and show all the marvellous silky skills that he possessed. Perhaps if he'd been Argentinian, the world of football would have been drooling over him as it did Ardiles and co. He was now well into his Liverpool career, having signed in 1970, but was still performing at the highest level, most often from the left wing, beating players at will and delivering superb passes and crosses for others to benefit from – a provider of the highest quality.

Dalglish very nearly added a second with another one of the turn and shoot efforts that he made look so easy, but this time his shot was wide. However, he doubled the lead after 20 minutes. As Spurs were having trouble putting passes together, the Reds had no such problems and were getting into full flow. One move led to a bombardment of shots being rained in on the Spurs goal from Dalglish, Ray Kennedy, then Case, who again mishit straight to Dalglish, who diverted it into the net.

Hughes had been hobbling around for several minutes and was replaced by Johnson, a forward for a defender, so Liverpool's attacking force was even more deadly now, especially with Heighway gliding past defenders as if they weren't there.

Spurs' new World Cup winners couldn't get into the match at all and regularly lost the ball in midfield as red shirts swarmed around them, and it was only going to be a matter of time before Liverpool added to their lead. This time it was Ray Kennedy, who headed in a deep cross from McDermott on 28 minutes, although it looked to have gone in off centre-half Lacy. Maybe all three goals had a stroke of fortune, but it was no more than Liverpool deserved, as they were running the Spurs defence ragged.

Although Spurs managed to create a couple of half-chances through Ardiles and Hoddle, the rest of the Spurs players didn't seem to be on the same wavelength. Meanwhile, Liverpool began to turn on the style just before half-time and were toying with Spurs, who struggled to get a touch in a move that resulted in a Souness drive being deflected just wide. Then new signing Alan Kennedy went on a run from left-back, and kept going right through on goal, but his shot was saved by the busy Daines.

At half-time, the scoreline remained 3-0, but in the second half Liverpool were to get even better. Heighway was now mainly operating from the left, having moved over when Liverpool made their substitution, and Spurs were struggling to contain him. Meanwhile Case was operating from right-back and his ball down the right flank after 48 minutes started a slick move that led to Dalglish's shot being saved by Daines, but the ball fell to Johnson to slot home.

Still Liverpool surged forward, Souness the next to try his luck with a powerful shot that Daines pushed over. You had to feel sorry for the Spurs keeper really as he was actually having a good match and keeping the scoreline reasonable ... at least for now. On 58 minutes Spurs again lost the ball in midfield. The ball found its way to Dalglish via Ray Kennedy, and he slipped a ball through to Johnson who put it through Daines's legs for number five.

Six minutes later and it was six goals for the Reds. Duncan, who had somehow just cleared one off the line with a brilliant overhead kick to prevent a Johnson hat-trick, then tripped the dangerous Heighway in the box for a Liverpool penalty. Up stepped the ever-reliable Neal to take the kick. Daines dived to his right to save but was adjudged to have moved too early ... it really wasn't his day. Neal made no mistake with the retaken kick.

Johnson very nearly claimed his hat-trick when he raced on to another great ball from Dalglish, but again Daines came to the rescue as he raced out to foil the striker.

Then on 76 minutes came the goal of the match, and quite possibly the best goal I've ever seen. I can watch it over and over again. It's not a spectacular shot or some piece of Messi-like wizardry, but simply brilliant awareness, turning defence into attack with incisive passing, first-time crossing and brilliant finishing.

All in a matter of seconds, a Spurs attack resulted in a Liverpool goal ... just like that. Clemence gave the ball to Ray Kennedy, who passed on to Dalglish. He quickly transferred the ball on to Johnson on the halfway line. Johnson turned and fed a perfect cross-field ball out to Heighway, who was racing down the left wing. Heighway, without breaking stride, hit a first-time cross deep into the Spurs penalty area where McDermott had somehow raced to meet it with a bullet-like header past Daines. Simply brilliant! Most players raced to congratulate McDermott, while Heighway calmly walked back down towards the halfway line ... not a hair out of place as ever.

And there it was, Spurs' biggest league defeat, which would have been much worse if not for Daines, who pulled off more saves in the remaining minutes of the match. And a real lesson for Ossie Ardiles and Ricky Villa in English league football at its best.

※ ※ ※

Before the end of September, Liverpool had been knocked out of the European Cup at the first hurdle, and it was their nemesis, Nottingham Forest, who put them out over two legs. Forest went on to lift the cup and then defended it in 1979/80, as English clubs began their domination of the trophy.

However, Liverpool still qualified for the 1979/80 European Cup by winning the league by a comfortable eight points over Forest, as well as reaching the semi-final of the FA Cup, where another arch-enemy, Manchester United, put them out, before going on to lose 3-2 to Arsenal in a memorable final.

It was to be a high-scoring season for the Reds, as in addition to the drubbing of Spurs, they beat Derby County 5-0 and Norwich City 6-0. They scored 85 league goals in the season, over 20 more than rivals Forest, and they ended with a positive goal difference of 69, conceding only 16 goals in 42 matches.

The title was won with two matches to spare after a 3-0 victory over Aston Villa. Their tally of 68 points (remember only two points for a win) was a record and a sure sign that this 11th title was not to be their last.

As for Steve Heighway, there was still more to come. He remained with the Reds for a further two years, totalling 475 appearances in all. He may have only scored 76 goals, but just how many he created, nobody knows. He was a wonderful servant for the Reds, winning four league titles, one FA Cup, two European Cups and two UEFA Cups.

He later spent some years coaching at the academy, bringing on such stars as Robbie Fowler, Michael Owen and Stevie Gerrard – not a bad legacy.

16

First League Cup

Liverpool 2 West Ham United 1
League Cup Final Replay
1 April 1981
Villa Park
Attendance: 36,693

Liverpool	**West Ham**
Clemence	Parkes
Neal	Stewart
A. Kennedy	Lampard
Thompson	Bonds
R. Kennedy	Martin
Hansen	Devonshire
Dalglish	Neighbour
Lee	Goddard
Rush	Cross
McDermott	Brooking
Case	Pike (Pearson)
Manager: Bob Paisley	*Manager:* John Lyall

YOU COULD hardly say that the 1979/80 season was a bad one for Liverpool, as they won the league title for the 12th time and reached the semi-final of both domestic cups. However, it was disappointment again in the first round of the European Cup as they were surprisingly knocked out by Dinamo Tbilisi, losing 3-0 away, having taken a 2-1 lead to Georgia.

Fast forward to 1980/81 and it was to be a different cup that Liverpool would first focus on, and one they hadn't won before, the League Cup. However, it didn't start well for them when they lost in the first leg of their opening match, 1-0 at Bradford City of the Fourth Division, despite having a full-strength team out, apart from an injured Dalglish. His absence was his first in 180 matches for the Reds but he was back to score two goals as they put things right in the home leg. Further goals from Ray Kennedy and Johnson brought about a comfortable 4-0 victory to allay any worries of an embarrassment.

Liverpool's defence of their league title had started okay, and goals soon started to flow both in the league and the League Cup. They hit four in each of the league matches against Norwich, West Brom and Brighton, and put five past Third Division Swindon Town in the third round of the League Cup, thanks to Lee (2), Dalglish, Fairclough and an own goal.

The cup draw was favouring Liverpool, as they next faced lower league opposition again in Third Division Portsmouth, winning comfortably, 4-1, with Johnson hitting a double in between goals from Dalglish and Souness.

An unlikely duo of Aston Villa and Ipswich had set the initial pace at the top of the league table, but by the end of November Liverpool had moved up to second behind Villa, although Ipswich had matches in hand, so it looked as if the defence of their title was going to be much tougher this season.

In the fifth round of the League Cup, Liverpool finally faced First Division opposition in mid-table Birmingham City but ran out comfortable 3-1 winners, with Dalglish, McDermott and Johnson the scorers. Perhaps Wembley was beckoning, as they were now into the semi-final, where they would face Manchester City over two legs.

Before the first leg, Liverpool suffered a crucial 2-0 defeat to Villa, but were still only two points behind them, with Ipswich looking likely champions with two matches in hand and only one point behind the leaders. However, the Reds were back to winning ways at Maine Road, as a crucial late goal by Ray Kennedy sealed a first-leg victory to set the Reds on course for Wembley.

Form then deserted Liverpool, as between the two semi-final legs, they lost two league matches and went out of the FA Cup to Merseyside rivals Everton. The league was now looking beyond them, so their focus domestically was on the League Cup.

The home leg against City was a struggle, despite having the one-goal advantage from the first leg. It looked easy enough when Dalglish put the Reds ahead on 23 minutes, but City equalised through Reeves and went in search of the all-important second goal. Twice they hit the woodwork in the closing minutes, but Liverpool's luck held and their quest for their first League Cup continued.

Maybe it was to be their year, the Wembley final being against Second Division West Ham, who would become champions by the end of the season and return to First Division football. Liverpool were firm favourites but it wasn't to be. No, you haven't misread the title of this chapter, it's just that the match ended 1-1 and went to a replay.

The first match was pretty dull, ending goalless and going into extra time. Even then there was no incident until three minutes from the end when referee Clive Thomas, who liked a bit of controversy, allowed a Liverpool goal by Alan Kennedy, despite teammate Lee lying in an offside position. Different rules back then of course, but Thomas had disallowed a West Ham goal in similar circumstances earlier. It looked as if Liverpool would lift the cup but, in the closing seconds, the Hammers were awarded a penalty when McDermott handled. Up stepped ace penalty taker Ray Stewart to earn the Hammers a deserved replay at Villa Park.

Before the replay, a league defeat to Arsenal left Liverpool languishing in sixth place as Ipswich led the table with a match in hand and looked almost certain champions.

%% %% %%

The Reds were in the middle of a busy spell of matches at the time of their replay against the Hammers in the League Cup Final on April Fools' Day 1981, with Clive Thomas back in charge. It's not too surprising that West Ham were showing themselves as too good for the Second Division when you look at their line-up. This was a team with pedigree and international players, such as Billy Bonds, Frank Lampard, Alan Devonshire and Trevor Brooking, as well as a young Paul Goddard, who was later to go on to star for Liverpool.

The replay kicked off with Liverpool in their changed strip of white shirts and black shorts, and they had the best of the early exchanges, Dalglish heading just wide from Lee's right-wing cross, then having his left-foot shot saved by Parkes. But as Liverpool applied further pressure, West Ham won the ball just outside their own penalty area. Brooking strode away before passing to Neighbour, who was racing down the right wing. He skipped past Hansen and put in a near-post cross, where Goddard met it with a firm header into the roof of the net. Just nine minutes gone, and the Hammers had snatched the lead against the run of play.

Liverpool went straight back on the attack, Rush robbing Bonds and setting Dalglish up, but his shot was inches wide. In fact, it was all Liverpool pressure now, with West Ham unable to get out of their own half, but they were defending stoically. In addition, keeper Parkes was keeping Liverpool at bay, diving to push away a rasping Lee drive from 25 yards on the quarter-hour mark. Then a quick Lee free kick sent in Rush, whose shot rebounded off the woodwork. Just a few minutes later, a Ray Kennedy header hit the bar and you wondered whether it was going to be one of those nights.

But then came a moment of Dalglish magic on 25 minutes. Neal and McDermott had exchanged passes down the Liverpool right before McDermott spotted Dalglish's darting run into the penalty area. McDermott chipped in a perfect ball, which Dalglish met with a volley on the turn that flashed past the onrushing Parkes into the net. It had taken a piece of individual brilliance to finally break through the West Ham rearguard.

Just three minutes later came a goal from Alan Hansen. He'd joined the Reds from Partick Thistle four years previously and worked his way into the team as Tommy Smith reached the end of his career. Despite his elegant defending and great use of the ball from the back, he wasn't renowned for his goalscoring, only netting 14 times in over 600 matches. However, tonight was as good a time as any to score one of his rare goals. After a Dalglish shot had been deflected behind, Hansen strode forward to head in Case's corner, albeit via a deflection off the thigh of Bonds, but no one was going to take this one away from Hansen.

West Ham now had to come forward, and very nearly equalised from a bending shot by Stewart that hit the side-netting, with most people thinking it had gone in. However, Liverpool controlled the rest of the first half to lead 2-1 at the break.

The second half started with the Hammers applying pressure as they sought the equaliser, but they never really threatened Clemence in the Liverpool goal. At the other end Parkes had to come to the rescue again when Case hit a powerful curling shot from a free kick. The West Ham keeper then produced a great fingertip save when Dalglish hit a shot on the turn in the penalty area.

West Ham's best chance to equalise came as McDermott made a rare slip, giving the ball away just outside his own penalty area. Brooking seized on it, cut inside, and sent a curling shot just wide. He hung his head as he trudged back, knowing that he should have scored.

Both teams were tiring now, as this replay had been played at a pretty frantic pace, and was certainly not a dull affair like the original match at Wembley. Both teams had half-chances but failed to convert them, as the Liverpool fans started to sing their traditional anthem in the closing minutes.

Then in the last 30 seconds, Case got in a mess in his own penalty area when he should have put his foot through the ball but allowed it to break to Cross, who hit a low shot that beat Clemence but also the far post by inches. It was agonisingly close as it rolled past the post, and the Liverpool players' and fans' hearts must have been in their mouths. Shortly afterwards, Mr Thomas blew the final whistle, the fans invaded the pitch, and Liverpool finally had their hands on the League Cup.

%% %% %%

Having lifted their first League Cup, Liverpool's chances of winning the league were forlorn, despite a 3-0 victory over Stoke, where Ronnie Whelan scored on his debut. However, they remained eight points adrift of Ipswich and their remote hopes of retaining their league title went as they failed to win any of their next three matches. Draws away at Nottingham Forest and Leeds sandwiched a 1-0 defeat at Anfield by Manchester United to leave the Reds in sixth place, as Villa took over top spot and were to go on to win the league.

Alan Hansen, who had scored the winner in the League Cup victory, was to go on to become a legend for the club over the next ten years, staying for the remainder of his career, playing 620 matches. He won a remarkable eight league titles, two FA Cups, three League Cups and three European Cups, and is one of the best defenders the club has ever seen.

Although he admitted to suffering from pre-match nerves, he was cool, calm and collected as he strode about the pitch, looking in complete control. He formed some great central defence partnerships with Phil Thompson, Mark Lawrenson and Gary Gillespie, and it was only injuries to his knees that stopped him prolonging his illustrious career. However, he went on to become a regular pundit on *Match of the Day*, forming a new partnership with Alan Shearer.

17

An Unlikely Hero

Liverpool 1 Real Madrid 0
European Cup Final
27 May 1981
Parc des Princes, Paris
Attendance: 48,360

Liverpool	Real Madrid
Clemence	Agustín
Neal	Cortés (Pineda 85)
A. Kennedy	Camacho
Thompson	Stielike
R. Kennedy	Sabido
Hansen	Ángel
Dalglish (Case 86)	Del Bosque
Lee	Santillana
Johnson	Navajas
McDermott	Juanito
Souness	Cunningham
Manager: Bob Paisley	*Manager:* Vujadin Boškov

IN 1980/81 there was to be no exit at the first hurdle of the European Cup as in the previous season. In fact, far from it. The Reds surprisingly only drew 1-1 in the first leg away at Finnish champions Oulu Palloseura, but put the Finns to the sword at Anfield with a massive 10-1 victory. Souness and McDermott both hit hat-tricks as the Reds ran riot, scoring six in the second half.

In the next round they faced Alex Ferguson's Aberdeen, winning both legs, 1-0 at Pittodrie after an early McDermott goal, and 4-0 at Anfield, with Neal, Dalglish and Hansen adding to an own goal. This was a decent Dons team too, containing Jim Leighton, Alex McLeish, Willie Miller, Gordon Strachan and Mark McGhee, but they were no match for their English counterparts.

Although their domestic form hadn't been looking too hot, in Europe it looked as if the Reds could be on the way to their third trophy. At the quarter-final stage they faced CSKA Sofia and had the job as good as done in the first leg at Anfield. Another Souness hat-trick and goals from Lee and McDermott helped them to a 5-1 victory, as Heighway put in an impressive performance, despite not having been picked much over the season. Then before the League Cup replay against West Ham, Liverpool disposed of the Bulgarian team with Johnson's goal giving them a 1-0 victory in the away leg to seal a 6-1 aggregate victory and a place in the European Cup semi-final against Bayern Munich.

The semi-final was to be a very tight affair. The Germans boasted an international line-up that included Klaus Augenthaler, Paul Breitner, Dieter Hoeneß and Karl-Heinz Rummenigge. Liverpool, meanwhile, had some injury problems for the first leg and were without key midfielder Souness, while several others were nursing knocks. They also lost McDermott injured during the match.

After early Liverpool pressure, the German defence held firm and restricted them to very few opportunities. Bayern were playing for a goalless draw, although they went close when Niedermayer hit the crossbar. However, they got what they came for and Liverpool faced a difficult trip to Munich, where they knew they needed to score.

When the Reds travelled to Munich for the second leg of the semi-final they had Souness and McDermott back in the line-up, but the team also included Richard Money and Colin Irwin in place of Alan Kennedy and Phil Thompson, as the season began to take its toll on the Reds. Then the injury hoodoo hit again, as Dalglish damaged his ankle after only nine minutes, to be replaced by Howard Gayle.

However, Liverpool produced a composed performance throughout. The first half was very tight, the German team knowing that an away goal for Liverpool could prove costly, and being reluctant to push too many players forward. Liverpool started the second half well but Gayle ran out of steam after 70 minutes and was replaced by Case, whose drive started to push the team forward.

All the goal action came in the last seven minutes, when Ray Kennedy scored the vital away goal on 83 minutes that would surely send Liverpool through. But Munich weren't done, as Rummenigge hit back four minutes later to level the tie and leave Liverpool hanging on to that away-goal lead, which they did, for a deserved place in the European Cup Final against the mighty Real Madrid.

Liverpool's remaining league matches were pretty irrelevant, as they were to finish fifth, their lowest league placing for ten years. What was important was getting key players back to fitness and making sure they incurred no further casualties. Fortunately, Thompson and Alan Kennedy recovered to play in the final league match, a 1-0 victory over Manchester City, but Dalglish was still absent, with only eight days to go before the final.

※ ※ ※

The Real Madrid team wasn't the Galácticos of recent years, although it did contain future Spain national manager Vincente Del Bosque, Uli Stielike and the wonderfully talented Laurie Cunningham, one of my all-time favourite players, who tragically died much too young.

Liverpool were back to full strength, as Dalglish returned to partner Johnson up front and they went into the match as marginal favourites to lift their third European Cup. They were also seeking to keep the cup in England for the fifth successive year. Meanwhile,

Real's pedigree was second to none, having won the first five competitions, then a sixth in 1966. However, it was 15 years since their last triumph.

Not unusually, the match didn't live up to the hype that surrounded the reputation of these two great teams, but Liverpool were perhaps no longer the team that had won the trophy twice previously and Real were nothing like their attacking team of old. They successfully adopted a man-to-man marking system in an attempt to stifle Liverpool's attacking prowess.

In the first half both teams struggled to create any clear opportunities. Liverpool's first effort was a long-range shot from Alan Kennedy that stayed low, but was parried away for a corner by Agustín. Meanwhile, Dalglish was being kept comparatively quiet, although he did manage one trademark shot on the turn, which didn't trouble Agustín too much. However, it was perhaps Real who came closest to scoring when Camacho chested down a Juanito pass before hitting a speculative lob that had Clemence scrambling as it went marginally wide. Dalglish then set up Souness for a 25-yard drive that went straight at the keeper, who spilled it but managed to recover it just in time as Souness charged towards him.

It was goalless at half-time and evenly balanced, with Liverpool having more of the possession but Real always posing a threat, although Cunningham was having a quiet match, as Neal kept him under control.

Early in the second half, Real had their best chance to take the lead, in what was clearly going to be a very close match. The Liverpool defence stopped, expecting an offside flag against Cunningham, but this allowed Camacho to run clear through the middle of the defensive line from an onside position. Clemence came out as the last line of defence, and Camacho chipped him. Those in red held their breath. Fortunately, the ball didn't dip soon enough, clipping the crossbar as it went out for a goal kick.

Liverpool, though, were still failing to create clear-cut chances, being restricted to long-range shots. McDermott hit one straight at Agustín, then soon after it was Lee's turn, but the ball nestled firmly in the keeper's midriff.

Then came the moment of the match on 81 minutes. Liverpool had a throw deep in Real's half on the left flank. Ray Kennedy threw to Alan Kennedy, who was making a strong and determined run forward. He chested the ball on, evaded the flailing leg of a defender and smashed the ball past Agustín from an acute angle at his near post. After the briefest of hesitations to make sure the ball had gone in, Kennedy continued his run to the large area behind the goal, straight towards the sea of manic Liverpool fans, as the Real defenders stood with their hands on their hips.

Real never threatened an equaliser, and it was Liverpool who nearly added to the scoreline when Dalglish made headway down the left wing and crossed. Although Agustín parried away his cross, it fell to Lee, who slipped it inside to the onrushing Souness, but the keeper managed to recover in time to save his rasping shot.

As the referee blew the final whistle, all those in red, both on and off the pitch, went crazy. Liverpool had won the European Cup for the third time in five years, with a goal from perhaps the unlikeliest of sources.

※ ※ ※

Alan Kennedy had been doubtful for the match after breaking his wrist just a few weeks previously, but fortunately for the Reds he recovered just in time to play a crucial role in this fantastic climax to the season.

He'd joined Liverpool from Newcastle in 1978 and was to stay at the club for eight trophy-laden years. This night's vital goal was one of 20 that he scored in over 350 matches for the Reds, during which he won five league titles, four League Cups and two European Cups.

He was the archetypal attacking left full-back, who always gave 100 per cent. What he may have lacked in finesse, he certainly made up for with pace and enthusiasm.

Although he'd missed a large part of this season with injury, his vital goals in both cup finals showed that he had the knack of scoring just at the right time. And as you will read later, his goal in the 1980/81 European Cup Final wasn't to be his only winning goal in this prestigious tournament.

18

Liverpool Earn Their Spurs

Liverpool 3 Tottenham Hotspur 1
First Division
15 May 1982
Anfield
Attendance: 48,122

Liverpool	Tottenham Hotspur
Grobbelaar	Clemence
Neal	Hughton
Kennedy	Miller
Lawrenson	Roberts
Hansen	Hazard
Thompson	Perryman
Whelan	Brooke
Dalglish	Falco
Lee	Villa
Rush	Hoddle
Souness	Crooks (Price 77)
Manager: Bob Paisley	*Manager:* Keith Burkenshaw

LIVERPOOL WERE back on top in Europe but they started 1981/82 having lost their mantle as champions of England, so were determined to win their 13th league title. However, it got off to a bad start, losing two and drawing one of their four opening matches.

It was then time to kick off the defence of the European Cup against Oulu Palloseura of Finland, the team they had beaten

11-2 on aggregate the previous season. This time it wasn't quite as emphatic, as the Reds ran out 8-0 victors, with a 1-0 win away and 7-0 at home. The second leg was an emotional match for the Reds, as it was on the day after the great Bill Shankly had died, and for a while during the second half the Liverpool fans sang his name.

League form wasn't improving, and by the time they faced AZ 67 Alkmaar of the Netherlands in the European Cup second round, they sat tenth in the league table, having won only three of their first ten matches. They had just drawn 3-3 with Brighton, having been 3-1 up with only ten minutes to go, before old boy Jimmy Case netted to start the Seagulls' comeback.

It was changing times for Liverpool, and it was clear that new players were taking some time to settle in. Ray Clemence had moved on to Spurs, to be replaced by Bruce Grobbelaar, Mark Lawrenson had arrived from Brighton, and Ronnie Whelan and Ian Rush were becoming more regular fixtures in the team. It was also changing times for the English league, as it was now three points for a win to encourage more attacking play and to make a win much more attractive than a draw.

At least Liverpool's form in cup competitions was better than their league form, as they demolished Third Division Exeter City 5-0 and 6-0 in the two legs of the opening match of their League Cup defence. Rush bagged four of the goals, as he started to form what was to become a devastating partnership with Dalglish.

The second round of the European Cup was a much tighter affair than expected. The away leg ended 2-2, as the Reds blew a two-goal lead. At home it was again 2-2 and looking as if extra time would be needed when Hansen popped up with another of his rare goals to seal the tie on 85 minutes.

The League Cup seemed to be providing some welcome relief from Liverpool's disappointing league form as they disposed of Middlesbrough 4-1 in the third round, then Arsenal 3-0 in extra time of the fourth-round replay, following a goalless draw at Highbury.

The new year thankfully saw a change in form, with the Reds going unbeaten in league and domestic cups for 11 matches. By the time they lost to Chelsea in the fifth round of the FA Cup in mid-February, Liverpool had moved up to third in the league table, with surprise leaders Southampton ahead of Manchester United. The Reds were only four points behind the Saints with a match in hand.

In the League Cup, Liverpool had reached the final for the second year in a row, as they defeated Ipswich 4-2 on aggregate, having also played them in the league in between the two legs, beating them 4-0. But their European Cup progress came to a juddering halt in the third round in Bulgaria. They were up against CSKA Sofia, who they had demolished 6-1 on aggregate the previous season. The Reds won the home leg 1-0, but were pegged back in Bulgaria as the match ended 1-0 to CSKA after 90 minutes to force extra time. It all went wrong, as the Bulgarian team scored in the first half of extra time and Lawrenson was sent off before the end, and Liverpool's hopes of retaining the trophy were dashed.

However, they did manage to retain the League Cup, now called the Milk Cup, defeating Spurs 3-1 in the final at Wembley in between the two CSKA matches. Like London buses, you wait for one, then two come at once, as the Reds were to make the League Cup their own for a period in the 80s.

It was difficult for me to choose between this and what was to be a league-winning victory against Spurs by the same scoreline later in the season, but having won the League Cup the season before, regaining their league title won the day for me. However, a trophy is a trophy, and the League Cup was a hard-fought one, Spurs leading from the 11th minute right through to the 87th minute when Whelan saved the day for the Reds. It was extra time again, and Whelan again, who scored in the first half to give Liverpool a

2-1 lead, which was added to by Rush a minute before the end to take the trophy back to Merseyside.

With all cups out of the way, Liverpool's focus was now on the league title. It was a double surprise at the top, as Southampton still led the way, with Swansea sitting second. Then came the usual suspects of Manchester United and Liverpool, both with matches in hand.

It was Liverpool's experience that was to hold sway, as they remained unbeaten for the rest of the season following their European Cup exit. In fact, they won their next ten league matches, conceding only four goals, and winning vital matches against Southampton and Manchester United. They now led the table by four points from Ipswich and had a match in hand, as they took complete control of the league.

Away draws at Spurs and Arsenal, although good results, meant that Ipswich were still in touch when Liverpool faced Spurs again, this time at Anfield, knowing that a win would seal the title with a match to spare.

※ ※ ※

For Spurs, Liverpool old boy Ray Clemence received a rapturous reception on his return to Anfield, but two of Spurs' key players, Archibald and Galvin, were absent as they attempted to get fit for the upcoming FA Cup Final, where Spurs would go on to defeat QPR after a replay.

The omens were good for Liverpool, as Spurs hadn't won at Anfield since 1912, and they didn't start the match like a team that was confident of breaking that hoodoo. Alan Kennedy was causing havoc down Liverpool's left and getting crosses in, one of which Dalglish somehow nearly bundled over the line while he was on the floor, but Clemence scrambled across his goal to save. Dalglish then turned provider, spreading the ball wide to Whelan, but his shot was straight at Clemence, who gathered safely.

Then came a moment of brilliance on 27 minutes, but not from a player in a red shirt. Spurs had created nothing of note and had the ball in the Liverpool half in a seemingly innocuous area. Villa laid the ball back to Hoddle, who was only just over the halfway line. He took the ball on a few yards, then let fly from 30 yards with a screaming shot that would have beaten Grobbelaar and Clemence if they had both been in the Liverpool goal. Suddenly, all the hard work since Christmas to lead the table was undone with one magical shot that could have taken the league championship to Portman Road.

Liverpool continued to press in the first half, but Clemence held firm and looked as if he was going to spoil Liverpool's day, as Spurs led 1-0 at half-time and the crowd began to sound a little anxious.

The second half, though, belonged to Liverpool, and the inevitable goal came after 51 minutes. From a deep Liverpool corner, Lawrenson rose above everyone to power a header over Clemence for the equaliser. It was a magnificent header from a player who had forced his way into the team during this season. Like his defensive partner Hansen, he wasn't a prolific goalscorer, only netting 18 times in over 350 matches, maybe none as important as this one.

The Kop was now in full voice as they sensed that their team would inevitably go on to win, especially as they were kicking towards the Kop in the second half. And it wasn't long before they were celebrating again, as their beloved Reds took the lead.

Dalglish played the ball forward, but it was headed clear as far as Lawrenson, who hooked the ball over his own head towards the Spurs penalty area. Fortunately, Dalglish had continued his run, and the Spurs central defence was nowhere to be seen. Dalglish controlled the ball with his right foot, slipped it on to his left, and guided it past Clemence to give Liverpool the lead on 55 minutes. Dalglish celebrated in front of the Kop as they went wild, while Clemence just looked rueful.

Lee had chances to seal victory, firstly after Rush had fed Whelan, whose mishit cross found him charging into the penalty area, only for him to smash his shot wide in his over-enthusiasm. Then he was brilliantly found in space on the right by Dalglish. Sammy this time tried a little finesse as he attempted a cheeky chip over Clemence, but he didn't get enough height on his shot.

Spurs never looked like posing any threat of an equaliser as Liverpool surged forward, looking for the decisive third goal. Eventually it came three minutes from time when Grobbelaar's long kick was headed clear by Miller, but only as far as Whelan. He chested the ball down into space, the Spurs defence absent again, and he smashed the ball with his trusty left foot past Clemence, who had no chance.

The goal sealed Liverpool's 13th league title, and their fifth in seven seasons. Bob Paisley was quoted as saying that this was the most difficult of the league championships that Liverpool had won, and when you look at their league positions during the season, it was clearly the introduction of some new faces in the new year that instilled life into their championship bid. In fact, for six of the line-up for this match, it would be their first league championship, but not their last.

※ ※ ※

Mark Lawrenson was one such player, and he was to go on to form a formidable defensive partnership with Alan Hansen, which is perhaps the best that the club has seen. He was at the club for seven seasons, winning five league titles, one FA Cup, three League Cups and one European Cup.

Apparently, Brighton had outbid Liverpool for his signature four years earlier, but eventually the Reds got their man, albeit at a nice profit for the south coast club, after Bob Paisley had seen him play well against Kenny Dalglish. Lawrenson was a great timer of a tackle and good on the ball, but struggled after an Achilles injury in 1987. He finished his playing career in lower league football, but then reformed his partnership with Hansen on *Match of the Day*, although I have to say that some of his jokes and puns, especially during match commentaries, leave a lot to be desired!

19

Reds in a Rush

Everton 0 Liverpool 5
First Division
6 November 1982
Goodison Park
Attendance: 52,741

Everton	Liverpool
Southall	Grobbelaar
Borrows	Neal
Bailey	Kennedy
Keeley	Thompson
Wright	Lawrenson
McMahon	Johnston
Heath	Hansen
Johnson (Richardson 74)	Dalglish (Hodgson 82)
Sharp	Lee
King	Rush
Sheedy	Souness
Manager: Howard Kendall	*Manager:* Bob Paisley

EVERY SEASON seemed to have Liverpool challenging for at least one title, and 1982/83 was to be no exception. It started with a trophy win, the Charity Shield, as the Reds again overcame Spurs at Wembley in a 1-0 victory. They then set about the defence of their league title with great intent, winning five of their first seven matches and drawing the other two.

During this period, they also commenced another assault on the European Cup, defeating Dundalk 5-1 on aggregate, but their league form then took a jolt with successive defeats, to Ipswich and West Ham, then a goalless draw with Manchester United to leave them third in the table behind United and West Ham.

Although Liverpool then went down to a surprise 1-0 defeat in the first leg of the second round of the European Cup away to HJK Helsinki, they went on a good run that saw them draw their next league match, then win nine consecutive matches in all competitions. This run included disposing of HJK Helsinki 5-0 at Anfield, with left-back Kennedy scoring twice to continue his good run of goals in this competition.

The winning run came to an end at Carrow Road when Norwich won by a solitary goal. However, by this time Liverpool were sitting at the top of the table, three points clear of Manchester United.

Within the winning sequence came a match that will remain with me for ever, as Ian Rush put Everton to the sword on their own patch. I remember listening to the commentary in my bedroom, where I had a huge second-hand stereo system made in Russia. The radio was so good that I remember once picking up a European match between Carl Zeiss Jena and Newport County broadcast from East Germany.

The Everton team for this match included a couple of Liverpool old boys in Kevin Sheedy and David Johnson, the latter having moved over Stanley Park at the end of the previous season, but it was to be his replacement up front for Liverpool who was to grab all the headlines on this day, and many times in the following few seasons.

Ian Rush had been signed from Chester City in 1980 for a then-world-record fee for a 19-year-old player of £300,000. He'd scored 17 goals in 39 matches for Chester, and was to go on to become a goal machine for the Reds, scoring almost 350 goals in 660 matches. This match was to be one of the highlights.

※ ※ ※

As the match kicked off, Everton actually started the brighter of the two teams, with Wright just unable to direct a McMahon free kick on target early on. Then Hansen brilliantly read a King pass, intercepting and gliding forward deep into the opposition half before placing a perfectly weighted defence-splitting ball for Rush on the Liverpool left. He took it in his stride and slotted it past Welsh countryman Southall to give the Reds the lead after only 11 minutes.

Just moments later, Rush was sent clear again, this time by a long pass from Lee. He smashed the ball past Southall, but it rebounded off the bar and away to safety. It was clear, even at this early stage, that it was going to be a long afternoon for the Everton defence as they struggled to cope with the pace and movement of Rush. In fact, they were often in a state of panic in their own penalty area, such was Liverpool's domination and cutting edge.

The match was being played at a frantic pace and could easily have been 5-0 to Liverpool at half-time. Southall saved brilliantly from Dalglish, who also missed a sitter when put in by Rush after a devastating Liverpool break. Dalglish then appeared to have scored the second when he headed past Southall and everyone raced back for the restart, as the linesman stood stoically with the flag behind his back. Everton players protested, so the referee consulted the linesman and they somehow decided it was offside. We'll never know why.

Perhaps the turning point of the match came in the 37th minute. Another through ball split the Everton defence and Dalglish got the better of the hapless Keeley and was in on goal before the defender hauled him back. Off he went, to leave Everton with only ten men, facing a rampant Liverpool.

The busy Southall then came to Everton's rescue again when he dived to keep out Lawrenson's header. It was all happening but still only 1-0 at the break, Howard Kendall deciding to reorganise his team for the second half, with future Liverpool player Steve

McMahon going into defence, but it didn't really help. On 51 minutes, Hansen again strode into the Everton half and played the ball forward to Rush, who collected and shot from the edge of the penalty area. This time the Reds had some luck, as a deflection took it past Southall for 2-0.

Then it was Lawrenson's turn to bring the ball out from defence, playing it to Rush on the left of the penalty area. His cross was met by Dalglish at the far post but somehow the ball stayed out of the goal. But not for long. On 55 minutes, Liverpool took a quick throw-in on the right, deep into the Everton half. Dalglish escaped everyone's attention to race down the right and slide the ball across the goal area for Lawrenson to convert easily at the far post. It was effectively game over, but not for Rush.

First, he had a goal disallowed for offside after a brilliant one-touch move on the Liverpool left. Then the Dalglish-Rush partnership simply proved too much for Everton as their movement and vision seemed telepathic at times. A Dalglish flick was just nudged out of the path of Rush as he closed in on his hat-trick, then Rush set up Dalglish for a powerful shot that went straight at Southall.

It seemed only a matter of time before the Welshman's goal was breached again, and it was that same devastating partnership that did the damage. Dalglish, on the halfway line, sent Rush through with a first-time pass. If there was ever one player that I would bet my house on in a one on one with the keeper, it would be Rush, and he made no mistake. His first shot beat Southall but rebounded off the post, but he calmly slotted in the rebound from an acute angle for his hat-trick and a 4-0 lead.

Everton must have been glad to see the back of Dalglish when he was substituted on 82 minutes, but their misery wasn't yet over. This time Lee sent Rush clean through on goal, and once again he did the business, taking the ball past Southall before slotting home for his fourth and Liverpool's fifth.

% % %

It was Liverpool's third 5-0 victory of the season, and a week later Rush scored another hat-trick as they beat Coventry 4-0 at Anfield. At the end of the season he was voted the league's most promising player, and this season was merely a portent of what was to come, as he won both the FWA and PFA Footballer of the Year awards, and the European Golden Boot the following season.

In his two sessions with the Reds he scored 346 goals and won a whole host of trophies, including five league titles, three FA Cups, five League Cups and one European Cup. Without doubt, Liverpool's greatest goalscorer to date.

After the crushing victory over Everton at Goodison Park, Liverpool's next 20 matches in all competitions saw them win 18 times. By mid-February they led the league table by a massive 15 points and had progressed to the fifth round of the FA Cup, where they were to surprisingly lose to Brighton at Anfield.

They were also to suffer the disappointment of a surprise exit from the European Cup to Widzew Łódź of Poland. The Reds lost 2-0 away to leave them facing an uphill task in the home leg, but they had overcome such problems before. It looked promising back at Anfield when a Neal penalty put them one up after only 14 minutes, but two goals from the Polish team put them well in control, with Liverpool needing four goals in the last 37 minutes. They managed to get two, to win 3-2, but the 4-3 aggregate defeat put their European dreams on hold for another year.

However, Liverpool continued to dominate the league, at one point leading by 16 points from Watford, with Manchester United still a threat in third. The Reds needed only five more points from their remaining seven matches to seal their 14th title. Strangely, they didn't win again, losing five and drawing two. Fortunately, Watford slipped up in their next two matches, and United's draw with Norwich meant that the Reds, despite having lost 2-0 at Spurs, were champions with three matches remaining.

Beating the Mancs at Wembley

Liverpool 2 Manchester United 1 (aet)

League Cup Final
26 March 1983
Wembley
Attendance: 99,304

Liverpool	Manchester United
Grobbelaar	Bailey
Neal	Duxbury
Kennedy	Albiston
Lawrenson	Moses
Whelan	Moran (Macari 69)
Hansen	McQueen
Dalglish	Wilkins
Lee	Muhren
Rush	Stapleton
Johnston (Fairclough 83)	Whiteside
Souness	Coppell
Manager: Bob Paisley	*Manager:* Ron Atkinson

AS WELL as a successful league campaign in 1982/83, Liverpool's defence of the League Cup also started well, with a Rush double giving them a 2-1 victory in the second round first leg against Ipswich at Portman Road, followed by a comfortable 2-0 victory in the second leg, with goals from Whelan and Lawrenson. This was followed by progress through two further rounds, with Johnston scoring the only goal of the match against Rotherham, then Lawrenson and Fairclough scoring in the 2-0 victory over Norwich.

Next up were the team they beat in the final two years previously, West Ham. It was another 2-1 victory, with a late Souness goal clinching a semi-final place, Hodgson having scored the first. The semi-final pitched them against another claret and blue team, Burnley, but the tie was won in the first leg at Anfield, with goals from Souness, Neal and Hodgson giving the Reds a comfortable 3-0 lead to take into the second leg at Turf Moor, where they lost 1-0. The 3-1 aggregate victory set up a Wembley final against the old enemy Manchester United.

*%. *%. *%.*

For Liverpool the League Cup Final of 1983 was the opportunity to avenge their 1977 FA Cup Final defeat to United that had prevented them winning the treble of league, FA Cup and European Cup. Victory would also mean that they would be the first team to win the League Cup three years in a row. However, United were on a good run, having lost only one of their previous 17 matches. They were sitting third in the league, and would prove to be tough opposition on final day, despite being without captain Bryan Robson.

After a cagey start to the final, Liverpool had the first opportunity when Rush robbed a dithering Wilkins before unleashing a shot that flew just too high. However, it was United who struck first. Referee George Courtney awarded them a disputed free kick in their own half, after Whelan appeared to play the ball rather than the man. The free kick was played square to McQueen, who hit it long to 17-year-old Norman Whiteside. He controlled it on his chest, then brilliantly turned Hansen, before unleashing a low drive from the edge of the penalty area that beat Grobbelaar. United were ahead after only 12 minutes.

Liverpool came straight back at them though, and Whelan should have done better with a shot after Bailey in the United goal had flailed at a Johnston cross.

As usual in a Liverpool–United match, the tackles were flying in. Souness and Moses had already had a crunching tackle early on in the centre circle, then Dalglish was clattered from behind by Duxbury on the edge of the penalty area. The free kick was played to Souness but his drive curved a yard wide.

Liverpool were looking the more dangerous and came close to an equaliser just before half-time when Whelan crossed low from the left and Rush directed it goalwards, but it hit Bailey and was cleared to safety by Wilkins. So, it remained 1-0 to United at the break, and it looked as if the Mancs were going to get the better of us yet again at Wembley.

The second half started at the same fast pace, with Liverpool particularly hounding Wilkins, not allowing him the time to pick his passes. Then another crunching tackle from behind on Dalglish, this time by Moran, led to a free kick from which the Reds fashioned a headed chance for Whelan, but he directed it straight at Bailey.

United were mostly playing on the break as Liverpool applied the pressure, and as one of their breaks came to nothing, Liverpool surged up the other end, resulting in Kennedy sending a rasping shot just over the bar. It looked only a matter of time before the equaliser would arrive, but Liverpool continued to be frustrated.

Even Rush wasn't his usual clinical self. As Liverpool broke quickly, this time through Neal, the ball found its way to Dalglish, with Rush steaming forward in acres of space on the left. Kenny's perfectly weighted pass surely meant Rush would score a trademark goal with his left, but he snatched at it, dragging it well wide.

United then lost centre-back Moran to injury on 71 minutes, to be replaced by the diminutive Macari. In those days, there was only one sub, so they had to reshuffle their defensive line, with

Duxbury moving in from right-back, and Macari dropping into the full-back berth.

This did United no favours, and just four minutes later the scores were level. Wilkins was again robbed as he dithered on the ball. Johnston found Lee, who played a square ball out to Kennedy. And guess what? That man did it again in a cup final. He took two paces forward with the ball and drove a low bouncing shot on goal that found its way past Bailey and in at the far post. He just loved scoring in cup finals.

Fifteen minutes to go for either side to find the winner. Liverpool introduced supersub Fairclough, but even he wasn't to become a hero this time. For United, it was another reshuffle when McQueen was injured and was sent up front out of the way, with centre-forward Stapleton now at centre-back. The nearest they came to scoring was when Grobbelaar went walkabout as Moses put in a deep cross, but Whiteside couldn't direct his header on target.

Then in stoppage time Liverpool broke quickly in numbers and had a three on one, with Whelan carrying the ball down the left. However, he made a hash of it and allowed Albiston to intercept, with Rush waiting to sew the match up. The final ended 1-1 and went to extra time.

United were effectively playing with ten men as McQueen hobbled about, so Liverpool were able to pick their attacks off easily. As Lawrenson robbed Whiteside on one such attack, Liverpool again passed the ball forward at speed down the right wing to Rush. He slipped it inside to Dalglish, who glided past Stapleton, but his low shot couldn't beat Bailey.

Then eight minutes into extra time came the goal of the match. Yet another feeble United attack came to nothing, and Liverpool broke down their right. The ball was played to Dalglish in the centre but his shot from distance was easily blocked. The ball fell to Kennedy, who quickly transferred it to Whelan, and went for the return pass. Whelan's attempted return hit the legs of the defender and went back to him, at which point he simply sent a brilliant, instinctive curling right-foot shot into the top corner of the net.

The onus was now on United to come forward, but it was Liverpool who continued to attack at the start of the second half of extra time, Fairclough coming inside from the right but driving his shot straight at Bailey. Fairclough was then put through by Kennedy but his shot under pressure flew over. Then when Dalglish put him away in a similar position, he again shot straight at Bailey.

McQueen, now returned to centre-back but not fully fit, did manage to leap for a header from a Muhren free kick, but sent it over the bar, as United only really looked like scoring from a set piece.

Then in the final minute Fairclough was sent clear through on goal, an even better opportunity than his previous two, but again he missed the target, perhaps an indication of his rustiness due to lack of first-team action. However, it didn't matter, as the final whistle sounded and Liverpool, after taking so long to lift their first League Cup, had now won three in a row.

Ronnie Whelan, a Dubliner, had scored twice in the previous season's League Cup Final against Spurs, and had done it again at the crucial time. He'd been a trainee at United before signing for Liverpool in 1979 and stayed with the Reds for 15 years, making the left of midfield position his own and scoring crucial goals on the big occasions. As well as being the hero of the last two League Cup finals, he would go on to win one more with the club, plus winning six league championships, two FA Cups and a European Cup.

21

This Time it's the Toffees

Liverpool 1 Everton 0
League Cup Final Replay
28 March 1984
Maine Road
Attendance: 52,089

Liverpool	Everton
Grobbelaar	Southall
Neal	Stevens
Kennedy	Bailey
Lawrenson	Ratcliffe
Whelan	Mountfield
Hansen	Reid
Dalglish	Irvine (King 70)
Lee	Heath
Rush	Sharp
Johnston	Richardson
Souness	Harper
Manager: Joe Fagan	*Manager:* Howard Kendall

THE EAGLE-EYED amongst you will have noticed from the line-up above that Liverpool fielded the exact same team for the 1983/84 League Cup Final replay as they had in the previous season's final. However, there was one significant change: a new manager, Joe Fagan, appointed from within the famous Boot Room.

After having been associated with the club for over 44 years, Bob Paisley decided to retire at the end of the 1982/83 season. He'd managed the Reds in over 500 matches, having taken over from Bill Shankly in 1974, and had won absolutely everything apart from the FA Cup. He'd also brought some fantastic players to the club, including the Scottish trio of Kenny Dalglish, Alan Hansen and Graeme Souness.

The man who became a Liverpool legend was a reluctant hero and a reluctant manager when asked to take on the role, but he went on to win six league championships, three European Cups, one UEFA Cup, three League Cups, and no fewer than six Manager of the Year awards. The question now was whether the Reds could continue this trophy domination without him.

Things didn't start well for the new boss, as Liverpool lost to Manchester United in the Charity Shield, 2-0 at Wembley, as the Mancs got revenge for their League Cup Final defeat. Early league form was okay, winning five and drawing two of their first seven matches, before losing to United again, this time 1-0 at Old Trafford.

It was then the turn of the League Cup, as Liverpool set out to win it for the fourth year in a row. Entering in the second round, they faced Third Division Brentford, with Rush scoring another double in the 4-1 away victory, adding to goals by Robinson and Souness. Without Rush in the second leg, the Reds still won 4-0, with goals from Souness, Hodgson, Dalglish and Robinson, to ease through. The goals had started to flow after a quiet start to the season, including a 6-0 thrashing of Luton in the league.

By Christmas, Liverpool were top of the league table by one point over Manchester United, despite a shocking 4-0 defeat away to Coventry, who were going well in fifth. The Reds had also struggled past Second Division Fulham in the League Cup, needing three matches and a Souness goal to see off their opponents 1-0 at Craven Cottage, after two 1-1 draws.

It wasn't vintage Liverpool form, but they were still in two cups and leading the league, with the FA Cup third round still to come, where they despatched Newcastle 4-0, but were to be knocked out by Brighton for the second season in a row in the next round. So, just the league, League Cup and European Cup treble to think about then!

Another replay was required in the League Cup fourth round to get past Birmingham City, Rush scoring two after Nicol had given them the lead, as they won the replay 3-0 at Anfield. Then yet another replay was needed in the quarter-final after a 2-2 draw at Hillsborough against Sheffield Wednesday. Rush again got a double at Anfield, either side of a Robinson goal, as Liverpool ran out comfortable 3-0 winners.

By the time of the League Cup semi-final, Liverpool still topped the league table but only by five points from Manchester United, who had a match in hand, with West Ham only a point further back, both also with a match in hand over the Reds. This season's title battle was clearly going to be a tight one.

The path to Wembley was also proving difficult, as the two-legged semi-final against Third Division Walsall, which everyone expected to be a walkover for the Reds, proved to be anything but. In the first leg at Anfield, Whelan appeared to have set the Reds on their way to Wembley with an early goal, but Neal scored at the wrong end to give Walsall hope. Whelan, who seemed to love scoring goals in this competition, scored again on 73 minutes, only for the West Midlands club to equalise a minute later to earn a 2-2 draw.

A week later, in the second leg, Whelan was on the scoresheet again, adding to Rush's goal to finally break Walsall's resolve in a 2-0 victory, and the Reds were on their way to Wembley for an all-Merseyside League Cup Final. If there's one thing better than beating the Mancs at Wembley, it's beating the Toffees.

However, before they could think about that, Liverpool had an important league fixture but fell to defeat at high-flying

Southampton at The Dell, which left the Reds in the precarious position of having just a two-point lead over Manchester United, who still had that match in hand and could go top with a win.

Next up, Everton at Wembley for the first, and not the last, cup final clash between the Merseyside rivals. In fact, it needed two matches just to settle this cup final, as the Wembley match ended goalless after extra time. However, it was far from dull, and Liverpool should have lifted the trophy at the first attempt. Rush was guilty of missing two good chances, although for their part, Everton perhaps should have had a penalty when Hansen appeared to handle a Heath shot in the penalty area, and they did put Liverpool's defence under a lot of pressure.

So, it was a replay at Manchester City's Maine Road, where Liverpool's hero was to be captain Graeme Souness. The Scot joined Liverpool in 1978 from Middlesbrough, having previously failed to prove himself at Spurs. His tough tackling in midfield and ferocious shooting was to become a trademark over the next six years for the Reds as he became a driving force for the team.

※ ※ ※

Liverpool put out the same starting XI for the replay, while Everton were forced into one change due to an injury to Kevin Sheedy, with Alan Harper taking his place. With similar line-ups, the replay was played at the same frantic pace as the Wembley final, not unusual in a Merseyside derby, as two of the best teams in the country battled it out.

Everton had the best of the early action, with Reid forcing a full-length diving save from Grobbelaar, but despite the non-stop action, Everton created few clear-cut chances in the first half, while Liverpool created just two; however, they took one of those, which turned out to be decisive.

In the 21st minute, Johnston knocked the ball back to Dalglish, who in turn played it back to Neal. He slipped the ball forward to Souness, who controlled and turned in one movement. The ball sat up nicely for him to strike it with his left foot from outside the penalty area. Perhaps Southall in the Everton goal was surprised at the early strike, but he got nowhere near the ball as it flew past his outstretched left hand.

Rush had a great chance to double the lead before half-time after being set up by Dalglish, but he blasted his shot over. Meanwhile, Everton didn't lie down, with Grobbelaar kept busy by Reid and Heath, and Richardson having his effort cleared off the line. The Liverpool defence was often under a lot of pressure, but Souness, in his defensive midfield role, was always there to pick up the pieces.

The second half saw Liverpool take more control, as Everton seemed to fade after their first-half efforts. Rush had another opportunity, but Southall produced a brilliant save to deny him. However, Everton were still dangerous, with Reid hitting a shot just wide at the other end.

Then with just 15 minutes remaining came Everton's best chance of forcing extra time when Reid sent Heath through on goal. Fortunately for the Reds, Heath delayed slightly, allowing Lawrenson to get back and clear the ball for a corner.

From then on, Everton attempted to apply pressure, seeking the equaliser, while Liverpool played on the break, creating chances for Dalglish, Souness, Johnston and Rush, but failing to take any of them to seal the match.

The final whistle meant that Liverpool had won their fourth successive League Cup, and the first trophy for Joe Fagan. For Souness it was one of many successes. In his six years at the club, he played over 350 matches, scoring 55 goals, most of them from outside the box. He won five league titles, three League Cups and three European Cups, then went on to have a successful career in Italy, and as a manager, particularly at Glasgow Rangers.

Souness returned to manage Liverpool in April 1991 but the team was on the wane and he had mixed success, winning just the one trophy, the FA Cup in 1992. However, he can take pride in bringing some great new talent to the fore at Anfield, some of which we will come across later in Steve McManaman and Robbie Fowler.

※ ※ ※

Liverpool may have won one trophy this season, but they still had their eyes on a treble as they returned to league action with two victories, beating Watford 2-0 and thumping West Ham 6-0, including two more Souness goals. However, the lead at the top remained at just two points from Manchester United, and two disappointing draws could have put pressure on the Reds, but United also slipped up, to leave the two-point advantage intact.

Rush was then at it again as he hit four goals in a 5-0 thrashing of Coventry that as good as sealed the league title. Southampton and Manchester United could still pip them by one point, but Liverpool drew their next match against Notts County to seal their 15th title, which they eventually won by six points from surprise runners-up Southampton.

However, there was one more trophy to play for, as Liverpool sought to bring home the European Cup for the fourth time. Not a bad first season for the new boss.

22

Brucie's Wobbly Legs

Liverpool 1 AS Roma 1 (aet)

(Penalties 4-2)
European Cup Final
30 May 1984
Stadio Olimpico, Rome
Attendance: 69,693

Liverpool	AS Roma
Grobbelaar	Tancredi
Neal	Nappi
Kennedy	Righetti
Lawrenson	Bonetti
Whelan	Nela
Hansen	Cerezo (Strukelj 115)
Dalglish (Robinson 95)	Falcao
Lee	Di Bartolomei
Rush	Conti
Johnston (Nicol 73)	Pruzzo (Cherico 63)
Souness	Graziani
Manager: Joe Fagan	*Manager:* Nils Liedholm

LIVERPOOL'S QUEST for the 1983/84 European Cup started with a trip to Denmark to face Odense Boldklub, where they came away with a 1-0 victory thanks to an early Dalglish strike. The return leg at Anfield was a much more comfortable affair, as two goals each for Dalglish and Robinson added to an own goal to give the Reds a 5-0 victory to book a place in the second round.

However, goals were in very short supply in the next round against Athletic Bilbao of Spain. In fact, things looked decidedly dodgy for the Reds after a goalless draw at Anfield in the first leg. It was again tight in Spain, until Ian Rush headed Liverpool to a 1-0 victory and a place in the quarter-final, where they would face Benfica three months later.

Benfica, managed by Sven Göran Eriksson, came to Anfield and were beaten by another solitary Rush goal, to leave the tie in the balance. However, with two goals from Whelan and one each for Johnston and Rush, the Reds stormed to a fantastic 4-1 victory in the Stadium of Light, for what must have been one of their best away wins in Europe at that time.

They then faced Dinamo Bucharest in the first leg of the semi-final at Anfield, again coming away with a 1-0 victory, this time courtesy of a Lee goal, which left a difficult trip to Romania to come two weeks later. However, in the second leg, an early Rush goal gave them a 2-0 aggregate advantage and, although Dinamo had levelled by half-time, Rush popped up again six minutes from time to seal the tie and a place in the European Cup Final, where they would face AS Roma on their own ground, the Stadio Olimpico.

Although Liverpool were facing their opponents on their own patch, they were at least returning to the scene of their first European Cup victory seven years earlier. Roma had yet to concede a goal at home in their European Cup run to the final that included victory over Scottish champions Dundee United in the semi-final. However, they must have feared Liverpool, who had won all of their away legs on their way to the final.

%% %% %%

On a warm summer's evening the smoke from the red flares drifted into the sky before the kick-off. Roma's fans vastly outnumbered the 12,000 Liverpool fans, but those following the Reds made themselves heard.

Once the match kicked off, the atmosphere was hostile every time a Liverpool player touched the ball and even more when they touched a Roma player. However, Liverpool's game plan was to quieten the crowd early on, and they did this to some extent by having most of the possession and not allowing Roma's players any time on the ball in a quiet start to the match.

Liverpool had one scare when they allowed the ball to travel across their own penalty area, but Grobbelaar was quickly out to beat Graziani to the ball. Meanwhile, although comfortable in possession, the Reds were creating nothing up front.

Then on 14 minutes, Tancredi, the Roma keeper, dropped a deep Johnston cross under pressure. Roma's Nappi panicked with his clearance (a case of Nappi rash), hitting it straight at the prone keeper and it found its way to the centre of the penalty area where Neal was on hand to slot it home. The Italian team claimed that the keeper had been fouled, and many referees may have agreed, but the goal stood.

Neal, the only survivor from the 1977 final, where he also scored, actually thought he'd scored again just a couple of minutes later but was rightly adjudged offside. But Liverpool were in control, with Souness dominating midfield with his strong tackling and great distribution. Roma huffed and puffed, were regularly offside, and had a few corners, but weren't threatening Grobbelaar's goal.

However, Brucie soon had to move smartly when Roma took a quick throw-in, catching the defence out. Grobbelaar, however, got down quickly to save at his near post. This seemed to give Roma confidence as they started to pressurise Liverpool in search of the equaliser, although they failed to create any chances as the first half wore on.

Liverpool, meanwhile, hadn't looked like adding to their lead but had one half-chance five minutes before the break when Rush got free on the left, but his shot was parried for a corner by Tancredi. However, it looked as though they would take their lead into the break, but that changed just one minute before half-time. Conti's first attempted cross from the Roma left was blocked but he hit the rebound straight into the goal area where Pruzzo looped a header over Grobbelaar to level the scores.

The second half started brightly, with both teams moving the ball around quickly, and Roma certainly looking the more dangerous. They had one half-chance on 52 minutes following another cross from the left, but the cross was a difficult one for Graziani to get a decent header on and Grobbelaar saved easily.

Liverpool needed to weather the storm, as the goal before half-time had definitely given Roma the confidence to attack more. However, the Reds started to regain their rhythm as a chess match started to develop, but they could still not create anything, as the Roma defence kept Rush and Dalglish in check.

Grobbelaar had one of his moments around the hour mark as he completely missed a cross, but the ball fortunately fell to Lawrenson, who headed it back to the keeper. Grobbelaar had joined the Reds in 1981 from Vancouver Whitecaps to replace Ray Clemence. He was an athletic keeper and a superb shot stopper, but a little unorthodox at times. While on loan from the Whitecaps at Crewe he apparently used to walk around on his hands during matches and was known to sit on the crossbar, something which, thankfully, Bob Paisley soon put a stop to when he signed for the Reds.

Brucie was certainly an early adopter of the role of sweeper-keeper and several times was out of his area in this match to foil Roma attacks, as they attempted the long through ball approach behind the Liverpool defence.

By halfway through the second half, it was becoming clear that neither team was really looking like scoring, and Liverpool's players were increasingly becoming frustrated at some of the typical Italian tackling and 'off-the-ball' tactics. Roma were breaking quickly, but

Liverpool's defenders, in particular Lawrenson, were always able to get in a covering tackle or interception.

In the last quarter of an hour, Liverpool started to regain some control, and Dalglish, who had been very quiet, nearly produced something with 12 minutes remaining, but his shot was saved by Tancredi. The keeper's fumble was hooked clear as Rush waited to pounce.

The Roman crowd were now sounding anxious, as Liverpool started to push their team back, looking for a late winner, as Roma struggled to maintain any possession. Then, with five minutes left, came Liverpool's big chance to win the cup. Dalglish slipped an excellent ball through to substitute Nicol, in a similar position to that from which Alan Kennedy had won the cup against Real Madrid. Unfortunately, Nicol couldn't do the same, as his shot was kept out by Tancredi and Rush was beaten to the rebound.

Roma looked tired as Liverpool came on strongly, but the Reds couldn't press home their advantage and the match ended 1-1 and went into extra time. This started with Liverpool still dominating possession, as Roma attempted to chase them down, although Grobbelaar again had to come out to intercept a through ball, this time cheekily taking the ball around a Roma player before playing an excellent ball forward.

Liverpool introduced Michael Robinson on 95 minutes, replacing the struggling Dalglish, hoping that this would give them more attacking power. However, it was Roma who had the next opportunity as they broke forward, but again Grobbelaar was out quickly to save at the forward's feet.

Into the second half of extra time the pace inevitably slowed as the players tired. It was going to take a mistake or a piece of individual brilliance to decide the match. Conti tried it for Roma as he cut in from the left, beating Neal and Lawrenson before unleashing a powerful drive that Grobbelaar saved at the foot of the post as it looked like creeping in.

Roma then seemed to gain a second wind as they pressurised Liverpool, forcing a few corners but they were unable to create any clear chances. However, with five minutes of extra time remaining they were looking the more likely to snatch it, as Liverpool's passing game started to let them down. Even Kennedy, the hero of previous cup finals for Liverpool, couldn't conjure anything.

In fact, nobody could conjure anything in the last few minutes as the match went into the lottery of a penalty shoot-out, with Tancredi in the Roma goal having the reputation as the best penalty saver in Italy. But then Liverpool had Brucie of course.

The penalties were taken at the end of the Roma supporters to make life more difficult for the Reds. First to step up was Steve Nicol, who had been impressive after coming on as a substitute. However, the youngster blasted his shot over the bar to the delight of the Roma fans. Di Bartolomei then smashed his penalty home to give Roma the early advantage.

Liverpool drew level when the reliable Neal calmly hit his penalty into the top corner, then Conti hit his shot over the bar to leave the scores level after two penalties each. Next up, captain Graeme Souness hit a powerful shot into the top corner, but Righetti then scored to make it 2-2. Liverpool's Ian Rush, on 49 goals for the season, calmly slid his penalty into the corner, sending the keeper the wrong way to make it 3-2 to the Reds.

Then came Grobbelaar's antics. As Graziani prepared to take his penalty, Brucie stood on the goal line looking like a puppet on a string as he wobbled his legs and hands. Whether it affected Graziani we will never know, but he blasted his penalty against the bar to leave it at 3-2.

If Liverpool could convert their next penalty, they would once again be European champions, and who else but Alan Kennedy could take it? Up he stepped, shot with his left foot to Tancredi's right, as the keeper went left. In it went, to give Liverpool a 4-2 victory on penalties.

The stadium was strangely almost deserted as Liverpool collected the cup, as Roma fans had already left, feeling disappointed. However, the jubilant Liverpool fans were still there to see their team lift their fourth European Cup.

※ ※ ※

Despite the loss of Bob Paisley, it had been business as usual for Liverpool under new boss Joe Fagan. The season had seen them lift the League Cup, secure the league title and now their fourth European Cup.

Bruce Grobbelaar stayed 13 years at Liverpool and what an impact he made at the club, where he will be forever remembered for his madcap antics, particularly this wobbly legs episode. He played over 600 matches and made some memorable saves and, it has to be said, a few memorable howlers. Despite criticism aimed at him, Liverpool thrived while he was there, and he played 317 consecutive matches during this successful period.

Claim to fame time: Brucie once tried to steal a cup of coffee my wife had bought while we were watching a Wales international at Wrexham's Racecourse Ground – that's as glitzy as my life gets.

23

Kenny in the Hot Seat

Chelsea 0 Liverpool 1

First Division
3 May 1986
Stamford Bridge
Attendance: 43,900

Chelsea	Liverpool
Godden	Grobbelaar
Wood	Gillespie
Millar (McAllister 80)	Beglin
Rougvie	Nicol
McLaughlin	Whelan
Jones	Hansen
Nevin	Dalglish
Spackman	Johnston
Dixon	Rush
Speedie	Lawrenson
Canoville	MacDonald
Manager: John Hollins	*Manager:* Kenny Dalglish

AFTER WINNING three trophies in 1983/84, the following season was to be the first since 1974/75 that Liverpool won no silverware. It started with losing the Charity Shield 1-0 to Everton, who were to have a great season, winning the league by 13 points from the Reds and reaching the FA Cup Final … painful for the red side of Merseyside.

Liverpool reached yet another European Cup Final but lost 1-0 to Juventus in a match that was completely overshadowed by the 39 deaths that occurred prior to the commencement of the match when fans clashed inside the dilapidated Heysel Stadium. My memory of the match was racing up to my bedroom to watch it, as I always try to avoid the boring build-up and tune in just as the match kicks off. However, I was met by the awful scenes that had unfolded as the officials debated whether to play the match. The decision was taken to go ahead, seemingly to prevent further problems if they let the fans out of the stadium.

Blame who you like – Liverpool or Juventus fans, the over-zealous policing, or the condition of the stadium – the loss of life is never worth it; it's a football match for goodness sake.

It resulted in English clubs being banned from European competitions for five years, and Liverpool for one year longer. Everton fans have never forgiven Liverpool for denying them the opportunity of challenging for the European Cup, not that they would have won it.

It was to be Joe Fagan's last match in charge. Kenny Dalglish became Liverpool's first player-manager in May 1985 and was to have a spectacular first season of his management career in 1985/86.

Liverpool had a great start to the season, winning six and drawing three of their first ten league matches, before entering the League Cup, where they beat Oldham 8-2 on aggregate. Following the second leg of the League Cup, the Reds then went on another good run, winning seven and drawing two, plus progressing through the League Cup against Brighton, then Manchester United. By early December, despite this impressive run, the Reds were still two points behind United in the league.

A dodgy run over Christmas and New Year, with no wins, saw Liverpool slip to third as Everton moved up to second, with United five points clear with a match in hand over both Merseyside clubs.

West Ham and Chelsea were also still in the hunt with matches in hand.

The League Cup also looked to be offering a great chance of silverware, as the Reds powered into the semi-final, beating Ipswich 3-0, although they then lost to the same opposition less than two weeks later in the league. This left their league title aspirations looking unachievable, as they were now fourth in the table, as Everton led the way, looking for their second consecutive title.

The Reds then lost for the first time in several years in the League Cup, as they went out over two legs to QPR, losing the first leg at Loftus road 1-0, then drawing 2-2 at Anfield. In between the two legs, what looked like a decisive match for the Reds in the league ended in a 2-0 defeat at Anfield against Everton, who now led the league. The Toffees had an eight-point advantage over Liverpool in third, with Manchester United separating them.

However, from this point on the Reds remained unbeaten for the remainder of the season. In their final 12 league matches, the Reds won 11, a goalless draw with Sheffield Wednesday being the only glitch. They scored 32 goals in the 12 matches, conceding only four, with some big wins: 6-0 against Oxford, 5-0 against Coventry and another 5-0 against Birmingham.

Liverpool hit top spot on goal difference after a McMahon double gave them a 2-0 win over Manchester City at the end of March, although Everton had a match in hand, and both clubs were progressing in the FA Cup, having been kept apart in the semi-final draw.

The league title race was now down to just the two Merseyside rivals and remained in the balance, both teams winning their next three matches, until Everton slipped up with a draw as Liverpool thrashed Birmingham. However, the Toffees still had that match in hand that could give them a one-point lead.

Then it was advantage Liverpool when Everton lost, slipping to third, as West Ham now sat four points behind the Reds with a match in hand. Liverpool needed a victory at Stamford Bridge in their last match of the season to secure the title, with West Ham and Everton still having two matches to play.

※ ※ ※

Chelsea had won only one of their last nine home matches, but they began the match well, putting early pressure on the Liverpool defence. However, they failed to create any chances, and once Liverpool started to get into the match, they looked the more likely to score.

MacDonald had an early chance after a Spackman slip, but his shot was well saved by Godden in the Chelsea goal. Then as Liverpool upped the tempo, the busy Johnston gained possession but his shot from a tight angle never really tested Godden.

The Reds would surely soon get the goal they deserved, and on 23 minutes it arrived, courtesy of their player-manager. Gillespie headed on a Johnston corner to Dalglish, who laid it back to Beglin. His shot was cleared off the line by Jones for a throw-in. From the throw, Chelsea cleared the ball as far as Whelan, whose second attempt to get the ball forward found Beglin, who flicked it over the defenders to Dalglish. King Kenny chested it down and coolly slotted home with his right foot to give Liverpool a vital lead. Cue the trademark Dalglish celebration of two arms aloft and beaming smile.

Chelsea tried to hit straight back, with Jones having a half-chance after a clever Dixon flick over the defence, but his header was tame and easily collected by Grobbelaar. At the other end, the Chelsea defence was looking very nervous, and it could have been 2-0 to Liverpool when Johnston pounced on their dithering defenders, but he fired his shot narrowly wide. However, Chelsea then started to apply some pressure in search of the equaliser, with Grobbelaar kept on his toes, but it remained 1-0 to the Reds at half-time.

Chelsea came out firing in the second half, putting a lot of pressure on the Liverpool rearguard, but it held firm. Chelsea appealed strongly for a penalty when Speedie went down under a Lawrenson challenge, but the referee had a good view and judged that Lawrenson had played the ball.

Neither team was creating any clear-cut chances as time marched on, but with quarter of an hour to go Dalglish had an opportunity to clinch the match and the league title when he received the ball from Rush. However, his attempted 25-yard chip over Godden also cleared the bar.

With ten minutes to go, Chelsea sent on another forward, McAllister, in place of a defender to try to save the match. This seemed to provide some momentum as they applied more pressure. Speedie had a half-chance but hit his left-foot shot well wide, then McAllister hit a driven shot across the goal area, but nobody was on hand to add the finishing touch.

That was Chelsea's best effort and, despite increasing pressure, was to be their last, as the referee's final whistle meant that Liverpool had won their 16th league title, in Kenny Dalglish's first season as manager. Everton pipped West Ham to the runners-up spot, before the two Merseyside clubs met in the FA Cup Final at Wembley.

24

Reds at the Double

Liverpool 3 Everton 1
FA Cup Final
10 May 1986
Wembley
Attendance: 98,000

Liverpool	Everton
Grobbelaar	Mimms
Lawrenson	Stevens (Heath 65)
Beglin	van den Hauwe
Nicol	Ratcliffe
Whelan	Mountfield
Hansen	Reid
Dalglish	Steven
Johnston	Lineker
Rush	Sharp
Mølby	Bracewell
MacDonald	Sheedy
Manager: Kenny Dalglish	*Manager:* Howard Kendall

WITH NO European action in 1985/86, Liverpool's main cup focus had to be the FA Cup, where they faced Second Division Norwich in the third round. As has often happened since, they made short work of the Canaries, smashing in five goals without reply, with five different scorers: MacDonald, Walsh, McMahon, Whelan and Wark.

In the fourth round, Liverpool faced a tough tie away at Chelsea, but came away with a 2-1 victory, with two goals in two minutes by Rush and Lawrenson, to progress to what looked an easy tie in the fifth round at Third Division York City, but they were held to a 1-1 draw at Bootham Crescent, needing a Jan Mølby penalty to level the scores. In the replay, it was equally as tough, as the match ended in the same scoreline, and the Reds needed extra time goals from Mølby and Dalglish to progress.

The quarter-final pitched the Reds against Watford at Anfield, the match ending goalless, but Liverpool came within four minutes of exiting the cup in the replay, falling behind to a John Barnes goal. However, another Mølby penalty forced the match into extra time, where a Rush goal put the Reds through to the semi-final.

Fortunately, the semi-final kept Liverpool and Everton apart, the Reds drawn to play Southampton at White Hart Lane. The match ended goalless, but Liverpool reached the Wembley final after Rush again came to the rescue in extra time, scoring a double for a 2-0 win. Meanwhile Everton progressed past Sheffield Wednesday for another Merseyside cup final, this time for the more prestigious FA Cup.

※ ※ ※

The first all-Merseyside FA Cup Final showed just how two sets of rival supporters can mix together, as Wembley was a sea of red and blue all over, rather than the usual segregation.

Although Liverpool started the match on the front foot, early on Grobbelaar had to be alert as he came to the very edge of the penalty area to hack the ball away from the onrushing Lineker. Then only seconds later, a dangerous cross into the Liverpool area was challenged for by Sharp, who looked to be pushed by Nicol. Everton players were furious, Sharp chasing the referee, who thankfully waved play on.

Lineker was looking dangerous as Everton got the better of things early on, trying to take advantage of his speed, but Lawrenson was no slouch himself and seemed to have his measure. Meanwhile, up the other end, the speed of Rush was also being countered by the pace of Ratcliffe in the centre of the Everton defence.

On 27 minutes, Dalglish, unusually, failed to control the ball deep in Everton's half. Reid picked up the loose ball, looked up, and sent a pinpoint pass forward to Lineker, who for once outpaced Lawrenson. Grobbelaar saved his first shot, but the ball rebounded back to Lineker who bundled the ball home, despite Grobbelaar's best efforts. The blue half of Wembley went wild as Lineker celebrated his 40th goal of the season.

Liverpool looked to immediately hit back, as MacDonald split their defence with a through ball for Johnston, but Mimms in the Everton goal was quickly out to smother Johnston's flicked shot.

Jan Mølby then started to control things in midfield, spraying passes wide to set up attacks. The Dane had joined Liverpool in 1984, and stayed for 11 years, oozing class in midfield with his superb vision and passing game. He may not have been the most mobile, but he had plenty of players around him to do the running. All he needed to do was control the ball, stride forward and pick his passes. However, despite his efforts, Liverpool failed to create any chances in the remainder of the first half and went in a goal down.

Everton started the second half brightly, with Steven driving a shot just wide of Grobbelaar's post, although the keeper had the shot well covered. However, Liverpool were soon back on the front foot, as MacDonald took a quick free kick on the left, although the ball was still moving, to set Rush free in the box. As he was challenged, Rush set the ball back for Dalglish, but he blasted his left-foot shot into row Z, which takes some doing at Wembley!

Then came a great chance for Everton to stretch their lead, as Liverpool dallied over a clearance. Hansen and Lawrenson gave the ball away on the edge of the penalty area to Sheedy, who got past both of them but pulled his right-foot shot across the goal and wide of the post, with Grobbelaar beaten.

Then it was Sheedy again who nearly doubled Everton's lead. Johnston handled two yards outside the penalty area, and Sheedy drove a low free kick in, which Grobbelaar did well to turn round the post for a corner.

Grobbelaar then had one of his wobbly moments as he came for a corner and fumbled it, but Liverpool were able to clear it. However, it was soon played back in and Grobbelaar, now in full panic mode, scrambled back to try to pick up the loose ball as it ran towards the goal line. There was a moment's indecision between him and Beglin, which nearly let Steven pinch the ball, but finally Brucie got his hands on it. What followed has been shown many times on TV, as Grobbelaar shoved Beglin in the chest, and the two appeared ready to face off. Liverpool were clearly rattled, and that little pantomime didn't help one bit.

However, Mølby was certainly not one to be rattled. On 57 minutes, Whelan intercepted a poor pass by Stevens and played it quickly infield to the great Dane. He took a few paces forward and spotted Rush's darting run, then played a perfectly weighted ball through for Rush to take the ball round the advancing Mimms and slot home the equaliser.

Suddenly the momentum changed for a few minutes as Liverpool surged forward, although it was all a bit frantic and came to nothing. Then it was Everton's turn again, in what was turning out to be a classic final. They tried the long-ball route for Lineker again, but this time his run was thwarted by Hansen, who hooked the ball clear but only as far as the edge of the penalty area, where Sharp was surging forward in support. The ball fell perfectly for him to send in a powerful soaring header. Grobbelaar, who had already come out to cover Lineker's run, appeared to be stranded, but he somehow scrambled back and leapt to tip the ball over the bar. Brucie was showing both sides of his character in this final, that's for sure.

Just how crucial a save this was soon became evident when, moments later, Beglin sent Rush away down the left wing. He slipped the ball to Mølby inside the penalty area, who took the ball past a defender and sent in a low cross to the far post where Johnston rammed it home to give the Reds the lead.

Everton immediately sent on Heath, a forward, for defender Stevens in search of the equaliser, but it was Liverpool who looked more likely to score. Whelan again picked up a loose ball in midfield, passing to Rush on the left, who knocked it back to Dalglish on the edge of the penalty area. Dalglish side-stepped to send the defence the wrong way, then slipped the ball inside to Mølby. The Dane took the ball past two defenders and only had Mimms to beat. Unfortunately, he didn't get the goal he deserved, hitting his powerful shot straight at the keeper's legs.

Liverpool were now in full flow, and Mølby was putting on a show, as he played one first-time ball wide into space for Whelan without even looking, but knowing that Everton had taken off their right-back and there would be acres of space. Whelan cut inside on to his right foot and sent a beautiful chip over the Everton defence into the path of Rush, who controlled and shot past Mimms for his second and Liverpool's third to seal the match with only six minutes remaining.

However, there was still time for Dalglish to send Rush clear on goal. As Mimms came out, Rush tried to chip him but didn't quite get the elevation to beat the keeper for his hat-trick. Soon after, the referee blew the final whistle and Liverpool had won the double for the first time.

%% %% %%

Although Rush's two goals were decisive in this cup triumph, it was the performance of Jan Mølby that set up the win, having a hand in all three goals. During his stay he won three league titles and two FA Cups, unfortunately missing out on European action due to the ban, where I'm sure he would have excelled.

Liverpool had, in fact, actually won a treble, as they won something I hadn't heard of until my research for this book. The

The league championship-winning Liverpool team of 1963/64

Liverpool players celebrating the club's first FA Cup trophy in 1965

Ian Callaghan and Kevin Keegan holding the 1974 FA Cup aloft after Keegan's two goals sealed victory over Newcastle

*The great
Bill Shankly
in familiar
pose in 1971*

*Supersub David
Fairclough scoring
the winner against
St Etienne in the
European Cup
quarter-final 1977*

*Veteran Tommy
Smith rises to
head home in the
1977 European
Cup Final
against Borussia
Möenchengladbach*

*Goalscoring hero Alan
Kennedy with the 1981
European Cup after victory
over Real Madrid*

Manager Bob Paisley with an array of trophies from the 1980/81 season

Bruce Grobbelaar showing no nerves in the penalty shoot-out against AS Roma in the 1984 European Cup Final

The victorious Liverpool team after beating Everton in the 1986 FA Cup Final

Ronnie Whelan and Kevin Ratcliffe before the 1989 all-Merseyside FA Cup Final

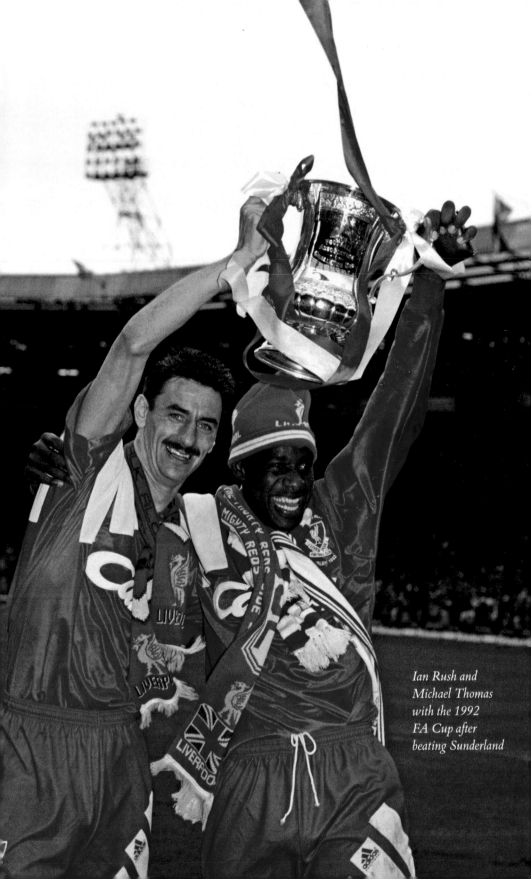

*Ian Rush and
Michael Thomas
with the 1992
FA Cup after
beating Sunderland*

Michael Owen celebrates his equaliser against Arsenal in the 2001 FA Cup Final

Liverpool players celebrate the 'golden goal' victory over Alavés in the UEFA Cup Final in 2001

Jerzy Dudek saves the penalty of AC Milan's Shevchenko to secure the Champions League in 2005

Liverpool celebrate their penalty shoot-out victory in the 2006 FA Cup Final vs West Ham

Adam Lallana's celebration after the dramatic added-time winner vs Norwich City in 2016

Dejan Lovren rises to head home in the last minute vs Dortmund in 2016

Divock Origi celebrates his goal vs Barcelona in the Champions League semi-final in 2019

Jordan Henderson lifting the Champions League trophy in 2019

Football League, to compensate those teams that had qualified for European competition but missed out through the ban, organised what was to be a one-off competition – the ScreenSport Super Cup. Liverpool progressed past Southampton and Spurs in the group phase, Norwich in the semi-final, then Everton in another all-Merseyside final, with two goals from Rush and one from McMahon.

So, Kenny Dalglish's flying start to management was very similar to that of Joe Fagan, but there was much more to come from King Kenny.

25

First Trip to Anfield

Liverpool 4 QPR 0
First Division
17 October 1987
Anfield
Attendance: 43,735

Liverpool	QPR
Grobbelaar	Seaman
Gillespie	Neill (Pizanti 77)
Venison	Dawes
Nicol	Parker
Whelan	McDonald
Hansen	Fenwick
Beardsley	Allen
Aldridge	Coney (Maguire 77)
Johnston (Walsh 86)	Bannister
Barnes	Byrne
McMahon (Lawrenson 86)	Brock
Manager: Kenny Dalglish	*Manager:* Jim Smith

EVERTON GOT their revenge in 1986/87 as they regained the title, with Liverpool in runners-up spot, as the Merseyside rivals maintained their domination.

In fact, after Dalglish's successful first season in charge, there was to be no silverware in his second season. They came close in the League Cup, but were denied their fifth success by Arsenal in the final, where a Charlie Nicholas double in reply to Ian Rush's opener took the cup south.

The following season started brightly for Liverpool, winning seven and drawing one of their first eight league matches and progressing through the second round of the League Cup. However, QPR had also started well and, having played two more matches, were leading the table by three points from the Reds going into the match at Anfield between the two.

I moved to North Wales in February 1987, so was a lot closer to Liverpool than when I lived in East Anglia. In those days, unless it was an all-ticket match, you could just queue up for admission, so off I went with Gwen, who I'd met soon after arriving in Wales. It was quite a long queue, and I hate queuing, but it was well worth it for my first visit to the great Anfield stadium.

After a disappointing 1986/87, Liverpool had invested during the close season, bringing in Peter Beardsley and John Barnes to play alongside John Aldridge, who had joined in January 1987. It was a formidable strike force, which I couldn't wait to see in action, especially Barnes.

England international Barnes cost £900,000 from Watford. He'd played a role in their climb from the Fourth Division to the First Division in just four years under Graham Taylor. He'd already made a good impression, creating his first goal for Liverpool after just nine minutes of his debut against Arsenal. He was to stay at Anfield for ten years, winning two league championships, one FA Cup, one League Cup, two FWA awards and one PFA Footballer of the Year award. He played over 400 matches, scoring over 100 goals, but set up many more for his strike partners.

Meanwhile, Aldridge was amongst the goals already and Beardsley opened his account in only his second match for the Reds. Barnes then scored his first in Liverpool's fourth match when they beat Oxford United. All three were already forging a strike force that can be talked of in the same breath as today's front three of Firmino, Salah and Mané.

‰ ‰ ‰

For the QPR match, Anfield was full to capacity, but thankfully we were there early enough to get in and were standing on the famous Spion Kop. Ian Rush, now at Juventus, was also in the crowd, and the Liverpool fans were singing his name loudly.

QPR were kicking towards the Kop in the first half and started the match on the offensive, forcing an early corner, which was easily dealt with. A few minutes later, Liverpool could have taken the lead when Beardsley cleverly slipped his marker to set up McMahon, but he dragged his tame shot wide.

Both teams were confidently playing the ball around, but Liverpool suddenly pounced on a QPR mistake, the ball finding its way to Beardsley, who put in a first-time cross. McDonald mistimed his jump and there was Aldridge waiting to pounce, but his weak header was straight at Seaman in the QPR goal.

It was then QPR's turn, as Parker robbed Beardsley and sent the ball forward to Bannister, whose 30-yard shot was tipped over by Grobbelaar. Both teams were there to attack and were showing why they occupied the top two places in the league, as the match ebbed and flowed.

Then came a moment of controversy and incredibly poor refereeing. Beardsley had been Liverpool's main creative threat, as his movement was allowing him to lose his man-marker. On this occasion it was his tenacity that won him the ball on the halfway line from Brock. He drove forward and slipped the ball through to Johnston who was on his right shoulder. Johnston took the ball on and drove in a powerful cross-shot from an acute angle that beat Seaman and went in at the far post. The players celebrated before realising that the referee hadn't allowed the goal but had given Liverpool a free kick, not allowing an obvious advantage. The boos rang out around Anfield.

Looking back at it now, I still can't see any infringement in the build-up.

However, it wasn't long before Liverpool actually took the lead. They were beginning to dominate possession, and Barnes, who had been kept quiet up to this point, found himself one on one with his marker. He drove to the byline and put in a low, hard cross, which was met by the onrushing Johnston, who rammed it into the net. Just four minutes to half-time and the Reds had finally taken the lead.

Liverpool started the second half confidently, with Hansen moving forward to send in a low shot from distance, but Seaman dealt with it comfortably. However, QPR's defenders were also pushing up, and right-back Neill drove in a cross that was met on the volley by left-back Dawes, and Grobbelaar had to get down quickly to save.

The Reds were soon back in control though, and I was seeing plenty of action from the Kop end as they sought the all-important second goal. It took a while to come, and QPR weren't happy with the referee this time. Liverpool were awarded a free kick on 65 minutes, close to the corner flag on the left. Barnes sent the free kick into the penalty area, which appeared to have been headed clear by Fenwick; however, we all saw, and thankfully the referee saw, that Fenwick had used his hand. The QPR players surrounded the referee to protest, but a penalty it was. Up stepped Aldridge to drive the ball into the top-right corner, giving Seaman no chance. For Aldridge it was 11 matches started and he'd scored in each one.

The Kop started to sing 'Liverpool, Liverpool, top of the league', as it seemed there was no way back for QPR now. To be fair, they gave it a go, and rattled Liverpool's defence once or twice. Dawes perhaps should have halved the deficit, having a clear header on goal, but only managed to direct it straight at Grobbelaar.

On 77 minutes, QPR made a double substitution in an attempt to rescue the match, but only two minutes later the result was put beyond all doubt by the brilliance of Barnes. Whelan won the ball in the QPR half as they failed to clear. He slipped the ball to Barnes, who played a deft one-two with Aldridge before sending a powerful right-foot shot into the top corner, with Seaman rooted to the spot.

Then six minutes later he scored an even better one, this time needing no help whatsoever. He won the ball on the halfway line and set off towards goal. As he reached the edge of the penalty area, a desperate QPR defender came sliding in, but Barnes easily side-stepped him, then cut inside another, before sliding his shot past Seaman into the corner. Simply brilliant, and typical of Barnes on his day. Maybe this wasn't quite as good as the one he scored for England against Brazil, but it wasn't far off.

My first Liverpool match could hardly have gone better, a 4-0 win, some brilliant goals, and the sun was shining. The win meant that Liverpool overtook QPR to go top of the table, and other than losing to Everton in the League Cup, they were unbeaten from the start of the season until March 1988, when they again lost to their Merseyside rivals, this time in the league.

Goals were also flowing, with the Reds scoring four or more on 12 occasions, one of those being a special win against Brian Clough's Nottingham Forest, who were sitting third in the league table.

26

Near Perfection

Liverpool 5 Nottingham Forest 0
First Division
13 April 1988
Anfield
Attendance: 39,535

Liverpool	Nottingham Forest
Grobbelaar	Sutton
Gillespie	Chettle
Ablett	Pearce
Nicol	Walker (Wassall 46)
Spackman	Forster
Hansen	Wilson
Beardsley	Crosby
Aldridge	Webb
Houghton (Johnston 85)	Clough
Barnes	Glover
McMahon (Mølby 78)	Rice
Manager: Kenny Dalglish	*Manager:* Brian Clough

IT'S ALWAYS nice to beat one of Cloughie's teams, but at least on this occasion he did have the good grace to admit that his team had been beaten by an exceptional performance. It may have been a young Forest side, but they were third in the table, so clearly no whipping boys. Liverpool attacked Forest from the kick-off, with Beardsley outstanding in the early stages, particularly one piece of skill where he dragged the ball back, bamboozling two Forest players before shooting on goal. Unfortunately, the quality of his shot didn't live up to what went before, and it flew safely wide of the goal.

Beardsley then released McMahon, who drove across the pitch, finally releasing the ball to Nicol, who was flying up the wing. He took a few paces infield before smashing a powerful shot from the angle, which Sutton parried away for a corner.

Given their early dominance, it's surprising that it took 18 minutes for Liverpool to open their account, but when they did it was like a knife through butter. Houghton collected the ball in midfield and strode on unchallenged. He slipped the ball inside to Barnes on the edge of the penalty area, ran on for the one-two, and calmly slid the ball past Sutton while the Forest defenders looked on. Football looks such an easy game sometimes.

Barnes then nearly set up a second, sliding an inch-perfect pass through to Beardsley, but Sutton pulled off an excellent save to deny him. However, it wasn't all one-way traffic as Webb set up Nigel Clough, whose low shot was pushed out for a corner by Grobbelaar.

Sutton in the Forest goal was performing heroics to keep the scoreline down. One move saw McMahon powering forward before sending a fierce shot in on goal, which Sutton parried. Barnes was following up and looked certain to score but his shot struck the post.

However, it wasn't long before Liverpool's second goal arrived, and it was another top-class effort. On 37 minutes, Beardsley, in his own half, turned away from two defenders and sent a superb 30-yard ball through the Forest defence for Aldridge, who was clean through on goal. As Sutton came out, Aldo just lifted the ball over him and into the net in true Ian Rush style.

Beardsley was running riot and Forest simply couldn't handle him. He nearly scored what would have been a hot contender for goal of the season when he again picked the ball up deep and set off on a mazy run. Defenders backed away as he approached the penalty area, then Beardsley cut between two of them, took it past another, before sending a rasping shot past Sutton, which unfortunately crashed against the bar and away.

Beardsley had signed from Newcastle for a British record fee of £1.9m at the start of the season and was instrumental in a lot of Liverpool's attacking play, linking up the midfield and forward line and finding gaps where many others didn't know they existed. He had a magnificent football brain and seemed to be a perfect fit in this stylish Liverpool team, exemplified by his performance in this match.

Barnes and Beardsley again came so close to creating Liverpool's third goal. The Reds had a free kick about 30 yards out, and Forest expected Barnes to send in a left-foot shot. However, he passed the ball into the penalty area to Beardsley, who flicked it into the path of Houghton. It was Sutton to the rescue again, this time with his feet, and Pearce cleared the ball for a corner to relieve the danger. Somehow, the score was only 2-0 at half-time but could easily have been four or five, as Liverpool were rampant.

In the second half the pattern continued. This time Houghton was providing the opportunity, crossing to the far post. The ball was headed clear but only as far as Beardsley, who jinked through the defence, only to have his shot saved by Sutton again. However, the keeper could do nothing about Liverpool's third goal. Barnes took the resulting corner quickly, passing to Houghton on Liverpool's left. He made his way along the goal line and pulled it back to the penalty spot, where Gillespie was waiting to smash the ball into the roof of the net with his left foot.

Webb did come close for Forest with a powerful shot but that and Clough's first-half effort were as close as Forest got to Grobbelaar's goal. Beardsley, meanwhile, got the goal his dazzling performance deserved on 79 minutes. Spackman passed to Barnes on Liverpool's left. At the corner flag Barnes nutmegged Chettle, tricked his way past Crosby, then pulled it back to the edge of the penalty area, where Beardsley gratefully rifled a shot into the corner of the net.

Spackman and Barnes were soon at it again when Spackman brought the ball from the halfway line unchallenged once more. This time he played a one-two with Barnes, before cutting the ball back for Houghton, but he snatched at his shot, sending it flying over the bar.

Spackman appeared to be taking over from Beardsley in slicing through the Forest defence. With two minutes to go, he again advanced, playing a one-two with Beardsley. This time his cutback found Aldridge, who made no mistake with his finish to make it 5-0 and a scoreline that reflected Liverpool's superiority on the night.

%%%

Not only was this a superbly dominant display by the Reds but the quality of the goals was outstanding. This thrashing of Forest saw Liverpool leading the league by 11 points from Manchester United, and they were to go on to win the title when they beat Spurs with five matches remaining to take their 17th league championship.

In all, the Reds played 50 matches in 1987/88 and lost only four times. Unfortunately, one of those defeats came in the very last match of the season, when they surprisingly went down to the Crazy Gang of Wimbledon in the FA Cup Final, which prevented the Reds winning another double. Even more unfortunately, John Aldridge set a record for being the first man to miss a penalty in an FA Cup Final!

Peter Beardsley's stay at Liverpool was relatively short, just four seasons, before Graeme Souness sold him to Everton. While at Liverpool, he established himself as an England international, making 59 appearances, and in his 175 appearances for the Reds he scored over 50 goals, helping them to three league titles and an FA Cup success.

The season had seen Liverpool come agonisingly close to winning the double for the second time, but 1988/89 was to be even more agonising, as the league title was to go down to the last few seconds. However, all that was to be completely overshadowed by the events at Hillsborough on 15 April 1989.

At the start of 1988/89, Liverpool gained revenge on Wimbledon at Wembley by winning the Charity Shield, with Aldridge scoring both goals in a 2-1 victory. However, despite a promising start, league form was inconsistent, the Reds sitting fourth at the end of October, with Norwich leading the way from Arsenal.

By the time Liverpool entered the FA Cup in January 1989, they were still fourth in the table, nine points behind leaders Arsenal and having played one match more, so the chances of retaining their league title looked slim. It was actually a strange-looking league table, with Norwich in second and Millwall in third.

The Reds had a comfortable win in the third round of the FA Cup, beating Carlisle United 3-0, then went on a fantastic run of 19 wins and three draws in their next 22 matches, with the goals starting to flow again. During this run, they went through the fourth and fifth rounds of the FA Cup, disposing of Millwall and Hull, then had successive league victories, 4-0 away at Middlesbrough and 5-0 against Luton at Anfield, where Aldridge hit a hat-trick. Then it was 4-0 again, this time against Brentford in the quarter-final of the FA Cup.

After the Luton mauling, the Reds were still only fourth in the table, ten points behind Arsenal but, importantly, with two matches in hand. However, six straight league wins saw them hit top spot on goal difference from the Gunners, having played the same number of matches.

Then came the events that will remain forever etched in the hearts of everyone on Merseyside when Liverpool met Nottingham Forest in the FA Cup semi-final at Hillsborough. Even though the true facts of what happened at Hillsborough have only recently come out, the important thing to remember is that 96 football fans lost their lives after going to support their team. Initially the blame was put on 'hooligan' Liverpool supporters for being drunk, despite their claims to the contrary, but nobody was listening. However, the families and friends of those who lost their lives never gave up the fight for the truth to be revealed.

The coroner's initial report in 1999 ruled the deaths as accidental. However, calls for a further investigation were successful, and in 2012 a report found that South Yorkshire Police had falsified reports in an attempt to cover up their ineptitude. They had claimed that Liverpool fans forced their way through a gate in an attempt to get into the ground, but it subsequently came to light that Chief Superintendent David Duckenfield approved the opening of the gate, which was inadequate to deal with the 2,000-plus fans waiting to enter.

As fans rushed to get in, with kick-off imminent, there was a crush, which the police then failed to manage effectively to ensure that rescue efforts were immediately put into action. The 2012 report found that at least 41 lives could have been saved if rescue efforts had been more efficient. The initial decision of accidental death in the coroner's report was overturned.

In 2014, a further inquest began, and Duckenfield finally admitted to lying about the opening of the gate, and admitted that his failure to close the main tunnel leading to the central pens directly caused the deaths. In 2016, the jury found that the 96 victims had been unlawfully killed and criminal charges were filed against six people, including Duckenfield and the Sheffield Wednesday club secretary, Graham Mackrell, who faced charges of breaching safety laws. Mackrell was found guilty but Duckenfield, at the time I was writing this book, was undergoing a retrial, after the initial jury failed to reach a verdict. In November 2019, he was cleared of manslaughter and walked free, so still no one has been held fully accountable for the tragic events of Hillsborough.

The rearranged FA Cup semi-final was played 22 days after the first match was abandoned and was an emotional night for everyone involved. Everton had beaten Norwich in the other semi-final, so how fitting it would be for there to be a Merseyside final.

The Reds were clearly determined to get to Wembley for the 96 fans who lost their lives and for their families and the city of Liverpool. They dominated the match from the start, with Aldridge putting them ahead after only three minutes. Although Forest grabbed an equaliser half an hour later, the Reds weren't to be denied. Aldridge scored his second, then a Forest own goal sealed Liverpool's place at Wembley to face the blue side of Merseyside in a fitting tribute to those who lost their lives.

However, before the final, Liverpool had three more league matches, in which they beat Forest again, followed by victories over Wimbledon and QPR. The league leadership was changing hands, depending on whether Arsenal had played an additional league match while Liverpool played in the FA Cup. However, the Gunners slipped up at home to Derby, losing 2-1, then drew at home to Wimbledon, leaving the teams on equal points but with Liverpool having a match in hand. The teams' goal difference was equal, but Arsenal were top due to having scored more goals. The most important factor in all this though, was that the two teams were due to meet in the last match of the season.

27

A City United

Liverpool 3 Everton 2 (aet)
FA Cup Final
20 May 1989
Wembley
Attendance: 82,800

Liverpool	**Everton**
Grobbelaar	Southall
Ablett	McDonald
Staunton (Venison 91)	van den Hauwe
Nicol	Ratcliffe
Whelan	Watson
Hansen	Bracewell (McCall 58)
Beardsley	Nevin
Aldridge (Rush 72)	Steven
Houghton	Sharp
Barnes	Cottee
McMahon	Sheedy (Wilson 77)
Manager: Kenny Dalglish	*Manager:* Colin Harvey

BEFORE WHAT was to be a dramatic climax to the league season came the emotional FA Cup Final between Liverpool and Everton. Once again, Wembley was a sea of blue and red mixed together in the crowd, and a one-minute silence was held before the match kicked off, as the Union flag fluttered at half mast. Everton kicked off their 11th FA Cup Final, equalling the record held by Arsenal

174

and Newcastle. Liverpool, meanwhile, were unbeaten in 22 matches since New Year's Day. A close match was predicted.

Everton started brightly, earning an early corner, from which McMahon had to clear from the far post, although the ball looked to be going just wide. Then Liverpool had their first attack, and how devastating it was. Nicol received the ball deep in his own half but quickly passed the ball 40 yards into the path of McMahon. He got away from Ratcliffe and had Aldridge free on his left, clean through on goal. McMahon squared the ball and Aldo did the rest, smashing it into the top corner past Southall in the Everton goal. Just four minutes gone, and the Reds were ahead.

Everton pressed forward immediately for the equaliser, while Liverpool attempted to hit them on the break, and should have made it 2-0 almost immediately after taking the lead. A quick break by Houghton and Whelan sent Barnes free on the left. His curling left-foot cross was perfect for Aldridge, but his powerful diving header was just wide as Southall looked on, with no chance if it had been on target.

The Everton threat mainly seemed to be long punts up to Sharp, but Hansen was easily picking up any loose balls and setting up further Liverpool attacks, mainly through Barnes, who nearly set up a goal as he slid a low ball across the goal area, but no one was there to add the finishing touch. Liverpool seemed to be finding it easy to open up the Everton defence, and were having no scares at the other end as the first half ticked on.

Aldridge could again have added to his tally when Houghton slipped him through, but he hit his shot wide, as Liverpool looked destined to score again before half-time. However, despite their pressure, it remained only 1-0 at the break.

The second half started a bit scrappily, with both teams guilty of surrendering possession. One such occasion saw Everton give the ball away deep in their own half to Beardsley, who scampered away from Everton's trailing defenders, bearing down on Southall.

Unfortunately, he hit his shot at Southall's legs, and the ball rebounded safely. I, and many others, began to wonder whether Liverpool would live to rue these missed opportunities.

Next up was Barnes, who seemed to be finding acres of space on Liverpool's left. He ran from his own half unchallenged to the edge of Everton's penalty area, sending a low shot past Southall, but also a yard wide of the post. Another chance gone begging. Immediately after this, Everton made what was to become a crucial substitution, sending on McCall for Bracewell with half an hour to play.

This change didn't lead to any immediate improvement for Everton, as Barnes again went close with a deflected left-foot shot, this time forcing Southall to save low to his right by the post. Soon after this, Liverpool took off Aldridge, bringing on Rush for the final 18 minutes, for what was to be an even more important substitution.

Everton now had to go for it, and began to look more dangerous, McCall sending in a cross for Sharp, but Grobbelaar comfortably saved his header. However, the danger signs were there, and Liverpool couldn't afford to switch off, as Everton started to send in more crosses, in their usual direct style.

Then with just one minute to go came the moment we all dreaded after having dominated most of the match and had several chances to secure a comfortable win. After one stupid Everton fan had been cleared off the pitch, Southall sent one final long clearance upfield. Watson headed the ball on to Cottee, who flicked it inside to Sharp. He played the ball wide and a low cross was sent in, where a mass of players filled the goal area. Grobbelaar got to the cross but couldn't hold it, and it was forced home by McCall. Wembley erupted, and more Everton idiots invaded the pitch in celebration. The referee's whistle went soon afterwards to indicate extra time.

As extra time kicked off, the Everton fans were singing loudly, but as at the start of the match, their team may have started brightly but Liverpool scored within four minutes of kick-off. Nicol, now playing from the left, sent in what looked like an innocuous cross towards Rush, who had his back to goal, and Ratcliffe right behind him. Rush did a Dalglish-like turn and shot, sending Ratcliffe the wrong way, and the Reds were back in front.

However, the lead only lasted eight minutes, as McCall came to Everton's rescue once again. A free kick from the halfway line was sent high into the Liverpool defence, where it was headed clear, but straight to McCall. He chested it down and sent a superb lobbed volley past Grobbelaar for 2-2.

Then one minute later it was that man Rush again, who seemed to love scoring against his Merseyside rivals. Liverpool started with the ball by their own corner flag on the left-hand side. Two passes later they were in the Everton half on the right-hand side. A few passes later McMahon passed it out to Barnes on Liverpool's left, as they moved Everton from side to side. Barnes sent in a curling cross to the edge of Everton's goal area, where Rush stooped to help the ball on its way with his head, past a forlorn Southall, to put Liverpool back in front again. The whistle soon went to end the first half of extra time, so just 15 minutes to go. Could the Reds hang on to the lead this time?

The second half started with chants of 'Rushie is back' from the Liverpool fans, as both he and McCall aimed to be the first player since Stan Mortensen in 1953 to score a hat-trick in an FA Cup Final.

Everton continued to pump high balls up to Sharp, but the Liverpool defence were dealing with these easily. At the other end, Houghton had a chance to put the result beyond doubt when he latched on to a blocked Rush shot. Southall's feet came to the rescue to keep Everton in the match.

A few minutes later, Southall saved again, this time charging out of his goal to block Rush's shot, as gaps started to appear in Everton's defence as they pushed forward in search of the equaliser.

Barnes was next to find space when he cut in from the left wing to force Southall into another save.

There was now only one team likely to score, as Liverpool dominated play. Southall seemed to be the only thing preventing them sealing the match, as he next stretched full length to fingertip away a low Beardsley drive. Everton provided no further threat as the clock ticked on until the final whistle went and the FA Cup was to be bedecked in red ribbons.

*% *% *%

One part of the double was in the bag, and next up for Liverpool was a home match against relegation-threatened West Ham. The gulf in league positions was emphatically displayed, as Liverpool tore the Hammers apart in a magnificent second-half display, winning 5-1. As important as the three points was the fact that the Reds had improved their goal difference. They now led the league by three points and their goal difference was four better than Arsenal's. However, with the two teams meeting just three days later, a 2-0 victory for the Gunners would seal the league title for them on goals scored.

I remember this match vividly. Arsenal knew what they needed to do, but Liverpool were perhaps caught between two stools. Do you attack and try to win the match or sit back and play for a draw, or even settle for a 1-0 defeat? It can't have helped that this was Liverpool's third match in six days, and they had been through extra time at Wembley.

Liverpool didn't really threaten to win the match, falling behind on 52 minutes to an Alan Smith goal. Arsenal just needed one more, but the clock ticked on ... and on ... and on. Houghton and Aldridge both spurned opportunities to equalise but it seemed that the title was going back to Anfield as 90 minutes was up.

Then it happened. Gaps seemed to appear in the Liverpool defence from nowhere as the ball was swept forward for Michael Thomas, who was suddenly clean through on goal. Surely not!

Unfortunately, yes … he scored with virtually the last kick of the league season to win the title for Arsenal.

The Liverpool players sunk to their knees, knowing they had thrown it away in the last few seconds. They weren't the only ones on their knees, as I was on mine, head in hands, in front of the TV, not believing what I was witnessing. Some of the players have said they have never fully got over that evening. I know I haven't.

28

Aldo's Last Stand

Liverpool 9 Crystal Palace 0
First Division
12 September 1989
Anfield
Attendance: 35,779

Liverpool	Crystal Palace
Grobbelaar	Suckling
Hysén	Pemberton
Burrows	Burke
Nicol	Hopkins
Whelan	O'Reilly
Hansen	McGoldrick
Beardsley (Aldridge 66)	Pardew
Gillespie	Thomas
Rush	Gray
Barnes	Bright
McMahon (Mølby 79)	Wright
Manager: Kenny Dalglish	*Manager:* Steve Coppell

AFTER THE disappointment of the end of the previous season, 1989/90 started well for Liverpool. Prior to the meeting with Crystal Palace at Anfield, the Reds had gained some element of revenge by defeating Arsenal in the Charity Shield and were unbeaten in their first four league matches of the season. Ian Rush was now first-choice striker ahead of John Aldridge, who regularly warmed

180

the bench. Personally, I thought at this stage that Aldo was the better player, as Rushie was past his prime, although he did prove me wrong by going on to score several more important goals. I guess Kenny knew what he was doing. Aldridge wasn't content with the substitute role, however, and had agreed a move to Real Sociedad, and the Palace match was to be his last for Liverpool.

I was fortunate that a work colleague, who was a Liverpool season ticket holder, couldn't go to the match, so I ended up with two tickets to see one of my favourite players in his last match for the Reds. However, I was disappointed to find that he was again not in the starting XI.

※ ※ ※

Liverpool started the match on the front foot, applying early pressure on the inexperienced Palace team, and this paid off after only seven minutes. Barnes cut inside from the left wing and shot with his right foot, but the shot was blocked. The ball came out to Whelan on the edge of the box and he made as if to shoot, but deftly laid the ball to his right, where Nicol was free. He curled his left-foot shot into the top corner, giving Suckling no chance.

McMahon had a chance to double the lead within a few minutes, as Liverpool's passing was proving difficult for Palace to manage. The midfielder was through on goal but hit his shot wide of the mark.

Palace were mainly trying to use the speed of Ian Wright on the break but were having little success. However, they came close to an equaliser when awarded a free kick about 30 yards out. The ball was touched to Thomas, whose powerful left-foot shot beat Grobbelaar but rebounded to safety off the foot of the post.

This only stung Liverpool into action, and McMahon made amends for his earlier miss by scoring a sensational goal on 15 minutes. After good work by Beardsley, Nicol sent McMahon through on goal in an almost identical position to the one he'd found himself in earlier. This time he chipped the onrushing Suckling brilliantly, and the ball nestled in the back of the net.

It really should have been 3-0 immediately afterwards, as McMahon sent Barnes through, only for Pemberton to take him down from behind. We all waited for the referee to award the penalty, but for some reason he awarded a corner. I don't think I've ever seen a clearer foul. Justice was nearly done when Hysén met the corner with a powerful header, but it went just wide.

It took a while for Liverpool to get their third, which didn't arrive until the stroke of half-time. Barnes played a ball into the penalty area, where left-back Burrows turned it into the path of Beardsley. He jinked his way through, only to be fouled from behind as he was about to shoot, but the ball fell kindly for Rush to smash it into the net for 3-0 at the break.

Standing on the Kop, I was to see plenty of action in the second half, as Liverpool immediately went on the attack. It took only 11 minutes for the Reds to add to their tally, when Barnes flicked on a Beardsley corner for Gillespie to head in at the near post.

The Kop was chanting, 'We want five', and it only took another five minutes before we were celebrating that fifth goal. Whelan took a free kick on Liverpool's right, passing to Beardsley, who played a quick one-two with Rush before firing the ball into the top of the net.

As Aldridge started to warm up on the touchline, I was hoping that I was going to see his farewell appearance for the Reds. I clearly wasn't the only one, as the Kop started chanting, 'There's only one Johnny Aldridge'. We were soon to get our wish in unusual circumstances.

Barnes strolled forward with the ball before sending Whelan through on goal. He was tripped from behind by Hopkins and the referee this time saw the foul and awarded the penalty. Suddenly, we all noticed activity on the touchline as Aldridge started to take off his tracksuit. Off went Beardsley and on came Aldo. Barnes, the usual penalty taker, slapped him on the bum in encouragement as he made his way forward, where the ball was already on the penalty spot. After clearing a speck of dirt in front of the ball, Aldo stepped back a few yards, ran up and sent the keeper the wrong way to score the most popular goal of the night. It was his 50th league goal for the Reds in his short stay.

Perhaps the excitement got the better of Liverpool, as almost immediately, after they had played a bit of one-touch football outside their own penalty area, Pardew nipped in and Hysén rashly brought him down. We weren't too worried about a comeback at 6-0 but cheered loudly when Thomas skied his spot kick well over.

Barnes then started to turn on the style, teasing the Palace defenders with his nimble footwork, although the Eagles did enjoy a period of possession as Liverpool eased off for a while. Not for long though, and Gillespie came close to scoring his second, only to be denied by Suckling.

Gillespie then started the move that saw Barnes threading a ball through for Rush, clear on goal. Suckling came out of the penalty area, bringing Rush down as he tried to take the ball past him. Free kick, and a booking for the keeper. Barnes stood over the ball, took one step, then curled a beauty over the wall and into the top corner for 7-0, with 11 minutes still to play.

Three minutes later it was 8-0. After Whelan had been fouled on Liverpool's left, Barnes swung in the free kick, which was headed out for a corner. Barnes took the corner quickly, swinging in another cross, which was met by a powerful Hysén header for his first goal in the First Division. The Kop was now getting greedy as we called for ten, but for now it was eight goals by eight different scorers, and eight minutes left to play.

Palace then had their best spell of the match. Bright came close when he stuck his boot out to try to divert a mishit shot, but it went just over. Then Pemberton had a shot from distance, but straight at Grobbelaar. Perhaps their best chance came when Gray cut inside

Hysén and was through on goal, but Grobbelaar saved with his feet to deny Palace any consolation for their miserable evening.

Liverpool weren't done yet though, and finished the night off nicely when they scored in the final minute. Steve Nicol, who had scored the first goal, spoiled the record of having different scorers of every goal when he bagged his second. Burrows sent in a low cross, which evaded everyone but Nicol at the far post. He tucked it away for number nine.

At the final whistle, John Aldridge came to the Kop, took off his shirt and threw it into the crowd, swiftly followed by his boots. What a match to bow out in, and I was so glad I was there. He only played 104 matches for the club but scored 63 goals in that time, a fantastic record of a goal every 1.65 matches, compared to Rush's 'inferior' 1.91. Aldo also holds the club record of having scored in ten consecutive league matches. In his short stay he won a league championship medal and one FA Cup, but he could have won so much more if he'd stuck around a bit longer.

※ ※ ※

This magnificent victory was part of an eight-match unbeaten run in the league that saw the Reds sitting top, again with the Gunners in close pursuit. However, four defeats in their next seven matches saw them slip to third, as Chelsea led the way. The rivalry with Arsenal was also gaining momentum as the Gunners had dumped the Reds out of the League Cup in the third round, although one of Liverpool's league victories in this poor spell was against Arsenal at Anfield.

What came next was another of those great runs of matches that Liverpool had become renowned for. Following their defeat to Sheffield Wednesday at the end of November, the Reds played 31 more matches, including an FA Cup run to the semi-final stage. The record read: won 19, drawn 10, lost 2, and only one of those defeats was in the league. The other defeat? Ironically, a 4-3 defeat by Palace in the FA Cup semi-final, when the Reds were hot favourites to reach the final yet again.

The run included 20 matches unbeaten, until Spurs beat them 1-0 at White Hart Lane, although the number of draws early in this run meant that Aston Villa were still well in contention for the league title, and actually led the league after the Spurs setback.

There were some outstanding performances too, notably beating championship rivals Chelsea 5-2 at Stamford Bridge, then 4-1 at Anfield, hammering Swansea 8-0 in the FA Cup after having drawn 0-0 at the Vetch, and a 6-1 victory in the final match of the season against Coventry City.

However, this final match was just the icing on the cake, as Liverpool had already sealed their 18th league title two matches previously when they beat QPR 2-1 to leave them nine points clear of Aston Villa with only two matches to play. Who would have thought that their search for a 19th league title would go on for so long?

29

A Thriller at Elland Road

Leeds United 4 Liverpool 5
First Division
13 April 1991
Elland Road
Attendance: 31,460

Leeds United	**Liverpool**
Lukic	Hooper
Sterland	Hysén
Whitlow	Burrows
Batty	Nicol
Fairclough	Mølby
Whyte	Staunton
Strachan	Beardsley
Shutt	Houghton
Chapman	Rush
McAllister	Barnes
Speed	Speedie
Manager: Howard Wilkinson	*Manager:* Ronnie Moran

LIVERPOOL STARTED 1990/91 the way they had finished the previous season, winning their first eight league matches, as well as getting through two rounds of the League Cup. The rest of the teams must have thought 'here we go again', as the Reds already had a six-point lead over Arsenal. The fifth match of this run was a particularly satisfying one, as the Reds put Alex Ferguson's

Manchester United to the sword, beating them 4-0, after having drawn with them to share the Charity Shield in the season's opener. However, the perfect start to the season was brought to an end with a 1-1 draw at Norwich, but the Reds still led the league comfortably for a few more weeks, until they came down with a bump after a 3-0 reversal at Arsenal, which reduced the gap at the top to just two points. Then a run of three draws meant that the lead had gone, and Arsenal were top on goal difference, although Liverpool had a match in hand.

Then came a match that was to change the season for the Reds and lead to Kenny Dalglish resigning as manager. Liverpool had drawn Everton at Anfield in the fifth round of the FA Cup, which ended goalless. Then came an amazing replay at Goodison Park that went to extra time and in which Liverpool led four times, only to be pegged back each time for a 4-4 draw.

The next morning, Kenny Dalglish announced that he wanted to step down from the manager's post with immediate effect, citing that he desperately needed a break from the stresses of management. Later, he admitted that the events of Hillsborough had taken a greater toll on him than he'd realised, and when you see pictures of him at that time, you can see the emotional strain etched on his face. It was affecting his personal life, so it was time to go.

Ronnie Moran stepped into the breach until a permanent successor could be found, having been at the club in one role or other since 1949, so he knew his way around. However, it didn't start well for him when the Reds lost their next three matches, including a defeat to Everton in the second replay in the FA Cup, and a 1-0 defeat to rivals Arsenal in the league that gave the Gunners a three-point advantage at the top of the table.

Despite a 7-1 victory over Derby County that temporarily took the Reds back to the top, two successive defeats and a draw saw them slip eight points behind Arsenal, albeit with one match in hand. The league title seemed to be heading to North London.

Then came another high-scoring match that started a three-match winning sequence that kept Liverpool's title hopes alive. Opponents Leeds were sitting fourth but 17 points behind leaders Arsenal, so with no chance of winning the league.

%. %. %.

On a bumpy Elland Road pitch, Leeds went on the attack from the start, with Shutt having the first attempt on goal, outpacing Staunton, who was, unusually, playing in the centre of defence. Shutt's shot was straight at stand-in keeper Mike Hooper, but he fumbled it, thankfully recovering the ball before the striker could get to it. Leeds kept this early pressure on, forcing successive corners, as Liverpool were unsettled in their reorganised defence.

However, the Reds sprang into action, with Barnes marauding down the left flank before sending in a wicked cross. Speedie arrived at the far post but couldn't quite make contact with an attempted diving header, as the Leeds defence struggled to keep pace with Liverpool's counter-attack.

Then, on 11 minutes, Liverpool took the lead following a free kick on the halfway line. The ball was fed to Rush in the penalty area, where he controlled it and laid it back to Barnes. After a bit of nifty footwork, Barnes chipped a perfect ball to the far post, where Houghton moved in unmarked to meet it first time to shoot past Lukic.

Just five minutes later it was 2-0 when Barnes played the ball forward to Rush, who allowed the ball to run through his legs to Beardsley and moved into the penalty area to receive the first-time ball from his strike partner. Rush took the ball past Lukic but was felled for a penalty. Up stepped Mølby to convert the spot kick, sending Lukic the wrong way.

It was turning out to be similar to the big victory over Manchester United earlier in the season, with the opposition forcing the pace but Liverpool scoring the goals when the opportunities arose. Liverpool's clinical finishing was proving the difference once again, as they showed on 25 minutes. Having had a goal disallowed for offside just a few minutes earlier, a similar situation saw Barnes free on the left after a brilliant pass by Mølby. Barnes stroked the ball towards the far post, where Speedie smashed the ball into the roof of the net for 3-0.

Just three minutes later it appeared that the match was well and truly over. This time Barnes exchanged passes with Mølby and Rush, before striding through unchallenged and sliding the ball past Lukic for number four. It was turning into a true masterclass, as the Leeds defence was being torn to shreds. Four goals in 28 minutes – how many more would they score?

Well, no more before half-time as it turned out. In fact, there appeared to be no sign of the goal fest that was to come during the early stages of the second half, and I'm sure that Liverpool would have quite happily settled for the 4-0 scoreline after 90 minutes.

Leeds were starting to make a fight of it at least, Speed having a volley at goal diverted by his own player, with Hooper scrambling across his goal. Then on 68 minutes came a goal that would change the direction of the match, although from the muted Leeds players' celebrations you wouldn't have thought it at the time. After Sterland and Strachan had made progress down the Leeds right, the ball came out to McAllister. His scuffed shot from distance was saved by Hooper but it fell to Chapman in the goal area, and he knocked it into the empty net to give the Leeds fans something to sing about.

Liverpool soon had a chance to reinstate their four-goal advantage when Rush was sent clear through on goal by Barnes, but he shot well wide. Then the Reds were made to pay for this rare miss when Leeds scored their second. After having a goal disallowed for a foul by Chapman on Hooper, Liverpool were starting to look rattled in defence, as Leeds applied pressure. A long throw-in deep into the Liverpool penalty area evaded the defenders and fell to the feet of Shutt, who turned and shot into the goal from close range.

As the noise levels in Elland Road were turned up another notch, it looked as if Leeds could stage a mighty comeback. However, the crowd were quietened when 4-2 became 5-2 just two minutes later. Barnes nodded the ball on to Rush, who back-heeled it into the path of Barnes, who had continued his run. Barnes coolly shot past Lukic to dampen Leeds' hopes. Or so we all thought.

The goals just kept on coming. Two minutes later, a rare misplaced pass by Mølby was immediately crossed into the Liverpool penalty area by Batty, and Chapman was on hand to head past Hooper to reduce Liverpool's lead to 5-3 in what was turning out to be a frantic ending to the match.

Then on 88 minutes came the goal that really gave Leeds hope. Chapman had been beaten to a cross by Hooper, but his punched clearance fell to Strachan. He brilliantly made his way to the byline before standing up a cross to the far post where Chapman was waiting to head in his third. The crowd went absolutely wild, as did the players, thinking that this could be the comeback of all time. Fortunately, there wasn't time for Leeds to snatch an equaliser and Liverpool breathed a sigh of relief when the referee blew the final whistle to end this classic match.

A week after the Leeds match, Graeme Souness was appointed as Liverpool's manager. The spectacle at Elland Road may have deserved inclusion in my book for its drama but, in the end, it counted for nothing, as two away defeats under the new manager handed the title to Arsenal, and Liverpool ended the season empty-handed.

30

Michael Thomas, All Is Forgiven

Liverpool 2 Sunderland 0
FA Cup Final
9 May 1992
Wembley
Attendance: 79,544

Liverpool	Sunderland
Grobbelaar	Norman
Jones	Owers
Burrows	Ball
Nicol	Bennett
Mølby	Rogan
Wright	Rush (Hardyman 68)
Saunders	Bracewell
Houghton	Davenport
Rush	Armstrong
McManaman	Byrne
Thomas	Atkinson (Hawke 78)
Manager: Graeme Souness	*Manager:* Malcolm Crosby

WITH EX-PLAYING hero Souness now in charge for his first full season, 1991/92 started full of hope that Liverpool would be able to regain the league championship from the grasp of Arsenal. However, this was no longer the Liverpool team of old, and they had started to show signs of weakness in the last few weeks of Dalglish's reign.

They started the season quite well and, for Souness, a 3-1 Merseyside derby victory at Anfield in the fifth match of the season must have gone some way towards winning the supporters over.

English teams had returned to European competition in the previous season, but for Liverpool, with the additional year's ban, it was their first time back, this time in the UEFA Cup. They had a comfortable first-round victory over the Finnish team, Kuusysi Lahti, 6-1 at home, then won 1-0 away.

However, their league form was stuttering, and by the time of the UEFA Cup second round, they were tenth in the table, as Manchester United and Leeds battled it out at the top. Then the UEFA Cup seemed to be beyond them when they lost 2-0 away to Auxerre, but on one of those great European comebacks at Anfield, a Walters goal seven minutes from time sealed a 3-0 victory to see them through.

In the third round they met Austrian team Swarovski Tirol, winning 2-0 in the away leg, but this was followed by an embarrassing defeat in the League Cup fourth round at Third Division Peterborough United, despite playing a full-strength team. However, the UEFA Cup run continued when they defeated Tirol 4-0 in the second leg, to go through 6-0 on aggregate.

It looked as though cup success may be the only route to silverware, however, as the Reds were still struggling in tenth position in the league, having drawn eight of their 17 matches, but things then improved by the time the Reds entered the FA Cup at the third-round stage in January 1992, having moved up to fifth in the table. Liverpool were only 11 points adrift, although this looked to be too much ground to make up in the final few months of the season.

The FA Cup third round brought a comfortable 4-0 victory at Crewe, Barnes hitting a hat-trick to add to McManaman's opener, but the fourth round was a closer encounter, as the Reds struggled past Second Division Bristol Rovers 2-1 in a replay. They had fallen behind in the first half but McManaman and Saunders scored after the break to prevent the giant-killing. They also needed a replay and extra time in the fifth round to get past Ipswich, finally coming through 3-2, with McManaman again on the scoresheet, along with Houghton and Mølby.

Unfortunately, European success in their first year back wasn't to be. Following a 2-0 defeat in the first leg away to Genoa, the Reds surprisingly succumbed 2-1 at home to lose 4-1 on aggregate. In between the two legs, they did progress to the semi-final of the FA Cup though, beating Aston Villa 1-0 at Anfield thanks to Michael Thomas's winner. Yes, that's Michael Thomas, the man who broke Liverpool players' and fans' hearts in 1989. He'd signed for the Reds only three months previously as an exciting young midfield player with an eye for goal ... as Liverpool knew to their cost.

In the FA Cup semi-final, Liverpool faced Second Division Portsmouth, with only the cup left to play for. Despite moving up to fourth in the league, they were 12 points behind Manchester United, and were to win only two more league matches in the remaining month of the season, slipping to a disappointing sixth, as Leeds became champions.

The FA Cup semi-final against Portsmouth at Highbury was to be a tough affair. It ended goalless after 90 minutes, but a major shock looked to be on the cards when Pompey took the lead with only nine minutes remaining of extra time. Liverpool were also down to ten men after McManaman left the field injured, with both substitutes having already been used.

However, with only three minutes remaining, Liverpool equalised through Whelan to save them from the possibility of a second successive season without a trophy.

The replay at Villa Park eight days later again ended goalless, even after extra time. Portsmouth, after defending valiantly, had nearly stolen the match three minutes from normal time but were unlucky to see McLoughlin's shot hit the bar. Now, after only six days previously having undergone triple heart bypass surgery, Graeme Souness was watching a penalty shoot-out from his hospital bed. Fortunately, Portsmouth missed three of their first four penalties to ease any stress, and successes for Barnes, Rush and Saunders meant that Liverpool won 3-1 for a place in the FA Cup Final against Second Division Sunderland.

%. %. %.

Although Graeme Souness was back in charge of team matters for the final, Ronnie Moran led the team out at Wembley. Also back was Steve McManaman, following a month's lay-off following that ankle injury in the semi-final.

Sunderland, who had previously won the FA Cup as a Second Division team, famously beating Dirty Leeds in 1973, settled well into the match, putting early pressure on the Liverpool defence. But suddenly, up the other end, Thomas was clean through after Houghton fed the ball through to meet his intelligent run. However, unlike when he scored for the Gunners against the Reds, he skied the ball over as the Sunderland keeper, Norman, went to ground.

Sunderland didn't sit back, which made it an open start to the match, as both teams broke forward quickly and positively. First Sunderland had a three-on-three break, but Byrne opted to shoot from distance, hitting it straight at Grobbelaar. Then Liverpool broke, and a dangerous Nicol cross was headed over his own bar by Armstrong, as Norman was left flapping. Although the corner was initially cleared, the ball was soon fed back into the penalty area, where Wright was still forward, nodding it down to Ian Rush. Unfortunately, he was stretching for his shot and Norman was able to gather the ball comfortably, low down to his left.

Liverpool then started to play the ball around, with Mølby controlling matters, and Sunderland were left chasing the ball for a while. However, the Reds weren't creating chances, and Sunderland, when they had the opportunity, piled men forward, looking dangerous. In fact, they came close to taking the lead when Rogan lashed in a low shot towards Grobbelaar's right-hand post. Taking no chances, Brucie got down to push it out for a corner, but had Liverpool fans worried when he collided with the post and needed treatment.

From the resulting corner Sunderland had another opportunity when Byrne found himself free a few yards out but he completely miskicked, much to the relief of the hordes of Liverpool fans.

Liverpool continued to look shaky in central defence. Although Wright won a header to clear the ball from a long Sunderland throw-in, Mølby played what was perhaps too cool a pass to Jones in the penalty area. Jones hesitated momentarily, allowing Davenport to shoot through his legs, but fortunately Wright was in the way to block the shot, with Grobbelaar seemingly beaten.

As well as looking dangerous going forward, Sunderland were well organised defensively, allowing Liverpool no room and tackling fiercely, as the Reds struggled to get to grips with them. Could another Sunderland cup final shock be on the cards?

Although Liverpool did improve in the closing minutes of the first half, they still didn't really threaten to score, although McManaman was beginning to get more of the ball and at least forced Norman into a save from a dangerous cross. Dean Saunders also got free moments later, but Norman saved his shot from distance comfortably.

Then just before half-time Liverpool should have been awarded a penalty. McManaman had switched to the right-hand side and ghosted past two tackles before heading to the byline. Bracewell slid in and took his legs away but somehow the referee failed to see the foul. So, it remained goalless at half-time, but perhaps the effort that Sunderland had put into the first half hour would lead them to tire in the second half.

It certainly didn't look like it when the second half kicked off though. Sunderland again won the ball in midfield and forced a corner, which Grobbelaar did well to punch clear. The ball was lobbed back in, but this time Grobbelaar made a clean catch. He quickly threw the ball out to Houghton on the Liverpool left. He took the ball forward before passing inside to Mølby, who took the ball to the halfway line, then sent a long ball out to McManaman on the right. He beat one man on the outside before cutting in and flicking a brilliant ball into the penalty area, where Thomas had got forward. Thomas let the ball bounce and, as it sat up, volleyed brilliantly over Norman for a stunning goal. As the camera panned to Graeme Souness, someone was sitting behind him, seemingly restraining him from getting up and jumping around.

The goal came just two minutes into the second half and the mood of the match seemed to change, as Liverpool's expected superiority began to tell. They were now winning challenges and passing the ball around more fluently. The switch of McManaman to the right was also paying dividends, as he had the beating of Armstrong and Rogan every time.

On the hour mark, the sun finally came out, and Sunderland were literally chasing shadows, as some of Liverpool's intricate play was mesmerising at times. However, they created no clear chances to increase their lead, and Sunderland were still in the match, with Byrne always a threat to the Liverpool central defenders.

On 66 minutes it looked as if Saunders had doubled the lead when he rose to meet a Nicol cross, but his header rebounded off the bar to safety. However, just a minute later the Reds finally killed the match off through Ian Rush. Again, the move started from deep in the Liverpool half, with Burrows winning the ball and passing to Nicol, who fed it on to Houghton. He moved it forward to Saunders, who had come off his marker to receive the ball halfway inside the Sunderland half. Saunders turned and ran at the defenders, slipping the ball to Thomas, who was again marauding forward. Thomas's first touch was a little heavy as he tried to take the ball past the defender, but it fell into the path of Rush, who was his usual deadly self, slotting the ball past Norman.

Five minutes later we nearly witnessed an extraordinary goal when Norman raced out to clear, beating Rush to the ball. The keeper's clearance reached the centre circle but went straight to Houghton, who hit it back first time over Norman. The keeper was struggling to get back to his goal but, fortunately for him, the ball bounced inside the goal area and went over the bar. Then Liverpool again nearly had a third when a scintillating break ended with Saunders forcing a fine save from Norman, as Sunderland appeared to be wilting.

Liverpool controlled the remainder of the match, with Sunderland gamely chasing but getting nowhere and the Reds looking as if they could score with every attack. However, despite their superiority, and Saunders coming close with a rasping shot in the final seconds, they failed to add to the scoreline and 2-0 it remained, to give Liverpool their fifth FA Cup.

Although there had been sparkling displays by McManaman and Saunders in the second half, it was Thomas who had ignited the spark that led to Liverpool's victory, scoring that superb goal and playing a large part in the second goal. His arrival from Arsenal may have been a surprise and not welcomed by many supporters but his opening goal in this match certainly improved his standing at Anfield. He stayed for seven years, making over 150 appearances but only scoring 12 goals, so not perhaps the goalscoring midfielder we expected, but we can forgive him that for helping the Reds to win the FA Cup.

31

Robbie's Four-Minute
Hat-Trick

Liverpool 3 Arsenal 0
Premier League
28 August 1994
Anfield
Attendance: 30,017

Liverpool	Arsenal
James	Seaman
Jones	Dixon
Nicol	Winterburn
Bjørnebye	Jensen (Linighan 75)
Ruddock	Keown
Barnes	Adams
Mølby (Thomas 57)	Campbell
Redknapp	Wright
McManaman	Smith
Rush	Merson (Davis 75)
Fowler	Schwarz
Manager: Roy Evans	*Manager:* George Graham

AFTER THEIR FA Cup success, what followed were two
years of struggle for Liverpool. In 1992/93, the first season of
the Premier League, they finished sixth, went out in the second
round of the European Cup Winners' Cup, the third round of

198

the FA Cup and the fourth round of the League Cup, as pressure grew on Souness.

The following season was even worse, as they slumped to eighth in the league, and again went out early in the two domestic cup competitions. Souness didn't make it to the end of the season, having resigned in January 1994 after an embarrassing defeat to Second Division Bristol City in the FA Cup. His replacement was another Liverpool stalwart, Roy Evans, who had originally joined the club as a 17-year-old player, and had been working with the reserve team.

The following season, 1994/95, started well, with a 6-1 victory away at Crystal Palace. Then next up it was Arsenal at Anfield for a sterner test of Liverpool's promising signs of improvement.

What follows is not an account of the match, as in other chapters, but simply a report on 273 seconds that destroyed Arsenal and showed the wonderful talent of 19-year-old Toxteth-born Robbie Fowler. He'd turned professional just two years previously and made his debut at the start of the 1993/94 season, scoring in a 3-1 victory over Fulham in the League Cup. In fact, he made a remarkable start to his Liverpool career, scoring his first hat-trick in only his fifth match, and netting 13 times in his first 15 matches.

*** *** ***

The start of the match against Arsenal showed no signs of what was to come, and the Gunners had coped easily with Liverpool's strike threat for the first 25 minutes. Then came a devastating spell of football and finishing that left Arsenal reeling, and the match over in terms of the result.

Goal 1 (25 mins 58 secs) – Fowler scored the opening goal from close range after a Redknapp free kick had fallen into his path via Rush.

Goal 2 (28 mins 42 secs) – Liverpool sprung forward from deep, with Jones passing to McManaman, who stormed forward through the Arsenal midfield before finding Fowler on the left of the Arsenal penalty area. Robbie squeezed his shot through Dixon's legs, beating the unsighted Seaman, and it went in off the far post.

Goal 3 (30 mins 31 secs) – Fowler completed his fast-fire hat-trick after Barnes had exchanged passes with Bjørnebye, before spotting Robbie's run into space. Barnes lifted the ball over the Arsenal defence, leaving Fowler with only Seaman to beat. Although his first shot was saved by the keeper, Robbie followed it up, controlled it before it went out for a corner, then tapped it into the net with his right foot from an acute angle.

Fowler's hat-trick in only four minutes and 33 seconds was the fastest in the Premier League until Sadio Mané scored a hat-trick in only two minutes and 56 seconds in Southampton's 6-1 win against Aston Villa on 16 May 2015. For the Reds, it was two matches, two wins and nine goals scored.

Fowler left Liverpool in 2001 to play for Leeds, then Manchester City, but returned to the Reds in January 2006, playing the 2006/07 season before moving on again. He played over 360 matches for Liverpool, scoring 183 goals, and should have achieved more than the measly 26 international caps that he did. During what was a lean spell for the Reds, he still managed to win an FA Cup, League Cup and UEFA Cup, while also receiving the PFA Young Player of the Year award in 1995 and 1996.

I recently had the pleasure of watching him play for Liverpool Legends against AC Milan, and was thrilled when he scored the opening goal, showing that he'd lost none of his predatory awareness in the box.

※ ※ ※

The Arsenal victory was the second of three straight wins for Liverpool in what was a very promising start to the 1994/95 season. In the League Cup, the Reds progressed past Burnley, 6-1 on aggregate, and Stoke City, 2-1, to set up a fourth-round clash with Blackburn Rovers, who by mid-October were sitting top of the

Premier League. Liverpool were down to fourth, but just six points adrift and still in the title race.

Kenny Dalglish had made his managerial comeback, and was now in charge at Blackburn. This was a team with Tim Flowers, Graeme Le Saux, Tim Sherwood, Chris Sutton and Alan Shearer, but they were no match for Liverpool in the League Cup as Ian Rush hit a hat-trick to seal a 3-1 victory. However, Kenny was to show his managerial credentials this season, as Blackburn went on to win the Premier League, with Liverpool improving on recent seasons to finish fourth.

In the League Cup fifth round, Liverpool were drawn at home to Arsenal, going through 1-0 and sealing a semi-final tie with Crystal Palace, who the Reds had beaten 6-1 in the first match of the season, but had only drawn with at home.

The semi-final was over two legs, with Liverpool claiming a narrow 1-0 advantage in the first leg at Anfield, Fowler scoring an injury-time goal. And it was the same man who sealed their place in the final when he struck at Selhurst Park after 27 minutes to make it 2-0 on aggregate, with no further addition to the score.

In their next match, the Reds were dumped out of the FA Cup in the sixth round by Spurs, so the League Cup was their only hope of silverware this season. Prior to the final, they had a couple of decent results, beating Manchester United 2-0 at Anfield and securing a goalless draw at Spurs, so confidence must have been high going into the Wembley final. Their opponents Bolton Wanderers were challenging for promotion from the Second Division, having been promoted from the Third Division only two seasons previously, so Liverpool were red-hot favourites.

It wasn't exactly a thrilling final or a great performance by the Reds, but these were hard times, so any silverware during this lean period was welcomed. Bolton should perhaps have taken the lead after 30 minutes and had other chances, but Steve McManaman was to make them pay by scoring a magnificent double to seal

Liverpool's fifth League Cup win and, with an improved league position over recent years, showed that they were potentially on their way back to the top.

%%%

Despite a couple of early league defeats in 1995/96, it certainly looked as though Roy Evans was starting to pull things around and would bring success back to Anfield. It was nice to win the League Cup, but the Premier League, FA Cup and a return to European glory were what the team and the fans really yearned for.

By the end of October, despite those two early setbacks, the Reds were third in the league, with Newcastle and Manchester United above them. There had been some good performances too, notably a 3-1 win away at Spurs, a 3-0 home win over champions Blackburn, a 5-2 home win against Bolton and a 6-0 crushing of Manchester City at Anfield. The latter match came only three days after Liverpool had beaten the same opponents 4-0 in the League Cup third round, having previously got past Sunderland in round two.

In Europe, the Reds were in the UEFA Cup and had a tough trip to play Spartak Vladikavkaz in Russia, but came through with a 2-1 advantage to take to Anfield. A goalless draw at home was enough to send the Reds through to play Danish team Brøndby in the second round. After a goalless first leg in Denmark, Liverpool looked set to progress, but were surprisingly beaten 1-0 at home as they appeared to be failing to get to grips with their return to European football.

Liverpool's promising form then went out of the window for a few weeks, losing three and drawing one of their next four league matches, and they were sent out of the League Cup by a resurgent Newcastle, now under manager Kevin Keegan.

Following this defeat, however, an excellent run to the end of the season saw the Reds play 30 matches, winning 18, drawing nine and losing only three times. This run saw them climb from seventh in the table to finish third, but they were never quite in contention for the title, as Newcastle seemed to be stretching away from them and Manchester United for most of the season. However, events at Anfield in April 1996 were to send Newcastle, and Kevin Keegan in particular, into total meltdown.

32

Newcastle Get the Collywobbles

Liverpool 4 Newcastle United 3

Premier League
3 April 1996
Anfield
Attendance: 40,702

Liverpool	**Newcastle United**
James	Srnicek
Jones (Rush 86)	Watson
McAteer	Beresford
Wright (Harkness 46)	Batty
Collymore	Albert
Barnes	Howey (Peacock 82)
Scales	Lee
Redknapp	Beardsley
McManaman	Ferdinand
Fowler	Ginola
Ruddock	Asprilla
Manager: Roy Evans	*Manager:* Kevin Keegan

DURING THE 1995/96 season, Liverpool fans were soon to see why the club had splashed out a British record fee of £8.5m for Stan Collymore from Nottingham Forest. Having already scored on his debut, he hit a hat-trick in the third round of the FA Cup

204

in a resounding 7-0 victory over Rochdale. In the fourth round he was on the scoresheet again as the Reds beat Shrewsbury 4-0 to set up a fifth-round tie against Second Division Charlton at Anfield. This one was much tighter, the Reds scraping through 2-1, thanks to goals by Fowler and Collymore.

The quarter-final took the Reds to Elland Road, where they battled to a goalless draw against Leeds. However, the replay was a much easier affair, a comfortable 3-0 win gaining them a place in the semi-final at Old Trafford against Aston Villa. Again, it was a comfortable 3-0 win for the Reds, which meant they would be facing the old enemy Manchester United in the final.

United were chasing the double, and Newcastle had got stage fright by this point in the season. The two Uniteds were now level on points and Liverpool were five points adrift but, with only seven matches remaining, their championship hopes were faint. Newcastle had a match in hand, but that match was at Anfield on what was to become a night to remember.

※ ※ ※

When you look at the Newcastle line-up, you can see why they were having a good season, with a strike force that included Peter Beardsley, Les Ferdinand, David Ginola and Tino Asprilla. They also had quality in Philipe Albert, David Batty and Rob Lee, but maybe this match showed why they wouldn't win the league, as their defensive quality didn't match up to their striking prowess.

The match got off to an exhilarating start when Fowler scored after just two minutes, and it all started from the other end of the pitch with a Liverpool goal kick. After several passes, the ball was worked out to the left wing to Collymore, whose deep cross was met by Fowler's headed goal, and Newcastle were stunned.

The Magpies may have been happy to settle for a point before the match, but now they knew they had to attack, and that's just what they did. First, Ferdinand worked the ball on to his left foot outside the penalty area but drove his shot straight at James in the

Liverpool goal. Then Ginola weaved his way inside before shooting, but again James wasn't troubled.

However, the Liverpool keeper was left embarrassed on ten minutes, when he somehow failed to save Ferdinand's fierce shot. From a Newcastle throw-in on their right, Asprilla tricked his way through, before pulling the ball back to Ferdinand. The striker controlled the ball with his back towards goal, then turned and shot straight at James. Somehow the ball seemed to go straight through the keeper's hands and in. Even Ferdinand couldn't believe it.

Liverpool were rattled, especially as the Newcastle forward line was putting pressure on their defenders as they tried to play the ball out from the back. Newcastle were now on the front foot, and on 14 minutes took the lead. After breaking down a Liverpool attack, Newcastle moved the ball forward quickly, and suddenly Ginola was through on goal after a Ferdinand pass. He slotted the ball past James to send the Newcastle fans wild. It had been a frantic first quarter of an hour, played at an incredible pace, and the atmosphere in Anfield was electric, as both teams showed their attacking intent and defensive frailties.

Liverpool started to gain more possession after falling behind, with Redknapp controlling things in midfield and spraying the passes around. In fact, it was Redknapp who next came close to scoring when he exchanged passes with Collymore before driving forward and unleashing a rasping shot that went just wide.

The frantic pace continued, which had an effect on some of the quality, as the ball was given away too often by both teams, as tackles were flying in. Fowler had a good opportunity to equalise after one such exchange when Redknapp's cross fell at his feet in the penalty area. Fowler quickly controlled and shifted the ball to his favoured left foot, but his instinctive shot went inches wide.

Liverpool started to dominate as the first half wore on, but Newcastle, now they were ahead, got more players behind the ball and defended stoutly, preventing any clear opportunities on goal.

Meanwhile, they created nothing themselves, being prepared to play on the break, but failing to make any inroads into the Liverpool defence, which was now looking more settled.

As half-time approached, the Reds missed a golden opportunity to equalise. After Asprilla had tripped himself over in the Liverpool penalty area, inevitably claiming a penalty, Liverpool broke quickly through McManaman on Liverpool's left. The ball was fed out to the right wing for McAteer to put in a deep cross. McManaman had continued his forward run and had a free header but chose to head it across rather than going for goal. Even then, they could have scored, as Fowler dived forward in an attempt to divert the ball goalwards, but couldn't quite reach it, so 2-1 to Newcastle it remained at the break.

In the second half, the pace didn't relent, and Newcastle came close to stretching their lead just two minutes after the restart. Ruddock played a loose ball out from the back, and Lee pounced on it, driving forward unchallenged. As he got into the penalty area, James came out to smother his shot.

Then it was Liverpool's turn to attack, McManaman being set free down their left. Unfortunately, he had no one to cross to, such was the pace of the attack, but he shot from a tight angle and forced Srnicek to parry the ball over for a corner. From the corner McManaman again tested Srnicek from distance, as Liverpool put the pressure on, trying to force the equaliser.

This pressure was starting to tell on Newcastle, who regularly gave the ball away as those in red shirts closed them down quickly, won the ball back and continued to attack in waves. The pressure nearly told on 53 minutes when Scales had a free header from a corner. He directed it on goal but also straight at Fowler, who attempted to redirect it past Srnicek but got way too much contact on it and headed it wide.

Then two minutes later Fowler made up for his miss, scoring to level the match at 2-2. After Ginola's shot had been blocked and fallen safely into the arms of James, Liverpool broke quickly, first through McAteer, then through McManaman on their right. He carried the ball into the penalty area, where four Newcastle defenders backed off, not knowing what he was going to do next. He simply squared it to Fowler, who met the ball with a left-foot drive past Srnicek.

Suddenly, the match was changing, and Newcastle knew they could no longer sit back, as inviting Liverpool on was asking for trouble. The Reds kept the pressure on, sensing the win, with Redknapp putting McManaman through with a long pass, but Srnicek raced out of the penalty area to head clear.

Then just two minutes after Fowler's equaliser, the match changed again. Beardsley did well to release Lee, who raced over the halfway line before splitting Liverpool's defence with a brilliant pass to Asprilla. Tino did the rest, slotting it past the advancing James to put Newcastle back in front, and send Kevin Keegan racing from his seat in celebration.

What should Newcastle do now? Sit back and try to protect their lead, knowing that Liverpool's attacking prowess would more than likely get the better of them, or continue to attack? For Liverpool, there was only one thing – attack. They continued to pass the ball around calmly, not panicking, and nearly created a carbon copy of Fowler's second goal, when McManaman again set him up, but this time his shot was straight at Srnicek. Then the roles were swapped as Fowler set up McManaman, but he hit a weak shot at the keeper.

On 68 minutes, the scores were level again, as Liverpool broke quickly once more when Asprilla lost the ball on the halfway line. McAteer, who was having increasing success on Liverpool's right, getting forward from his right-back berth, put in a low curling cross to the far post, behind the Newcastle defence, where Collymore crept in to knock it past Srnicek for 3-3.

With the atmosphere red hot, Liverpool continued to surge forward in search of their fourth goal, but Newcastle were still dangerous on the break, particularly through Ginola and Asprilla. However, there now looked to be only one team likely to score and, on 75 minutes, the Reds couldn't have come closer. McManaman put in yet another cross, this time low to the edge of the goal area, where Fowler somehow got a foot to it, but it deflected off Howey and went agonisingly wide.

However, Liverpool couldn't relax and, just minutes later, Ferdinand outmuscled Harkness but James was quickly out to block his shot. Newcastle's chances were rare though, and Liverpool continued to attack the Kop end, Barnes forcing his way through and bringing a good save from Srnicek as the pulsating tempo of the match continued.

On 86 minutes, Liverpool showed their intent to win the match when they sent on Rush for left-back Jones. They now had a forward line of Collymore, Fowler and Rush, with McManaman pulling the strings behind them, relishing his free role.

Given the way the match had gone, it was amazing that there had been no further goals for a whole 22 minutes, as the match reached its climax. Keegan was looking tense on the bench, now perhaps happy to take a point to narrow the gap on Manchester United. However, if he was happy with the draw, he didn't get this message across to his players, as they surged forward, seeking the winner.

And they had their chance. Liverpool fans' hearts were in their mouths when Ruddock fouled Asprilla on the edge of the penalty area with only three minutes remaining. Ginola and Asprilla stood over the ball, both capable of producing that moment of brilliance that would surely seal the match for Newcastle. However, Asprilla tapped it square to Ferdinand, whose shot sailed well over the bar.

Liverpool were soon back on the attack though, Redknapp shooting from distance and forcing Srnicek to punch clear. But the clock was ticking down and the match moved into stoppage time, seemingly heading for a draw, as the ball went back to James in the Liverpool goal.

The keeper bowled it out to Ruddock, and Liverpool quickly moved forward again, surely for the last time. The ball was worked up to Barnes, 30 yards out. He interchanged passes with Rush but, as they got into the penalty area, they got in each other's way in their desperation to score. The ball was at Barnes's feet, and he looked up to his left and saw Collymore moving forward. Barnes slid the ball wide, into Collymore's path, and Stan controlled it with his right foot before driving a fierce left-foot shot past Srnicek to leave the net bulging.

What a fitting climax to a fantastic match. The Kop went absolutely crazy, Collymore went on a lap of honour and Kevin Keegan sat with his head in his hands. Just a minute later the referee ended the match and Liverpool had won one of the greatest matches ever witnessed at Anfield.

‰ ‰ ‰

Despite the thrills and spills of this match, it meant that Manchester United remained top of the league. Liverpool's faint hopes of the title disappeared when they lost their next match to Coventry. Manchester United, as they did back then, continued to win, and Newcastle continued to blow their chances. The Red Devils won the league by four points, with Liverpool third, 11 points behind them.

Unfortunately, the Mancs also got the better of Liverpool at Wembley, winning 1-0, in what has to be the most boring FA Cup Final ever. I have to admit that I wasn't even bothered when Eric Cantona scored with five minutes to go, as I just wanted the match to be over, it was that bad.

As for Stan Collymore, he didn't stay long at Liverpool, leaving after just two seasons in which he scored 35 goals in 81 matches and forged a deadly partnership with Robbie Fowler. Although he won no honours for the Reds, he will always be remembered fondly for having scored the winner in the Newcastle match and sending Kevin Keegan into meltdown.

33

Owen's Late, Late Show

Liverpool 2 Arsenal 1
FA Cup Final
12 May 2001
Millennium Stadium, Cardiff
Attendance: 72,500

Liverpool	Arsenal
Westerveld	Seaman
Henchoz	Dixon (Bergkamp 90)
Babbel	Keown
Hyypiä	Adams
Carragher	Cole
Smicer (Fowler 77)	Ljungberg (Kanu 85)
Murphy (Berger 77)	Grimandi
Hamann (McAllister 60)	Vieira
Gerrard	Pires
Heskey	Henry
Owen	Wiltord (Parlour 76)
Manager: Gérard Houllier	*Manager:* Arsène Wenger

ONCE AGAIN, we jump a few seasons, during which Liverpool underwent several changes of personnel, another change of manager and very little silverware to show for it.

The 1996/97 season saw them finish fourth in the league, as Manchester United and Newcastle occupied the top two spots again. The season had started really well, with the Reds unbeaten in the league in their first eight matches and sitting top, but a defeat at Old Trafford put paid to the great start. However, Liverpool were still well in with a shout of their first Premier League championship until late April, but they lost at home to the Red Devils again to leave them five points adrift.

It also looked as though European success was beckoning, as Liverpool strode through to the semi-final of the European Cup Winners' Cup, entering as losing cup finalists as Manchester United had won the double the previous season. However, a heavy 3-0 loss away at Paris Saint-Germain (PSG) in the first leg couldn't be overcome, and despite a 2-0 home victory, the Reds ended with nothing to show for a promising season.

The following season, 1997/98, was nothing to shout about, as Arsenal won the double, with Liverpool 14 points behind in third. The closest to success in this season was a League Cup semi-final, which they surprisingly lost to Middlesbrough.

At the end of the season, a new face appeared in the management set-up when Gérard Houllier arrived to join Roy Evans as joint-managers. It was a surprise decision to go down this route, and it wasn't a successful one, lasting only four months until Evans stood aside. Houllier immediately brought Liverpool old boy Phil Thompson in as his assistant.

However, if Liverpool thought they would get back to winning silverware in 1998/99, they were to be severely disappointed. A seventh-place finish in the league and early exits from domestic and European cup competitions led to a bit of an overhaul in personnel, most notably the arrival of Sami Hyypiä to strengthen the defence. But even this didn't bring immediate success, as 1999/00 went by with nothing to show for it. They did improve to fourth in the league, but were 24 points behind champions Manchester United.

Surely 2000/01 would bring something to celebrate for Liverpool, who were fed up with seeing Arsenal and Manchester United dominate most of the domestic trophies. It certainly looked like being an improved season, as by the end of October, the Reds were third in the league, having just beaten Everton 3-1. Only Manchester United and Arsenal (who else?) were above them. However, two league defeats in November saw Liverpool slip to fifth.

Being in Europe, which I cover in the next chapter, meant that Liverpool entered the League Cup in the third round, where they saw off Chelsea 2-1, then annihilated Stoke 8-0 away in the next round, with Fowler hitting a hat-trick. But a league defeat to Ipswich saw them slip to sixth and starting to lose touch with runaway leaders Manchester United.

It seemed as though cup success would be Liverpool's only hope of silverware, which was reinforced when they beat Fulham 3-0 in the League Cup quarter-final, and kicked off their FA Cup venture with a 3-0 win against Rotherham. However, it looked a bit shaky for a while at the League Cup semi-final stage when Crystal Palace led 2-1 after the first leg at Selhurst Park. The second leg, though, was a completely different story as two goals from Danny Murphy helped the Reds to an empathic 5-0 victory and a place in the final against Birmingham City.

Before this, the Reds had tough FA Cup challenges to deal with. They progressed by defeating Leeds 2-0 at Elland Road, with late goals from Barmby and Heskey, then Manchester City 4-2 in the fifth round – Litmanen, Heskey, Smicer and Babbel scoring the goals.

Next up was the League Cup Final against Birmingham City at the Millennium Stadium, Cardiff. This was a dull affair, but it looked as though Fowler's 30th-minute goal was enough to seal the match as it entered its closing stages. However, in the third minute of stoppage time, Henchoz gave away a penalty, which Purse converted to take the match into extra time.

Unsurprisingly, there were no further goals, so the cup was to be decided on penalty kicks. Liverpool scored their first, but

Birmingham missed to give the Reds an early advantage. Two successes for each team left the score at 3-2 to the Reds, but then Hamann missed and Birmingham levelled things up at 3-3, which soon became 4-4. The pressure was now on Jamie Carragher, who stepped up to make it 5-4 to Liverpool. Birmingham now had to score, but Johnson missed, to give Liverpool the League Cup, 5-4 on penalties. It was their sixth League Cup and their first trophy since 1995.

The FA Cup quarter-final provided Liverpool with a local derby against Tranmere Rovers at Prenton Park, where goals from English quartet Murphy, Owen, Gerrard and Fowler gave the Reds a 4-2 victory to put them into the semi-final at Villa Park. There they faced surprise package Wycombe Wanderers of the Second Division in what should, on paper at least, have been a comfortable match. However, Liverpool were made to battle, and with 12 minutes remaining there was no score, and a surprise looked on the cards. Fortunately, Liverpool's strike force of Heskey and Fowler came up trumps, but Wycombe didn't give up, pulling one back on 88 minutes. The Reds held on, though, to reach their second cup final of the season, where they would face the old enemy of Arsenal.

%% %% %%

On a hot afternoon in Cardiff, Liverpool, playing in gold shirts, started brightly enough in the FA Cup Final, but the early exchanges lacked any quality, and neither team created any early chances. Arsenal perhaps looked the more dangerous, with Pires and Henry looking lively, and it was Henry who nearly broke the deadlock on 17 minutes when Vieira won the ball on the halfway line and Henry was put through on goal by Ljungberg. He rounded Westerveld and looked certain to score but Henchoz got back to block the shot. Henry claimed for handball, and replays showed that he had a very good case, as the ball clearly struck the defender's arm before going out for a corner. The referee actually gave a goal kick.

Minutes later, Liverpool created their first chance of the match when Heskey flicked on Babbel's long throw-in. Owen pounced on the loose ball, but his shot was blocked. The ball came to Gerrard outside the penalty area, but his shot flew over. And that just about sums up the action from the first half, which failed to live up to its billing, as so many cup finals do.

Three minutes into the second half, Liverpool came close to opening the scoring from a Murphy free kick, with Heskey's header forcing a reaction save from Seaman, who was sporting a ridiculous ponytail. However, Liverpool were mostly second best to Arsenal, who came close to scoring when some intricate play sent Henry through, but Westerveld did well to block his close-range shot. However, the ball rebounded to Cole, who looked certain to score a rare goal, but his poked shot was cleared off the line by Hyypiä.

Liverpool were living dangerously, and again required a goal-line clearance on 68 minutes to deny the Gunners. Again, Henry was denied but the ball broke to Ljungberg, who chipped it over Westerveld, only for Hyypiä to be on hand to save the day.

However, Arsenal were not to be denied four minutes later when Westerveld's poor clearance went straight to an opponent. The ball was fed to Pires, who slipped it through to Ljungberg. The Swede rounded the keeper before slotting home to give the Gunners a deserved lead after they had come so close on several occasions.

Just six minutes later, Arsenal should have had the match won when Henry easily beat the hapless Henchoz and was through on goal. Westerveld saved brilliantly but the ball came back to Henry. He mishit his second shot, but it was still creeping in before Hyypiä appeared to produce his hat-trick of goal-line clearances.

Almost immediately Liverpool made a double substitution, bringing on Berger and Fowler in an attempt to turn the tide, and six minutes later they were on equal terms. Liverpool had a free kick on their left wing, which was taken by McAllister. His cross was twice challenged for in the air before the ball fell for Owen, who hooked it into the net for a typical deadly finish. Just seven minutes left to play and Arsenal must have been cursing their missed chances.

The goal seemed to spark Liverpool into life, with Berger having a shot blocked by Keown only a minute after Owen's equaliser. Arsenal looked shell-shocked, so could Liverpool take advantage and complete a smash and grab act and take the cup back to Merseyside, despite having been under the cosh for most of the match?

Well, of course they could. On 88 minutes, it was that man Owen again. This time he completely outpaced Dixon down Liverpool's left after being sent free by a brilliant Berger pass. Owen fired the ball across the face of goal and in at the far post to turn the match completely on its head.

In fact, Liverpool had a good chance to extend the lead in injury time when Fowler was denied by Seaman, but this miss didn't matter, as the referee soon blew his whistle to signal the end of the match and an unlikely comeback win for Liverpool to seal their sixth FA Cup. It was also great revenge for the FA Cup Final defeat to the Gunners in 1971.

The goals for Owen made it eight in his last four matches, and he was to go on to score over 150 goals in just under 300 matches during his seven years at Liverpool, in which he won one FA Cup, one League Cup, one UEFA Cup and the PFA Young Player of the Year. He also won the European Player of the Year in this season and went on to score 40 goals in 89 matches in a stellar international career.

For the Reds it was two cup successes in the season. Could they now go one better and complete a treble by taking the UEFA Cup?

34

McAllister's 'Golden' Show

Liverpool 5 Deportivo Alavés 4 (aet)
UEFA Cup Final
16 May 2001
Westfalenstadion, Dortmund
Attendance: 48,050

Liverpool	Deportivo Alavés
Westerveld	Herrera
Henchoz (Smicer 56)	Contra
Babbel	Eggen (Alonso 22)
Hyypiä	Karmona
Carragher	Téllez
Murphy	Geli
Hamann	Moreno (Pablo 64)
Gerrard	Cruyff
McAllister	Tomic
Heskey (Fowler 64)	Desio
Owen (Berger 79)	Astudillo (Magno 46)
Manager: Gérard Houllier	*Manager:* José Manuel Esnal

THE 2000/01 season was to be a golden one for Liverpool in more ways than one and would end in an amazing climax in the UEFA Cup Final after some closely fought ties in the early rounds.

In the first round, Liverpool faced Rapid Bucharest, a Barmby goal the only one of the tie, which sent the Reds through to face Slovan Liberic of what was then Czechoslovakia. In the second round first leg at Anfield, Liverpool won 1-0, thanks to a late Heskey goal, but then fell behind early on in Czechoslovakia. However, goals from Barmby, Heskey and Owen brought about a comeback to win 3-2 on the night and to reach the third round to face Olympiacos.

This first leg in Greece was another tight match, ending 2-2, Barmby and Gerrard providing the goals, but the Reds finished the job at home through Heskey and Barmby for a 2-0 victory to reach the fourth round, where they would face AS Roma. This time the tie was won in the first leg at the Stadio Olimpico, where Liverpool pulled off a magnificent 2-0 victory thanks to a double strike from Owen. Despite a 1-0 home defeat in the return leg, the Reds progressed to the quarter-final to face Porto.

The first leg of the quarter-final was in Portugal, where the Reds fought out a goalless draw, which they followed up with a 2-0 win at Anfield in the second leg. Owen was on the scoresheet again to add to Murphy's opener, which set up a semi-final against the famous Barcelona. This Barça team included Frank de Boer, Phillip Cocu, Carles Puyol, Luis Enrique, Marc Overmars, Pep Guardiola, Rivaldo and Patrick Kluivert. However, despite this star-studded line-up, the Spanish team couldn't score in the first leg at the Camp Nou, and Liverpool held out for a goalless draw.

At Anfield in the second leg, Barcelona added a couple more star names to their ranks, Michael Reiziger and Emmanuel Petit, in what turned out to be a more exciting match than the one at the Camp Nou. Two minutes before the break, Kluivert handled a McAllister corner to give Liverpool a penalty, which McAllister duly converted to give the Reds the edge in the tie. McAllister had signed from Coventry City on a free transfer at the start of the season, although he should have signed for Liverpool much earlier than he did but ended up at Leeds after leaving Leicester. He was a bit of a surprise signing at this late stage of his career, but had been brought in to add experience to Liverpool's midfield, and was to turn out to be a canny bit of business.

Despite some Barça pressure in the second half, Liverpool defended excellently, and the Reds were into their third cup final of the season, where they would face more Spanish opposition, Alavés, in Dortmund.

※ ※ ※

When I said previously that many cup finals fail to live up to expectations, the UEFA Cup Final of 2001 wasn't one of them, as it exceeded anyone's wildest dreams of how it might turn out. And it did my blood pressure no good at all.

I'd never heard of Alavés, and thought cup final success would be a formality, given Liverpool's experience and top-quality personnel. The only familiar name in the Alavés line-up was that of Cruyff, in this case Jordi Cruyff, son of the great Johan. However, he never lived up to his father's name, as he proved during a disappointing spell at Manchester United.

Liverpool looked like blowing Alavés away early on, but kept letting them back into the game, and it was to turn out to be an extraordinary match that was to be decided in equally extraordinary circumstances.

Liverpool got off to an absolute flyer, scoring after only four minutes. After Heskey had been fouled on Liverpool's right, McAllister swung in a pinpoint free kick, which was met with a powerful header by Babbel for the opener.

Alavés were clearly shaken, struggling to put two passes together after their disastrous start. Liverpool, meanwhile, were buoyed by their early goal and were dominating possession. The Spanish team's frustration came to the fore after ten minutes when Astudillo flew into Heskey with a terrible two-footed tackle that would have resulted in a red card in today's game, but he got away with a yellow.

Then Alavés's night got worse on 16 minutes when they gave the ball away while passing out of defence. The ball was quickly fed by

Hamann to Owen, who spotted Gerrard's forward run, sending a perfectly weighted pass into his stride. He took the ball under his control and stroked it past Herrera, and it looked like a landslide could be on the cards.

Despite continuing pressure, Liverpool failed to finish Alavés, who were still struggling and made an early substitution to try to stem the tide by reverting to four at the back instead of three. Just a few minutes later they were back in the match when a deep cross by Contra was headed in by the substitute, Alonso, at the far post.

Suddenly, Alavés were fired up, as were their supporters, as the flares were set off in the crowd. It was now Liverpool's turn to look a little shaky, as Alavés enjoyed more possession and started to look more dangerous going forward. On the half hour, only a timely interception by Babbel prevented Moreno getting a shot in at the far post after Henchoz had misjudged his leap and completely missed his header. The resulting corner was cleared for a second one, which was again cleared, but only as far Téllez, whose shot was saved by Westerveld.

On 36 minutes, Alavés had a great chance to draw level when Herrera's long drop-kick was nodded on for Moreno, who cut inside, leaving Henchoz on the floor. With only Westerveld to beat, Moreno took too long over his shot, allowing the keeper to close him down and deflect it for a corner. Again, Liverpool failed to deal well with the corner, and Westerveld was called into action to save a shot by Tomic.

It was amazing how quickly the match had turned around, and the Reds were struggling to get to grips with Alavés. However, the Spanish team would regret their missed chances when Liverpool extended their lead four minutes before half-time. McAllister won the ball in his own half, and Hamann sent a brilliant long ball through to Owen. Herrera rushed from his goal and Owen skipped round him and advanced towards the edge of the penalty area. The keeper then had a rush of blood, first trying to handle the ball outside his area, then grabbing Owen and finally tripping him after he'd got into the area, taking him down for a certain penalty.

Up stepped the reliable McAllister, the dead-ball expert, to slot the ball into the corner, just out of the keeper's reach. There was probably an element of relief in the Liverpool supporters' celebrations, as the Alavés pressure looked to have been in vain. It was 3-1 at the interval, and Liverpool looked to be back in control.

Well, they were back in control for all of three minutes of the second half, as the match continued to sway one way, then the other. Tomic turned Carragher five times on the Alavés right wing before putting in a cross with his left foot, which Moreno met with a fine header to make it 3-2 and give Alavés the perfect start to the second half.

They were now outplaying Liverpool and what had looked like being an easy night for the Reds was now anything but, and it was about to get worse. Just three minutes after Moreno's goal, Henchoz committed a foul just outside the penalty area. Despite having six players in the defensive wall, Moreno's scuffed shot went underneath their feet as they jumped, leaving Westerveld with no chance. Alavés were now well and truly back at 3-3 and looking as if they would go on to win the cup, as Liverpool were all over the place.

The Alavés equaliser seemed to spark some life into Liverpool though, and they started to play with more urgency, realising they were in a match. However, they failed to create any chances, and the Alavés defence was looking a lot more secure than it had in the first 25 minutes. Therefore, on 64 minutes, in an attempt to find that all-important next goal, Liverpool sent on Fowler to replace Heskey, while at the same time Alavés surprisingly took off two-goal hero Moreno for midfielder Pablo.

Houllier's decision to bring on Fowler was justified just nine minutes later. McAllister brought the ball forward from the halfway line before sliding it to Fowler, who was moving in from the left wing. Fowler continued to come inside, while Owen waited for the pass. However, Robbie held on to the ball, the defenders stood off, and he passed the ball into the net with his right foot. A great substitution for the Reds, but would Alavés regret taking off Moreno and bringing on the more defensive Pablo now that they needed a goal? From the looks that Moreno was giving his manager, you could tell what he thought about it!

Having scored one goal and set up two others, McAllister's impact on this match was already obvious, but he was now controlling things in midfield, using his experience to calm things down, hoping to see the Reds through the final quarter of an hour to cup success.

As the clocked ticked down towards 90 minutes, it looked as though Liverpool had finally seen Alavés off. Owen went off, to be replaced by Berger, as Liverpool looked to play more conservatively. The Spanish team even resorted to trying to con the referee when Magno dived in the penalty area, but he was just given a yellow card for his trouble.

With only three minutes remaining, a long-range effort by Magno had Westerveld stretching to palm it away, then a minute later Alavés were claiming for a penalty again when Westerveld stretched to palm the ball away from Magno for a corner. He'd clearly played the ball rather than the man, and the referee rightly waved away their protests. However, from the corner, Cruyff climbed above the Liverpool defence to head in the equaliser.

The match went into extra time, which could be decided by the 'golden goal'. In other words, whichever team scored first would be champions, but if there was no further score, it would be a penalty shoot-out. This idea had been introduced with the idea that teams would be more attacking during extra time, seeking to score the golden goal, but it actually backfired in practice, as many teams were so scared of conceding a goal that extra time became more defensive.

However, as neither team seemed to know how to defend, they continued to press forward in the first period of extra time. Alavés had an early goal disallowed for a clear offside, then Téllez was shown the yellow card after his rugby tackle on Fowler prevented him from sliding a pass through for Smicer, who would have been clear in on goal.

Eight minutes into extra time, Magno regretted his earlier yellow card for diving, when he scythed Babbel down and was shown a second yellow, followed by the red. Liverpool now had the advantage of an extra man for the remaining 22 minutes, if it went that far of course.

They started to dominate possession and Alavés looked happy to sit back, hoping to take the match to penalties, and although Fowler had a goal disallowed for offside just before half-time, they looked in no danger of conceding at this point.

In the second period of extra time Liverpool again dominated possession and nearly scored the golden goal just one minute after the restart. Herrera came out to collect a Gerrard cross but completely missed it. However, his attempt seemed to put Fowler off, and he failed to get his head to the cross, with the goal begging.

Despite having an extra man, Liverpool still couldn't find the breakthrough, and soon they had two extra men when Karmona dragged Smicer back on Liverpool's left wing to receive his second yellow card. With only four minutes remaining, hopefully a gap would appear somewhere for Liverpool to snatch the golden-goal victory.

McAllister stood over the free kick, which was only a couple of yards from the byline, so would have to be a cross rather than a shot at goal. Alavés brought everyone (well, what was left of them) back to defend the free kick. McAllister stepped up, crossed into the goal area, the ball flicked the top of Geli's head, and there it was in the back of the net. Liverpool had the golden goal, and there was no way back for Alavés this time ... the match was all over, and

Liverpool had won the UEFA Cup, to go with the League Cup and FA Cup this season.

McAllister was clearly the man of the match, being involved in all but one of Liverpool's goals and had been a shrewd signing by Houllier. This season's three trophies were his only ones with the Reds, but he made a magnificent contribution in his two-year stay.

35

Dudek to the Rescue

Liverpool 2 Manchester United 0
League Cup Final
2 March 2003
Millennium Stadium, Cardiff
Attendance: 74,500

Liverpool	**Manchester United**
Dudek	Barthez
Henchoz	Neville
Hyypiä	Silvestre
Riise	Veron
Carragher	Brown (Solskjær 74)
Murphy	Ferdinand
Hamann	Beckham
Gerrard	Keane
Heskey (Baros 60, Smicer 89)	Scholes
Diouf (Biscan 89)	van Nistelrooy
Owen	Giggs
Manager: Gérard Houllier	*Manager:* Alex Ferguson

ALTHOUGH 2001/02 saw further improvement, with Liverpool finishing as runners-up in the league to double winners Arsenal, the season was to end with no major silverware, which was disappointing after the three cup wins of the previous season.

The season had started early, as the Reds had to go through a Champions League qualifying round, which they did successfully.

They then beat Manchester United in the Charity Shield, so at least they won something in the season, but they were to go out early in both domestic cups.

They did progress through the Champions League group phases, of which there were two in those days, but surprisingly went out at the quarter-final stage to eventual runners-up Bayer Leverkusen.

At the end of March 2002, the Reds actually led the Premier League by a point from Manchester United and two points from Arsenal, although the Gunners had two matches in hand. A first Premier League title for Liverpool was still a possibility, and they only lost one more match all season, but Arsenal were unstoppable and ended up winning the title by seven points.

However, the improvement in league position provided hope for 2002/03. But then hope never won anything. A series of disappointing results against teams they would have expected to beat left the Reds down in fifth position and out of the Champions League qualifying places by the end of the season.

They also failed to get out of the group stage of this season's Champions League, so went into the UEFA Cup, but they had at least got through their first match in the League Cup, defeating Southampton 3-1 in the third round, with goals from Berger, Diouf and Baros.

In the UEFA Cup third round, the Reds defeated Vitesse Arnhem 2-0 on aggregate to raise hopes of more European glory. Then on the domestic front they beat Ipswich in the fourth round of the League Cup following a penalty shoot-out after a Diouf equaliser had earned them a 1-1 draw.

In the next round they beat Aston Villa 4-3 in a thriller at Villa Park. Villa led through a 23rd-minute penalty before Liverpool took control through goals by Murphy, Baros and Gerrard. Hitzlsperger pulled one back for Villa before a Dublin shot deflected in off Henchoz with only two minutes remaining to level the scores at 3-3. The Reds weren't done though, and Murphy added his second to steal the match in the 90th minute.

In the semi-final, Liverpool faced Sheffield United in a typical bruising encounter against a Neil Warnock team. In the first leg at Bramall Lane, Liverpool looked to be in control when Mellor gave them the lead on 34 minutes, but a late rally by the Blades saw them score twice in the last quarter of an hour to take the advantage to Anfield.

The return leg was an ill-tempered affair, mostly on the touchline between Phil Thompson and Neil Warnock, but also on the pitch, where there were some meaty challenges to say the least. Liverpool levelled the tie at 2-2 when Diouf scored after only seven minutes but that was to be it for the 90 minutes, so the match went into extra time. If there were no further goals, Liverpool would go through on away goals, but they sealed the win when Owen scored early in the second period of extra time to take Liverpool to a final against Manchester United in Cardiff.

Although the Reds progressed through the next round of the UEFA Cup against Auxerre, they were to be surprisingly knocked out by Celtic after having secured a 1-1 draw at Celtic Park. Nobody could have predicted the 2-0 home defeat that saw them exit European competition. However, that was still to come. For now, all eyes were on the Millennium Stadium for the League Cup Final between the two north-west enemies.

%% %% %%

At the time of this match, Liverpool were down in seventh place in the league, while Manchester United were second, but would go on to win the title once again. United had already won at Anfield earlier in the season, so they went into the final as favourites.

The atmosphere in the stadium as the teams emerged was electric, made noisier by the fact that the roof was closed, and there was a fireworks display to welcome the players on to the pitch.

United had the better of the early exchanges, although it took 12 minutes for the first shot to arrive, courtesy of Giggs, but Dudek dealt with it easily. Liverpool, meanwhile, despite having their fair share of possession, were creating nothing of note, and even at this early stage it looked like being another one of those dull finals that would be decided by a single goal or maybe go to extra time.

On 20 minutes though, United very nearly took the lead when Keane collected the ball on the halfway line and fed it to Scholes. He passed the ball wide to Giggs on the United left, who fired a first-time, low cross into the goal area where van Nistelrooy was at full stretch. He managed to get his right foot to the ball to direct it goalwards, but it went a couple of inches wide.

It took 36 minutes for Liverpool to have their first serious attempt on goal when Murphy fired one over the bar, but only three minutes later they were ahead after what can only be described as a moment of Gerrard magic (mixed with a little bit of good fortune). Murphy drove forward before passing to Owen, who had moved out wide on Liverpool's left. He knocked the ball back to Riise, who then pushed it further back to Gerrard. There seemed to be nothing on when Gerrard received the ball 30 yards out, but he unleashed a fierce right-foot shot that took a deflection off Beckham and looped over Barthez and into the top corner.

It was just what this dull match needed, and suddenly it sparked into life. First, Carragher and Diouf combined down Liverpool's right, and Diouf crossed, but Heskey couldn't quite get on the end of it. United immediately counter-attacked through Giggs on their left. Gerrard looked to have got back to block the cross but Giggs maintained possession and cut back on his right foot, before sliding a square ball for Veron. The Argentine met the ball on the run, hitting it first time towards Dudek's top-left corner, but the keeper leapt to punch it away. The ball fell straight to Scholes, who drilled in a low shot, but Henchoz was on hand to clear it off the line and over the bar. I think that's the first positive contribution from Henchoz that I've mentioned in this book, but he did have some good points.

Just before half-time, United had a free kick in David Beckham territory, but his curled shot was easily saved by Dudek. It remained 1-0 to Liverpool at the break, but United could perhaps count themselves unlucky not to be at least level, but who cares?

Liverpool had the first opening of the second half when Owen should have done better, but failed to get a shot in after getting the better of Brown. However, neither team threatened to score until 58 minutes when an attempted Beckham cross was deflected before being headed into the Liverpool penalty area. The ball fell for van Nistelrooy, who turned smartly before firing a shot on goal, but again Dudek pulled off a fine save to deny United the equaliser.

Three minutes later, Liverpool had the chance to double their lead when they counter-attacked through Baros, having been sent away by Gerrard. Baros carried the ball forward into space, as Gerrard sprinted forward on his right. Baros cut inside before cleverly slipping the ball to Gerrard, who shot on the run but too close to Barthez, who was able to get his left hand to the near-post shot and deflect it for a corner.

The second half was already turning out to be better than the first, and Dudek saved well from Scholes, who had been set up by Veron. The keeper then denied van Nistelrooy again.

With only ten minutes remaining, United were throwing everything at Liverpool, and the defenders were struggling to get the ball clear, with Riise miskicking a right-foot clearance up into the air. The ball fell for van Nistelrooy, who chested it down before turning and shooting in one action. Somehow, Dudek got down to his right to push the ball clear, as it started to turn into a one-man show for the Reds.

Just six minutes later, the match was all over when Owen sealed the victory for Liverpool. Silvestre gave the ball away on the halfway line, leaving Hamann to surge forward, Liverpool having a two on one, as United had pushed so many men forward. Hamann committed the remaining defender before slipping the ball to Owen.

If you had to put your mortgage on anyone in a one on one with the keeper at that time, it was Owen, who took the ball forward and slid it past Barthez for 2-0.

The Reds could have scored twice more in the remaining minutes, Smicer somehow contriving to miss an open goal after an excellent Murphy cross, then Owen having a shot blocked by Ferdinand. United had had their chances but Dudek had stood firm and the cup was Liverpool's for the seventh time.

Jerzy Dudek was Liverpool's hero of the match, and having seen him recently in a legends match, he was still performing heroics. The Pole signed for Liverpool from Feyenoord in 2001 and had his critics, but he was undoubtedly a fine keeper. He played for the Reds for nearly six years in over 180 matches, winning not only this League Cup, but an FA Cup and a Champions League, where he would perform even more heroics as you will soon read.

36

No Greek Tragedy

Liverpool 3 Olympiacos 1
Champions League Group Phase
8 December 2004
Anfield
Attendance: 42,045

Liverpool	Olympiacos
Kirkland	Nikopolidis
Finnan (Josemi 85)	Pantos
Hyypiä	Anatolakis
Riise	Schürrer
Traore (Sinama-Pongolle 46)	Venetidis (Maric 84)
Carragher	Georgiadis (Rezic 70)
Kewell	Kafes
Gerrard	Stoltjdis
Alonso	Djordevic
Nunez	Rivaldo
Baros (Mellor 78)	Giovanni (Okkas 87)
Manager: Rafa Benitez	*Manager:* Dušan Bajevic

THE NEXT season, 2003/04, was another disappointing one for Liverpool, finishing fourth in the league, which was won by Arsenal, and again not making significant progress in the domestic and European cup competitions. This led to the departure of Gérard Houllier at the end of the season, to be replaced by Rafa Benitez, who had brought the La Liga title to

Valencia after a 32-year wait. Could he deliver Liverpool's first Premier League title?

He certainly didn't get off to a flying start, as the Reds won only five of their first 11 matches of the season in all competitions, including a defeat in Greece to Olympiacos in the group phase of the Champions League. At this point they were down in 11th in the Premier League, having just lost to eventual champions Chelsea.

Their form didn't really improve, although they did progress through the third and fourth rounds of the League Cup, but coming into their final match of the Champions League group phase against Olympiacos, the Reds needed to win by two clear goals to be certain of progressing to the knockout phase.

※ ※ ※

Inevitably, before the match, there was plenty of talk about the Saint-Etienne match and the need to win by two clear goals, but Olympiacos weren't in the same class as the French team from 1977, so confidence was high coming into the match.

That confidence looked well founded when Liverpool started strongly and Baros scored in the opening minutes, but his goal was disallowed for pushing. Sami Hyypiä should then have done better with a header from Gerrard's corner, and although the Reds continued to pile on the pressure, winning a succession of corners, they had nothing to show for it. It started to look as though it may be a frustrating evening ahead.

Gerrard was having an eventful night, coming close to scoring an own goal when Rivaldo whipped in a brilliant free kick. Gerrard had to get something on the ball to prevent a clear header on goal for his opponent, but his own header had Kirkland worried as it just cleared the bar. Then Gerrard instinctively diverted Alonso's free kick towards the Olympiacos goal, thinking he'd scored, and turning away in celebration, only to find that his shot had rebounded to safety off the post.

On 26 minutes, Liverpool's night became even more difficult when Olympiacos took a surprise lead against the run of play. The Greek team were awarded a free kick just outside the penalty area after a foul by Hyypiä, and up stepped Rivaldo. He may have been ageing by this time, but he still had stupendous ability with the dead ball in particular.

Kirkland must have known what was coming, and to be honest it was far from being Rivaldo's greatest free kick, but the Liverpool keeper was rooted to the spot as the Brazilian's left-foot shot nestled in his bottom right corner, having found its way through a gap in the defensive wall.

Liverpool now needed three goals in the remaining 64 minutes. Plenty of time, of course, but they also needed to ensure that they didn't throw everything at Olympiacos and risk conceding another goal.

Gerrard had another 'nearly' moment when he continued his run into the penalty area after passing the ball wide to Riise, who struck a shot with his left foot that went across the face of goal and just inches away from Gerrard's outstretched boot. However, Liverpool never threatened to score for the rest of the first half and went into the break a goal down and needing three second-half goals to avoid going out of the competition.

Benitez decided to bring on Sinama-Pongolle at the start of the second half to replace Traore, hoping that the additional forward player would bring results. It was to turn out to be a night of inspired substitutions by Benitez, in this case when the young Frenchman scored the equaliser within two minutes of the restart. Kewell held off a challenge on the Liverpool left and got to the byline before putting in a low cross to the near post, where Sinama-Pongolle nipped in to side-foot home to give the Reds hope.

Gerrard then thought he'd put the Reds ahead when he latched on to a Baros knock-down and volleyed his shot at goal. The keeper, Nikopolidis, got down to it but somehow let it slip under his body and into the net, but unfortunately Baros had been harshly penalised for his aerial challenge and the goal was disallowed.

Kewell had a great chance to put the Reds ahead when Sinama-Pongolle turned provider, putting in a deep cross to the far post where the Australian rose unopposed but directed his header straight at Nikopolidis. The frustration was growing as the clock ticked on, and Benitez was growing increasingly agitated on the sidelines.

However, the gaffer played another trump card when he sent on Mellor in the 78th minute to replace the tiring Baros. Two minutes later, Sinama-Pongolle was tripped about 30 yards from goal, and Alonso played the free kick into the box. Liverpool had good claims for a penalty for a foul, but the referee ignored their appeals. However, they didn't waste time complaining and Sinama-Pongolle crossed the ball to the far post where Nunez rose to direct a powerful header on goal. Nikopolidis pulled off a remarkable save but Mellor was on hand to knock in the loose ball to really set the Kop roaring. Ten minutes to go and just one more goal needed.

Kewell soon had the opportunity for Liverpool's third when Nikopolidis spilled Gerrard's forward ball at his feet, but he took too long in trying to get the ball on to his left foot, allowing the keeper to recover and gratefully grab the ball before he could get his shot away.

Olympiacos were now in panic mode, and gave away a needless throw-in near their own corner flag as the clock ticked down to just four minutes remaining. Carragher, whose pressure had forced the throw-in, got forward again and sent a cross into the penalty area, where Mellor leapt to knock the ball back to Gerrard, coming forward from midfield. Gerrard cut across the ball, and it flew past Nikopolidis, the ball not rising more than two feet off the floor, to give the Reds a 3-1 lead.

Gerrard's remarkable goal gave the Reds the two-goal cushion they needed, and they comfortably saw the rest of the match out to progress through to the knockout stages of the Champions League, when it looked as if all was lost. There were two unlikely heroes in Sinama-Pongolle and Mellor, but of course it was Steven Gerrard who was the hero of the hour, as he was to turn out to be on so many occasions for the Reds.

%. %. %.

A few weeks after the Olympiacos drama, Liverpool defeated Watford 1-0 at Anfield in the first leg of the League Cup semi-final, thanks again to a Gerrard goal, then repeated the feat at Vicarage Road, with Gerrard again the goalscoring hero.

However, it was to be another season where the Reds never threatened in the Premier League, often losing to seemingly inferior opposition, such as Southampton, Crystal Palace and Birmingham, to finish fifth at the end of the season. They also went out early in the FA Cup, losing to Burnley in the third round.

Back in the Champions League, Liverpool's first knockout match pitted them against Bayer Leverkusen, the Reds pulling off a stunning 6-2 aggregate victory by winning both legs 3-1, Luis Garcia scoring three goals over the two ties. Unfortunately, in between the two legs, the Reds came unstuck in the League Cup Final against Chelsea, losing 3-2. It looked as though they were on for another League Cup trophy when Riise got them off to a flyer by scoring in the first minute, and they held on to their lead until the 79th minute. Gerrard then scored again, but unfortunately for him and the Reds it was at the wrong end this time, and the match ended 1-1 after 90 minutes, with Chelsea coming out on top after extra time.

So now the Champions League was all that was left if Liverpool were to claim any glory in 2004/05. However, up next were the giants of Juventus, a formidable opponent, coached by Fabio Capello. The first leg at Anfield got off to a great start when Hyypiä gave the Reds the lead after only ten minutes, and Garcia made it two just 15 minutes later. However, Juventus improved in the second half and pulled one back through Cannavaro, to leave the tie in the balance going to the Stadio delle Alpi.

The second leg was as tense as they come. Juventus knew they only needed one goal to go through, but the Reds held firm, despite the absence of Gerrard. Watching it, you felt that Juve must create at least one clear-cut chance, but Liverpool were superb on the night and kept them at bay, with Dudek having a much quieter night than expected. It was a brilliant performance, and sometimes you just don't mind watching a 0-0 draw.

The semi-final saw an all-English tie, as Liverpool faced their League Cup victors Chelsea, managed by Jose Mourinho. The first leg, at Stamford Bridge, saw another goalless draw, a good result for the Reds, but Alonso's yellow card with only three minutes remaining meant that they would be without the key midfielder in the return leg.

The second leg at Anfield ended 1-0 to the Reds and was decided by a controversial goal that many still talk about today … many Chelsea fans that is. After only four minutes, Baros was put through by Gerrard and beat Chelsea's keeper, Cech, to the ball. The keeper brought Baros down for a clear penalty, but the referee allowed play to continue, as Garcia prodded the ball towards goal. The ball deflected off Terry, then Gallas tried to clear it away before it crossed the line. There was no goal-line technology back then, and the officials adjudged that the ball had crossed the line and awarded the goal, amidst massive Chelsea protests. Interestingly, the referee later said that had Liverpool not scored, he would have awarded the penalty and given Cech a red card, which may have been worse for Chelsea. It was the only goal of the tie, and Liverpool were through to the final of the Champions League to face AC Milan in Istanbul, in what was to be an unforgettable match.

37

The Miracle of Istanbul

Liverpool 3 AC Milan 3 (aet)
(Penalties 3-2)
Champions League Final
25 May 2005
Ataturk Stadium, Istanbul
Attendance: 72,059

Liverpool	AC Milan
Dudek	Dida
Finnan (Hamann 46)	Cafu
Hyypiä	Maldini
Riise	Stam
Traore	Nesta
Carragher	Pirlo
Kewell (Smicer 23)	Gattuso (Costa 112)
Gerrard	Seedorf (Serginho 85)
Garcia	Kaká
Alonso	Crespo (Tomasson 85)
Baros (Cisse 85)	Shevchenko
Manager: Rafa Benitez	*Manager:* Carlo Ancelotti

ALL THROUGH the Champions League, I'd watched the matches while sitting in the same seat on the sofa. I'm not particularly superstitious, but I made sure I was sitting in the same spot for the final.

What harm could it do?

However, it seemed as though my lucky seat wasn't working when AC Milan scored in the first minute and Liverpool looked shell-shocked. After Liverpool surrendered possession from the kick-off, Traore gave away a free kick wide on Milan's right. Pirlo sent in a low free kick and Maldini smashed home a spectacular volley, which Dudek probably never saw. Just 50 seconds on the clock, and any game plan that Liverpool had was already well and truly out of the window. They had gone 297 minutes of the Champions League without conceding a goal before this, but at least they had 89 minutes to do something about it.

They responded immediately, with Riise having a fierce shot blocked, then Hyypiä climbing to send in a header, which unfortunately went straight at Dida in the Milan goal. However, Milan subdued any hope of any immediate equaliser as only Italian teams can do, and with Hamann surprisingly left on the bench in favour of the more attacking but injury-prone Kewell, the class of Pirlo and Kaká in midfield was already beginning to flourish, while Gerrard and Alonso were invisible for the Reds.

On 13 minutes, it was nearly 2-0 when Seedorf's corner was headed towards goal at the near post by Crespo. Fortunately, Liverpool had Garcia guarding the post to clear the danger. Meanwhile, Liverpool were struggling to get a foothold in the match, while Milan were playing with arrogance, with Shevchenko making some dangerous runs in behind the Liverpool defence.

Kewell, who had been limping for a few minutes, left the pitch after just 23 minutes, but still Hamann remained on the bench, with Benitez preferring to replace Kewell with Smicer. The gamble on Kewell hadn't paid off, but with Liverpool only one down, the more attacking option of Smicer over Hamann at that stage was perhaps understandable.

The match became a bit scrappy for a while, with both teams guilty of giving the ball away, and defences being in control. Then Shevchenko thought he'd doubled Milan's lead on 28 minutes when he got in behind the Liverpool defence and slid the ball home, but the flag was up for offside to spoil his celebrations. The Reds may have been lucky, as it appeared that a Liverpool player, while making a challenge, had played the ball to Shevchenko. However, the danger signs were there, and it seemed only a matter of time before the Ukrainian avoided the offside trap.

Liverpool's only opportunities were falling to Garcia outside the penalty area, but he didn't have his shooting boots on, and the Reds hadn't threatened to score as the first half moved into its final minutes. At least it looked as though they would get to half-time just one down, but a quick Milan break soon put paid to that. Liverpool had claims for a penalty for handball by Nesta turned down, and he soon set his team on the attack. Quick passing and moving and Shevchenko was away on the right of the Liverpool penalty area. His low cross was met at the far post by Crespo, and it was 2-0 after 39 minutes.

Five minutes later things got worse when Crespo scored again. Kaká received the ball in midfield and immediately saw Crespo's forward run. The Brazilian played a brilliant ball through to split the Liverpool defence and Crespo coolly lifted his shot over Dudek for 3-0 after 44 minutes. If Liverpool were shell-shocked after the first-minute goal, I don't have the words to explain how they must have felt at this point.

Apparently, Everton and Manchester United fans were celebrating in the bars at half-time, and it's rumoured that Liverpool players overheard Milan celebrating in their dressing room. I seriously considered giving up my 'lucky' seat for the rest of the match but decided to stay put. You never know what might happen, and I wouldn't want to scupper Liverpool's chances of a comeback by not being in the right seat.

Clearly Benitez had to do something to change things at half-time, as Milan's clinical passing and moving was ripping Liverpool's defence to shreds. The decision was made to introduce Hamann into midfield, Finnan making way, so Liverpool moved to a back three and bolstered midfield, in the hope that the likes of Garcia, Gerrard and Alonso could get into the match more and at least salvage some pride and avoid a real hammering.

The change didn't seem to stem the tide at the start of the second half, as Milan continued to attack, and Liverpool's defence looked shaky. However, the Reds did have their first serious strike on goal since the first few minutes of the match, when Alonso drove a low shot just wide.

Milan still looked the more likely to score though. First the excellent Kaká looked to be racing clear, until rudely interrupted by a Hyypiä foul just outside the area. From the resulting free kick Dudek pulled off a good save to deny Shevchenko. But then things changed. Just one minute later, Riise crossed and Gerrard powered home a header to make it 3-1 on 54 minutes. At last the Liverpool fans had something to cheer, while Gerrard ran back to the halfway line waving his arms upwards to rouse his team.

Just two minutes later it was Milan's turn to be shell-shocked as Liverpool scored again. The referee waved play on rather than award Milan a free kick for offside when a Liverpool attack broke down, but the Reds won a throw-in wide on their left. It was taken quickly, and the ball fed square to Hamann, who fed it square again to Smicer, about 25 yards from goal. He hit a low shot that Dida got his hand to, but he failed to prevent the ball going in just inside the post. Game on!

Milan were rattled and Liverpool needed to take advantage, as the atmosphere inside the Ataturk Stadium reached fever pitch. It was now all Liverpool as they went on the attack looking for the equaliser. Talk about a match of two halves!

Then the miracle started to look possible when a ball into the penalty area reached the feet of Baros, who cleverly flicked it inside for the onrushing Gerrard, who looked certain to score from six yards before he was taken down from behind by Gattuso. The referee pointed to the spot despite the usual Italian protestations of innocence. It should have been worse for Milan, as it looked a certain red card offence, but the referee saw it differently.

The Milan protests continued as Alonso calmly placed the ball on the spot. The Spaniard was always a cool player and was another one whose hair never seemed to be out of place when he was playing. He stepped up and put his shot firmly to Dida's right, but the keeper guessed correctly and pulled off a brilliant save, only for the ball to come back out to the Spaniard, who smashed the rebound into the roof of the net for 3-3 on 59 minutes. The comeback had been achieved within a six-minute period, and still with 31 minutes remaining. Surely Milan were there for the taking now.

The whole flow of the match had now changed, and Liverpool were the team playing with confidence, Riise sending in a rasping left-foot shot that Dida managed to parry and retrieve. Hamann's introduction had freed up Gerrard to get forward more and he was the driving force behind much of Liverpool's best work. However, they failed to get the immediate fourth goal that surely would have sunk Milan, and the Italian team gradually started to recover and play their way back into the match.

In fact, it was Milan who came closer to scoring a fourth when Dudek spilled a Kaká cross but Traore was on hand to clear Shevchenko's shot off the line. Then moments later, Crespo played the ball in to the near post for Shevchenko, but Carragher put in a brilliant tackle to deny him a shot on goal.

With five minutes remaining, Liverpool played their last card, bringing on Cisse to replace the tiring Baros, who had just been shown a yellow card as he became increasingly frustrated with the officials' decisions and the manhandling he was receiving, particularly from Nesta. Meanwhile, Milan replaced two-goal hero Crespo with Tomasson, and Seedorf with Serginho. However, the changes didn't bring about a dramatic finish to the match, which moved into extra time.

Milan started to dominate possession during the first additional period, with Tomasson just failing to connect with a deep cross that Traore seemed to misjudge. Cafu was still bombing up and down the right flank, and having watched him recently in a legends match, he was still doing the same at 49 years of age. Meanwhile, Liverpool's passing game had deserted them and they invited further pressure by giving the ball away too often. Perhaps the efforts of the second half were beginning to tell, with Smicer receiving treatment for cramp just before the break.

Into the second period of extra time, Liverpool's back three appeared to have become a back five, with Cisse left alone up front to chase any opportunities that came his way. Milan seemed to be having a resurgence, with Kaká chasing a ball down their left flank and putting in a dangerous low cross that Carragher did well to stretch for and clear away, injuring himself in the process and becoming the second player to receive treatment for cramp. Benitez had no more substitutions left but Milan had one more change to make, bringing on Costa for Gattuso.

Milan continued to dominate, and with four minutes left Dudek produced heroics to prevent Shevchenko from scoring what must surely have been the winner. The Pole had been pretty shaky in goal so far, flapping at some crosses and failing to hold shots, but he made up for it with a superb double save from the Ukrainian, first from a point-blank-range header, then getting up quickly to block the follow-up shot. It was a pivotal moment, with Shevchenko left holding his head in his hands.

The Reds had one final opportunity when they were awarded a free kick 25 yards from goal as extra time moved into injury time. Was there to be one final twist? No, as they made a complete hash of the free kick and the match ended 3-3, going to a penalty shoot-out.

Milan took the first penalty kick, Serginho stepping up and blasting his shot well over the bar. Hamann then scored for Liverpool to give them a 1-0 advantage. Up next was Pirlo, the dead-ball king, but Dudek dived to his right to pull off an excellent save. Cisse sent Dida the wrong way to give Liverpool a 2-0 lead, before Tomasson scored Milan's first. Riise was up next for the Reds, the man with a fearsome left-foot shot, knowing that a goal would virtually clinch the trophy, but he decided to place his shot and Dida dived to his right to palm the ball away.

However, Liverpool still had a 2-1 advantage, with both teams having taken three penalties. Milan's fourth was taken by Kaká, who calmly scored, despite Dudek trying the Grobbelaar wobbly legs routine. Smicer maintained Liverpool's advantage when he sent Dida the wrong way, meaning that Shevchenko, the ace marksman, had to score or Liverpool would be European champions for the fifth time. He strode up and placed the ball towards the middle of the goal, but Dudek had dived to his right. However, the keeper stretched out his left arm and managed to palm the ball away to seal a miraculous win for the Reds against all the odds, and all while I was sitting in my lucky seat.

It was an extraordinary match and rightly called the 'Miracle of Istanbul', and the parade around Liverpool was equally as extraordinary, many still with a feeling of disbelief that they had actually just witnessed such a comeback in a major final. It still makes my spine tingle when I watch it back.

38

The Gerrard Final

Liverpool 3 West Ham United 3 (aet)
(Penalties 3-1)
FA Cup Final
13 May 2006
Millennium Stadium, Cardiff
Attendance: 71,140

Liverpool	West Ham United
Reina	Hislop
Finnan	Scaloni
Hyypiä	Ferdinand
Riise	Gabbidon
Carragher	Konchesky
Kewell (Morientes 48)	Benayoun
Gerrard	Fletcher (Dailly 77)
Alonso (Kromkamp 67)	Reo-Coker
Sissoko	Etherington (Sheringham 85)
Cisse	Ashton (Zamora 71)
Crouch (Hamann 71)	Harewood
Manager: Rafa Benitez	*Manager:* Alan Pardew

FOLLOWING THE drama in Istanbul, Liverpool had an early start to 2005/06 as they had qualified for the Champions League thanks to their victory over AC Milan, but had to enter at the first qualifying round stage. They were drawn against Total Network

Solutions of Wales and went through comfortably, winning both legs 3-0. They then won both legs in the second round against FBK Kaunas of Lithuania, before facing Bulgaria's CSKA Sofia in the third round, winning 3-1 away in the first leg.

All this was before the Reds kicked off their Premier League campaign, once again hoping to seal their first title, but again coming up short as they finished third, with Chelsea taking the title, nine points clear of Liverpool.

In the Champions League, the Reds lost to CSKA in the second leg but still went through to the group phase, 3-2 on aggregate. They won the group to qualify for the knockout stage, where they faced Benfica, but it wasn't to be a successful defence of the cup, as the Reds surprisingly went out to the Portuguese team, losing at home and away in a 3-0 aggregate defeat.

There was some cup success early in the season though, as Liverpool faced CSKA Moscow in the European Super Cup in Monaco. It took a Cisse equaliser eight minutes from time to save the match for the Reds and take the final into extra time, where two further goals, from Cisse and Garcia, sealed the win and another trophy for the Anfield cabinet.

In the domestic cups, the Reds went out in the third round of the League Cup to Crystal Palace, so all eyes were on the FA Cup when the third round got underway in January 2006. In a thrilling match at Kenilworth Road, Liverpool beat Championship team Luton Town 5-3. After Gerrard had given the Reds the lead on 15 minutes, Luton fought back to lead 3-1 and it looked as if a shock was well and truly on the cards. However, Liverpool regained control, with Sinama-Pongolle and Alonso both scoring twice to see the Reds safely through.

In the fourth round, Liverpool faced Portsmouth at Fratton Park, Gerrard and Riise scoring to seal a 2-1 victory, but then they were drawn to face rivals Manchester United at Anfield in the fifth round, a team that Benitez had failed to beat in his previous four attempts. However, it was fifth time lucky for Rafa, as a Crouch goal was enough to see Liverpool through.

The quarter-final away to Birmingham City saw yet another incredible scoreline, as the Reds were rampant. They got off to a flying start, scoring twice in the first five minutes through Hyypiä and Crouch, then Crouch was on target again before half-time. The match was as good as over, but Liverpool didn't hold back, Morientes, Riise and Cisse, plus an own goal, finishing off a magnificent 7-0 victory.

In the semi-final, Liverpool faced Chelsea yet again, this time with no doubt over the legitimacy of the goals, as Riise and Garcia sealed a 2-1 victory and a place at Cardiff's Millennium Stadium in the final to face West Ham, who had been promoted from the Championship the previous season.

The Reds were firm favourites going into the match and had beaten West Ham at Upton Park only two weeks previously. However, the Hammers gave as good as they got in the final and many would argue that they should have taken home the cup.

%%% %%% %%%

The cup final started with both defences on top in the early exchanges, and it wasn't until the 21st minute that the first opening appeared, and it led to the opening goal. West Ham found space down their right when Ashton found overlapping right-back Scaloni. Harewood was unmarked in the penalty area, and Scaloni's low cross was heading his way, although Reina looked likely to intercept it. However, Carragher was racing back and intercepted first, but unfortunately his attempted clearance ended up in the net to give the Hammers the lead.

Suddenly the tempo of the match changed, but Liverpool still hadn't fashioned a decent effort on goal when West Ham doubled their lead on 28 minutes with another 'scruffy' goal. Etherington's tame left-foot shot from the edge of the penalty area looked to have been gathered by Reina, but he fumbled it straight to Ashton, who had the simple task of tapping it into the goal. West Ham players and fans were delirious, while Liverpool fans couldn't believe the circus-like performance of their defence and keeper.

However, Liverpool had shown in Istanbul that they never knew when they were beaten, and they thought they had hit back within two minutes when Gerrard's clever quick free kick found Crouch, who slotted the ball past Hislop in the West Ham goal, but he'd been flagged offside. It was a very tight decision, but two minutes later the Reds were on the scoresheet through Cisse.

Again, it was Gerrard the provider, as his long raking pass into the West Ham penalty area was met by Cisse on the volley for an excellent goal. Oddly, Cisse was wearing one red boot and one white one, this goal scored by a wonderful technique with the red one.

Liverpool began to play with more confidence after their goal, but Ashton, who had been a doubt for the Hammers because of injury, was leading their line well, and came close on 36 minutes when his cross-shot went just wide. However, that was as close as either team came to adding to the scoreline in the first half.

Within a minute of the restart, West Ham could have been 3-1 ahead when Etherington broke down their left and crossed low to Harewood, whose shot was blocked by Reina. The Liverpool keeper then atoned for his earlier blunder by getting up quickly from his save to block Benayoun's shot.

Those saves proved even more important nine minutes later when Liverpool equalised through the increasingly influential Gerrard. Riise was fouled be Reo-Coker halfway into the West Ham half and the free kick was eventually crossed into the penalty area by Alonso, where it was nodded down by Crouch for Gerrard to pounce and drive it home. Liverpool had achieved another cup final comeback, were now in the ascendancy and looked certain to go on to victory.

However, West Ham wouldn't lie down, as both teams continued to attack, and the match became very open. More goals looked certain, but the source of the next goal was as unexpected as its method. On 64 minutes, West Ham played the ball wide on their left to Konchesky, the left-back, and his deep cross was mishit but looped over Reina and in at the far post. A complete fluke to add to an own goal and goalkeeping blunder, but the Hammers were back in front and Liverpool had it all to do again.

Suddenly, it was end-to-end stuff, with Liverpool pushing forward in search of an equaliser and West Ham breaking quickly when they had the opportunity, with Benayoun pulling the strings in midfield.

On 71 minutes Benitez gambled on a different formation, bringing on Hamann for Crouch and pushing Gerrard further forward. This was a similar move to that night in Istanbul, which had provided the catalyst for the memorable comeback. Could it work again? Certainly not immediately, as Liverpool had plenty of the ball but failed to create any clear chances, and West Ham defended well, particularly through Gabbidon.

The pace of the match was also beginning to tell, with three players, Riise, Gerrard and Harewood, all down with cramp at the same time in the 84th minute. Gerrard definitely looked to be struggling two minutes later when he grimaced in pain after striking a free kick over the bar. Then Cisse, wearing yellow boots in the second half, was the next to suffer cramp with only two minutes remaining, as Gerrard still hobbled about the pitch, clearly not fully fit.

However, Liverpool's own Captain Marvel wasn't finished yet. As the stadium announcer was stating that there would be four added minutes, a cross from Liverpool's left was knocked out of the penalty area where Gerrard was waiting. From 35 yards he powered a low shot that flew past the right hand of Hislop to take the match into extra time. A superb goal to cap a superb performance ... made one, scored two.

Liverpool mostly dominated extra time, Riise going close with a typically powerful long-range effort with his left foot, and Hyypiä hitting a right-foot shot just wide after turning two West Ham defenders and beating another. Meanwhile, players were dropping like flies with cramp, Harewood in particular struggling to walk, but West Ham had already used all their substitutes.

With just two minutes remaining, West Ham went close when a free kick was headed towards goal by Harewood, and Reina, at full stretch, fingertipped it against the post. The rebound fell to Harewood, who could hardly move, and he fluffed his big chance to be a cup final hero, as the match ended 3-3.

The destination of the cup would be decided on a penalty shoot-out and decisions needed to be made about who was mentally fit and physically fit to take them. First to step up was Hamann for Liverpool, who scored easily. Zamora, one of West Ham's substitutes was next, and Reina continued his heroics with a fine save low to his right to give the Reds the advantage. This was short-lived, though, when Hyypiä's penalty was saved by Hislop and 40-year-old Teddy Sheringham levelled things up.

Gerrard, who seemed to have overcome his cramp, sent Hislop the wrong way to make it 2-1 to Liverpool, before Konchesky sent his penalty kick down the middle of the goal but only found Reina's outstretched boot, which kept the kick out. Riise blasted his penalty down the middle successfully to make it 3-1 to the Reds, so Ferdinand needed to score to keep the match alive, but Reina saved to his right again and the cup was Liverpool's.

%. %. %.

Reina had proved to be a hero after his first-half blunder, but this was Steven Gerrard's final. There are so many matches that could feature him as the match-winner, but for me this was the ultimate, particularly with that stunning 90th-minute goal. He proved to be one of Liverpool's greatest players over his 16-plus years at the club, during which he also won 114 England caps.

Gerrard won two FA Cups, three League Cups, one Champions League and one UEFA Cup with the Reds, as well as being voted the PFA Young Player of the Year, the PFA Player of the Year, the FWA Player of the Year and the PFA Fans' Player of the Year (twice). He played over 700 matches for the Reds, scoring 186 goals, but he also seemed to score when it really mattered, and on several occasions was the driving force behind Liverpool comebacks.

Despite overtures from Chelsea on two occasions, Stevie G remained a one-club player before his retirement from top-level football, with only Jamie Carragher and Ian Callaghan ahead of him in the appearance list. After a brief spell in the MLS with Los Angeles Galaxy, he returned to Liverpool to coach the under-18s before taking the management reins at Glasgow Rangers. I wonder what odds you could get on his being the next Liverpool manager, especially as his contract in Scotland expires at the same time as Jürgen Klopp's with the Reds?

39

Champions League Record Breakers

Liverpool 8 Besiktas 0
Champions League Group Phase
6 November 2007
Anfield
Attendance: 41,143

Liverpool	Besiktas
Reina	Hakan
Hyypiä	K. Serdar (Higuaín 62)
Riise	Djatta
Aurelio (Babel 63)	Üzülmez
Arbeloa	Ibrahim
Carragher	Mehmet (Ricardinho)
Gerrard (Lucas 72)	Delgado
Benayoun	Cisse
Mascherano	Ö. Serdar (Tandogan 46)
Voronin (Kewell 72)	Koray
Crouch	Bobô
Manager: Rafa Benitez	*Manager:* Saglam Ertugrul

AS FA Cup winners, Liverpool kicked off the 2006/07 season in the Charity Shield, defeating Chelsea 2-1 to lift what was to be their only trophy of a frustrating season. They again finished third in the Premier League and went out of the domestic cups early, but the Champions League at least brought another final appearance, after winning a penalty shoot-out against Chelsea in the semi-final. However, in the final in Athens, AC Milan got their revenge for Istanbul, beating the Reds 2-1.

Liverpool made a good start to 2007/08, remaining undefeated in their first 11 matches in various competitions, including a 6-0 trouncing of Derby County and a 1-1 draw away at Porto in the first match of the Champions League group phase. The unbeaten run came to an end in the next Champions League match though, with a 1-0 home defeat to Marseilles, and qualification for the knockout stage looked a forlorn hope when they went down 1-0 to Besiktas in Turkey. Coming into the return match with Besiktas, the Reds were bottom of the table and desperately needed to win to stand any chance of progressing.

※ ※ ※

At Anfield, Liverpool nearly got off to a great start when Crouch nodded the ball down to Voronin, but he placed his shot wide. Crouch then had a chance of his own but headed wide from Riise's cross, and Benayoun hit a shot into the side-netting after a slick move had cut the Besiktas defence apart.

However, Liverpool's intentions were clear … all-out attack, and it didn't take too long for the first goal to arrive. Voronin slid the ball to Crouch outside the Besiktas penalty area. The big man seemed to be surrounded by defenders, but one slid in and diverted the ball goalwards, leaving Crouch through on goal. Although the keeper saved his first effort, the ball fell kindly for Crouch to put the Reds ahead after just 19 minutes.

Liverpool continued to attack, and Riise was unlucky not to score when his header from a corner was cleared off the line. In fact, at this stage, there was no sign of the goal deluge to come, as the clock ticked past the half-hour mark. Then enter Yossi Benayoun. The Israel international had performed brilliantly for West Ham against the Reds in the 2006 FA Cup Final and came to Anfield one year later for £5m. He stayed for three seasons, making over 100 appearances and scoring 29 goals, three of them in this match.

His first perhaps had a stroke of good fortune after Liverpool were controversially awarded a throw-in that appeared to last come off Riise. The Norwegian left-back took a quick throw from about three yards further on to set Voronin free on the left wing. His cross was beautifully controlled by Benayoun and slotted past Hakan in the Besiktas goal. It remained 2-0 at half-time but the match was already completely under Liverpool's control.

Within 11 minutes of the restart the match was over and Benayoun had grabbed a hat-trick. First, Voronin and Riise combined again, this time Voronin sliding Riise in on the left. His powerful shot was parried by Hakan, but Benayoun was on hand to knock in the loose ball. Then four minutes later it was 4-0 after Besiktas made a mess of trying to play the ball out of defence, Djatta being forced into a foul on Voronin on the edge of his own penalty area. Gerrard lined up the free kick, sent in a low shot that Hakan should have gathered easily but again spilled straight to Benayoun, who gratefully knocked the ball into the empty net. Not the most difficult of hat-tricks, but a case of being in the right place at the right time.

On 69 minutes Gerrard got on the scoresheet himself as he drove forward from midfield and played a one-two with the excellent Voronin before smashing the ball past Hakan, who this time had no chance. Five goals, and Voronin had been involved in each one in what was his best performance in the red shirt.

Benitez decided to ring the changes, bringing on Babel, Lucas and Kewell, as Voronin got a well-deserved rest, and within six minutes of the arrival of the latter two, all three substitutes were involved in making it 6-0. Kewell, on the left wing, played the ball inside to Lucas, who switched the ball wide to Benayoun on the right wing. His low cross was neatly diverted in by Babel, who got in front of his marker for a nice back-heeled finish.

Just three minutes later, it was Babel again, this time with a freaky goal. A long ball pumped forward from Liverpool's defence looked innocuous, but Babel chased, putting the lone defender Ibrahim under pressure. His attempted clearance hit Babel and looped over the hapless keeper to make it 7-0.

Babel had a great opportunity for his hat-trick shortly afterwards when Kewell put in a cross from the left wing and Babel had a free header but sent it against the bar and the ball bounced clear. However, there was still time for one more goal, as Crouch, who had started the scoring, finished off a Champions League record-breaking scoreline of 8-0. Benayoun was the provider, sending in a pinpoint cross from the right wing, which Crouch nodded past Hakan to seal a magnificent night at Anfield.

※ ※ ※

The Besiktas match kick-started Liverpool's Champions League campaign, as they defeated Porto 4-1 at Anfield and Marseilles 4-0 away to progress to the knockout stages. The goals were also flowing in the FA Cup, with a 5-0 defeat of Luton and a 5-2 victory against non-league Havant & Waterlooville, although the visitors actually led 1-0 and 2-1, before another Benayoun hat-trick prevented what would have been a major upset.

However, in the league, despite losing few matches, Liverpool had drawn too many and were hovering around fourth place, where they were to finish at the end of the season. They then exited the FA Cup in an embarrassing home defeat to Barnsley, so the Champions League was again the only trophy to play for.

They progressed through the first knockout round by defeating Inter Milan 3-0 on aggregate. Kuyt and Gerrard were on target in the 2-0 home leg victory, while Torres scored the only goal of an impressive victory in the San Siro. They then faced Arsenal in the quarter-final, Kuyt scoring the equaliser in a 1-1 draw at the Emirates, so Liverpool were favourites to progress to yet another Champions League semi-final.

40

Another Dramatic Finale

Liverpool 4 Arsenal 2

Champions League Quarter-Final Second Leg
8 April 2008
Anfield
Attendance: 41,985

Liverpool	Arsenal
Reina	Almunia
Hyypiä	Clichy
Aurelio	Gallas
Carragher	Senderos
Skrtel	Touré
Gerrard	Diaby (van Persie 72)
Alonso	Fábregas
Mascherano	Flamini (Gilberto 42)
Torres (Riise 87)	Eboué (Walcott 72)
Crouch (Babel 78)	Adebayor
Kuyt (Arbeloa 90)	Hleb
Manager: Rafa Benitez	*Manager:* Arsène Wenger

ARSENAL CAME into the Champions League quarter-final second leg knowing that they must score at least once to progress to the semi-final, after drawing 1-1 at the Emirates, but then Liverpool were never a team to play for a goalless draw, so goals were virtually guaranteed at Anfield. They didn't take long to come either, and it was advantage Arsenal after just 13 minutes, following a frantic start to the match. Hleb played in Diaby just inside the Liverpool penalty area but his first touch looked to have taken him too wide, and with the tight angle there seemed no way he could score, but his drilled shot went between Reina and his near post to give the Gunners the lead. Not the best piece of goalkeeping, and Arsenal were now ahead on aggregate.

Liverpool immediately pressed forward but were leaving themselves vulnerable to Arsenal's counter-attacks, nearly paying the price when Diaby got free on the left wing and sent in a cross to the unmarked Adebayor. Fortunately, Reina just managed to get a decent punch on the ball as the two challenged for it and the ball broke kindly to Gerrard to take it clear of danger.

The Reds continued to apply pressure, with Gerrard's attempted cross deflected towards goal, forcing an awkward save for Almunia that led to a corner kick. Gerrard's deep corner was met with a brilliant header by Hyypiä that flew into the net and the scores were level after 30 minutes, both on the night and on aggregate. This was Sami Hyypiä's third Champions League quarter-final goal for the Reds, and the big Finn didn't score that many in his ten years at Anfield, netting just 35 times in his 464 matches. However, his job was stopping them at the other end, and the classy centre-back is one of the best the club has ever seen.

Despite the end-to-end action, there were no more goals before the break, although Arsenal did lose the influential Flamini to injury. It was, therefore, all to play for in the second half of a match that could still go to extra time and penalties.

Liverpool started the second half strongly, Crouch doing well to control, turn and shoot from the edge of the penalty area, but Almunia saved easily. Then Torres left his marker for dead on Liverpool's right wing and put in a low cross that found its way out to Aurelio, whose shot from distance was off target but struck Crouch and bounced agonisingly wide of the goal. The Reds had upped the tempo and the typical European night atmosphere began to ring around Anfield.

It seemed that Liverpool would surely soon take the lead, but they had to wait until the 69th minute, although it was well worth the wait. Crouch flicked on a long ball to Torres who controlled it on the left side of Arsenal's penalty area. There didn't seem to be too much danger at this point, but Torres pirouetted, came inside the defender and unleashed an unstoppable shot into the top corner to give the Reds the advantage.

Liverpool now led the tie 3-2 but another Arsenal goal would see the Gunners go through on away goals, and Adebayor had that opportunity within minutes of Torres's goal. A low through ball somehow evaded Liverpool's central defenders and found Adebayor racing through on goal. He decided to take a first-time shot and only managed to guide the ball wide when he had all the time in the world to control the ball first. Was that Arsenal's big chance gone?

Arsenal had brought on Walcott on 72 minutes in search of some inspiration, but Liverpool, who had brought on Babel six minutes later, seemed to have the match under control as they continued to attack. From one such attack on 83 minutes, Gerrard tried a speculative shot from long range but failed to make good contact with the ball. Arsenal gained control through Walcott and broke quickly. In fact, they broke incredibly quickly, as Walcott ran the length of the pitch, gliding past four Liverpool players as though they weren't there. I remember screaming at the TV for someone to just take his legs when he first started his run and accept the inevitable yellow card, but they simply couldn't get near enough to him.

Walcott carried on into Liverpool's penalty area where the defence was outnumbered three to two. He cut the ball back and Adebayor was this time more composed, sliding the ball past Reina to level the scores and give Arsenal the advantage with just a few minutes remaining. As with the never-forgotten Michael Thomas goal all those years before, my head was in my hands, but you have to accept it was a wonderful piece of play by Walcott at his best.

Two minutes later, the tie was turned on its head again. Arsène Wenger had been gesticulating to his team to keep calm after Adebayor's goal, but with Babel running at him and past him in the penalty area, Touré clearly hadn't got the message, as he clumsily brought him down for a Liverpool penalty at the Kop end. Who else would you want in such a pressure situation other than Steven Gerrard, who placed the ball, ran up and struck it into the top corner to give the Reds a 3-2 lead and break Arsenal hearts.

And there was still time for more. Arsenal had a free kick in their own half, which they pumped towards the Liverpool penalty area in a last forlorn hope of an equaliser. Liverpool won the header and immediately released the ball forward, where only Fábregas had been left to defend against the pacy Babel. The Dutchman outsprinted the Spaniard and put the ball past Almunia for a superb finish to the match, a 4-2 victory on the night and a 5-3 aggregate scoreline. Yet another magnificent night of European football, and yet another dramatic finale.

*% *% *%

Unfortunately, Liverpool were not to reach the Champions League Final this time. They faced another English team in the semi-finals … Chelsea yet again. After a 1-1 draw in the first leg at Anfield, a Drogba-inspired Chelsea won 3-2 at Stamford Bridge after extra time to go on to an all-English final against Manchester United, which they lost on penalties.

Liverpool's Champions League quarter-final goal specialist Sami Hyypiä went on to make over 100 appearances for his country, and with Liverpool won two FA Cups, two League Cups, one Champions League and one UEFA Cup. Perhaps not the huge haul that his career deserved, but he was a wonderful player for the Reds and still looks good when playing for the Liverpool Legends today.

41

Torres Tames Madrid

Liverpool 4 Real Madrid 0

Champions League First Knockout Round
10 March 2009
Anfield
Attendance: 42,550

Liverpool	Real Madrid
Reina	Casillas
Aurelio	Pepe
Arbeloa	Ramos
Carragher	Cannavaro (van de Vaart 64)
Skrtel	Heinze
Gerrard (Spearing 73)	Diarra
Alonso (Lucas 60)	Gago (Guti 77)
Babel	Sneijder
Mascherano	Raúl
Torres (Dossena 83)	Robben (Marcelo 46)
Kuyt	Higuaín
Manager: Rafa Benitez	*Manager:* Juande Ramos

IN 2008/09, Liverpool made another good start to the season, remaining unbeaten for 16 matches until a 2-1 reverse at Spurs, which saw them slip from top spot on goal difference from Chelsea. They also progressed through a tough group phase of the Champions League against Atlético de Madrid, PSV Eindhoven and Marseilles.

Having won their Champions League group, Liverpool would have hoped for an easier match than Real Madrid in the next round, but the Galácticos had finished runners-up to Juventus, so a trip to the Bernabéu beckoned in the first leg. This was a Real Madrid team boasting Casillas, Ramos, Cannavaro, Marcelo, Raúl and Higuaín to name but a few, so for Liverpool, without the influential Gerrard, to come away with a 1-0 victory after a late Benayoun goal was some achievement, and of course it made them favourites to progress with the home leg to come.

※ ※ ※

Goalscorer Benayoun was out injured for the second leg but Gerrard returned to the team to replace him, as Anfield witnessed another one of those magical European nights.

Madrid needed to score, and Liverpool weren't going to sit back and play for the goalless draw, so the match started at a frantic pace, Torres going close early on after a pass from Gerrard found him on the edge of the penalty area. Torres's brilliant turn completely fooled Cannavaro, but the Spaniard's shot was well saved by Casillas in the Madrid goal. From the resulting corner, Madrid headed clear and the ball fell invitingly for Mascherano 25 yards out. Although never a prolific goalscorer, he sent in a rasping volley and Casillas was forced to save brilliantly again, as Liverpool piled on the pressure.

However, Casillas could do nothing on 16 minutes when Torres gave Liverpool a deserved lead after woeful defending by Madrid. A long clearance from the Liverpool defence was allowed to bounce by Diarra, wrong-footing the Madrid central defenders. Torres and Kuyt pounced as Pepe went to ground, and the ball fell kindly for Kuyt, who simply laid it back for Torres to knock into the empty goal. Pepe, probably one of the dirtiest players I've ever seen, complained that Kuyt had fouled him, but the referee saw no problem and the goal stood.

Liverpool now had a 2-0 aggregate advantage and Madrid had it all to do. This was Torres's only goal of the match, but he was already running the Madrid defence ragged and would continue to do so all night. The Spaniard had joined the Reds from Real's city rivals Atlético de Madrid in 2007, so he would have enjoyed his performance against his arch-rivals, having also grown up as an Atlético fan.

Liverpool were now swarming all over Madrid, winning every challenge and soon came close to doubling their lead after Gerrard had won the ball in typical fashion. Eventually the ball fell to Torres in the penalty area, and he completely mesmerised the Madrid defence before sending in a cross that was met by Gerrard on the half-volley but unfortunately too close to Casillas.

The Reds were not to be denied their second though, as a long ball found Arbeloa wide on the right, and his attempted chest-down was adjudged by the assistant referee to have been handled by Heinze, although it clearly hit him high on the shoulder. However, there was no VAR and Liverpool had a penalty, which Gerrard converted to make it 2-0 after 28 minutes.

Madrid had so far created nothing but Sneijder came close to pulling one back when he nearly surprised Reina in the Liverpool goal by shooting direct from a free kick some 30 yards out. Reina reacted quickly to dive to his right and push the ball out for a corner.

It remained 2-0 at half-time but Liverpool weren't prepared to sit back and invite Madrid on, despite the Spanish team needing three goals and the Reds having a match at Old Trafford in four days' time. Just two minutes into the second half it was definitely game over for Madrid, when Gerrard scored his second on his 100th European appearance.

Again Liverpool won the ball in midfield, this time through Mascherano, and it was fed out to Babel on the left wing. He lined up his defender, took him on the outside and sent in a low cross that Gerrard allowed to go across his body, hitting it on the half-volley with his right foot into the roof of the net. It was a wonderful goal that summed up Liverpool's performance so far, as Madrid's players looked disconsolate.

Liverpool did sit back a little after the third goal and after a tricky run by Marcelo, Ramos put in a cross that Raúl nearly scored from, but he couldn't control his shot. However, it was too little, too late for Madrid by then.

Gerrard was denied a hat-trick when Casillas saved his shot after brilliant build-up work involving Alonso, Torres and Babel had again torn the Madrid team apart. Soon after, the Liverpool captain made way for Jay Spearing, as Benitez was comfortable enough to rest key players ahead of the United match, and the youngster was soon in the action, winning the ball in midfield, which led to Torres sending in a superb curling shot that had the excellent Casillas saving yet again.

Torres then made way on 73 minutes for Andrea Dossena, and it was the Italian who put the icing on the cake within ten minutes of his arrival. Liverpool broke quickly and the ball was fed up to Babel, now playing down the middle. He played the ball wide to Mascherano on the right and his first-time low cross was met by Dossena, who rifled in a left-foot shot via the arm of Casillas to seal a marvellous 4-0 victory over the giants of Spain.

42

Rounding Off the Perfect Week

Manchester United 1 Liverpool 4

Premier League
14 March 2009
Old Trafford
Attendance: 75,569

Manchester United	Liverpool
van der Sar	Reina
Evra	Hyypiä
Ferdinand	Aurelio
Vidic	Carragher
O'Shea	Skrtel
Park (Giggs 74)	Gerrard (El Zhar 90)
Carrick (Scholes 74)	Riera (Dossena 68)
Anderson (Berbatov 74)	Mascherano
Ronaldo	Lucas
Rooney	Torres (Babel 80)
Tevez	Kuyt
Manager: Alex Ferguson	*Manager:* Rafa Benitez

JUST FOUR days after trouncing the Galácticos, Liverpool faced table-topping Manchester United in a crucial match. Chelsea and Liverpool were both four points adrift of United, who also had two matches in hand, so a victory for the Red Devils in this one would almost certainly put Liverpool out of the title race. No one could have expected the result that kept the Reds in the hunt for their first Premier League title.

Alonso was out of the United match with injury, and Liverpool also lost Arbeloa during the warm-up, so into the team came now-veteran Sami Hyypiä.

The early exchanges provided moments of danger at both ends, through Park for United and Torres for Liverpool, but the defences appeared to be on top, and it looked like being a tight match. However, just 23 minutes into the match United were awarded a penalty when Reina rashly raced out of his goal to try to get to the ball before the onrushing Park but only managed to bring the South Korean down according to the referee. Replays show that the keeper pulled out of the challenge, but Park cleverly made sure there was some contact, as all good forwards do. Reina dived the right way but couldn't get a hand to Ronaldo's accurate penalty kick that was tucked right into the corner of the net.

United's lead didn't last long though – just five minutes – and it was that man Torres again, who was having an excellent week. Vidic, who was to have a torrid match, allowed Skrtel's long punt downfield to bounce. It went over his head, and the advancing Torres sped past the central defender and was clean through on van der Sar in the United goal. The Spaniard calmly took the ball on before sliding a left-foot shot past the Dutch keeper.

United came back at Liverpool, Park in particular posing a threat, and Carrick hitting a shot wide from distance, but it was Liverpool who took the lead a minute before half-time when Torres and Gerrard linked up and Evra took Gerrard down just inside the penalty area. Captain Gerrard picked himself up and hit his penalty firmly to van der Sar's right. The keeper guessed correctly but, as with Ronaldo's penalty, the accuracy was such that the keeper stood no chance. Liverpool took a 2-1 lead into the break.

United came out strongly in the second half in search of the equaliser but Liverpool held firm. However, they were thankful for the woodwork when Ronaldo made a run down the right wing and sent in a mishit cross that fooled Reina and struck his near post. Fortunately, the keeper was first to react to the loose ball.

United came close again just past the hour mark after a good move involving Anderson, Park and Tevez, which sent Ronaldo free on the left. His deep cross was met by Rooney's far-post header across goal, which Tevez couldn't quite get on the end of.

On 74 minutes, Alex Ferguson made a triple substitution in an attempt to save the match, but only two minutes later Vidic's nightmare afternoon got even worse when he fouled Gerrard, who had been put through on goal by a clever Kuyt flick, and the referee showed the Serbian the red card. At least Torres couldn't torment him any more for the remainder of the match.

The foul was just a yard outside the penalty area and up stepped Aurelio to curl a brilliant free kick over the defensive wall and into the net as a static van der Sar looked on in disbelief. United down to ten men and Liverpool ahead 3-1 ... the week was getting better and better for some of us.

Gerrard had a great opportunity to add the fourth after good work by Dossena in providing a ball into the penalty area for Babel resulted in a deft back-heel by the Dutch player to the free Gerrard. Somehow Stevie G managed to blast his left-foot shot well over the bar.

However, there was to be a great finale to the match in the final minute as Reina's long goal kick went over the midfield and suddenly Dossena was racing in on goal alongside O'Shea. Dossena won the foot race and, as van der Sar had advanced too far from his goal, the Italian delivered a beautifully judged lob over the keeper's head and into the net for his second goal in two matches to round off an emphatic 4-1 victory. They were, in fact, the only two goals

Dossena scored for the Reds, but he could hardly have picked two better opponents to score against.

%% %% %%

The goals were flowing for Liverpool, as in their next match they best Aston Villa 5-0, so in the space of 12 days it was three wins, 13 goals scored and just a dodgy Ronaldo penalty conceded. However, it was a simple 1-0 victory at Fulham that saw the Reds hit top spot in the league by two points, although United still had two matches in hand.

A 3-1 setback against old rivals Chelsea in the first leg of the Champions League quarter-final brought Liverpool's winning run to an end, but the goals kept coming as Liverpool next beat Blackburn 4-0. However, Manchester United had won one of their extra matches, so now led the league by one point, with one match in hand.

Unfortunately, although Liverpool continued to score plenty of goals, they also started to concede, resulting in consecutive 4-4 draws. The first was in the second leg against Chelsea in the Champions League, after the Reds had led 2-0 and looked as though they may be going through, but a Frank Lampard double sent the Blues into the semi-final.

Liverpool's next match should really read Liverpool 4 Arshavin 4, as the Arsenal forward was unplayable in an incredible match, in which Torres and Benayoun both scored two for the Reds. This draw took Liverpool back to the top of the table, but only on goal difference, and United now had two matches in hand.

The Reds could do no more than win their final six matches, which they accomplished, scoring 14 more goals and conceding only two; however, as expected, United didn't slip up, taking the title by four points, but Liverpool appeared to be mounting a serious challenge for their first Premier League title.

43

Arsenal Gunned Down

Liverpool 5 Arsenal 1
Premier League
8 February 2014
Anfield
Attendance: 44,701

Liverpool	Arsenal
Mignolet	Szczesny
Touré	Sagna
Cissokho	Mertesacker
Skrtel	Koscielny
Flanagan	Monreal (Gibbs 61)
Gerrard (Ibe 76)	Arteta
Coutinho	Wilshere
Henderson	Oxlade-Chamberlain
Sterling	Özil (Rosický 61)
Suarez (Aspas 86)	Cazorla
Sturridge (Allen 66)	Giroud (Podolski 60)
Manager: Brendan Rodgers	*Manager:* Arsène Wenger

I GUESS that the observant amongst you will have noticed that we've jumped to 2014, so all that promise of 2008/09 came to nothing. In fact, 2009/10 saw the Reds slump to seventh in the league and fail to get out of the group phase of the Champions League. They did make it to the semi-final of the Europa League but lost to Atlético de Madrid on away goals.

The end of the season saw the departure of Rafa Benitez, to be replaced by quite possibly the worst manager Liverpool have ever had, Roy Hodgson. Thankfully, he didn't last long, as a terrible first half of 2010/11 saw the Reds win only seven of their 20 league matches, losing nine, which left them 12th in the table. Hodgson didn't see out the season, and Kenny Dalglish stepped in to take over temporarily, managing to take them up to sixth by the end of the season.

Dalglish remained in post for 2011/12 but Liverpool had their worst league finish since 1993/94, finishing eighth. However, the domestic cups provided some relief, as the Reds won their eighth League Cup in a dire final, beating Cardiff City on penalties, and getting to the final of the FA Cup, before going down 2-1 to Chelsea, Drogba again proving to be their nemesis.

Despite having brought some silverware back to Anfield, Dalglish called it a day at the end of the season, to be replaced by Brendan Rodgers, who had been doing an excellent job at Swansea, and had a reputation for delivering attractive football. However, there was no immediate improvement, with the Reds finishing seventh in the league in 2012/13 and not having a sniff at any cup success. Ironically, Swansea went on to win the League Cup, thrashing Bradford City 5-0 in the final.

There were, though, some signs of the attacking style to come, with Liverpool beating Norwich 5-2 and 5-0, Swansea 5-0 and Newcastle 6-0. In particular, the strike partnership of Suarez and Sturridge was deadly and, once again, hopes were being raised of that first Premier League title now that Rodgers's style was bedding in.

The following season, 2013/14, was to be a thriller, as moneybags Manchester City were now the team to beat, and Liverpool looked to climb out of mediocrity to put in a really serious challenge for the title. They had the advantage of no European football, due to their lowly finish in the previous season's league table, so there was no better opportunity for the Reds to win their first Premier League title.

They got off to a good start, winning their first three league matches, but by the beginning of December it looked like another disappointing season when a 3-1 defeat to Hull City left them in fourth place in the league, seven points behind leaders Arsenal.

Despite a good run of form during the winter months, Liverpool were still fourth, now eight points behind the Gunners, and seven behind Manchester City, who also had a match in hand. Liverpool's next match was a big one, at home to league leaders Arsenal, and a chance to close the gap.

※ ※ ※

Arsenal hadn't lost at Anfield in seven years but Liverpool were in good form at home and were simply too good for the Gunners right from the start, taking the lead in the very first minute through the unlikely source of Martin Skrtel. The uncompromising Slovakian central defender was in his sixth season at Anfield and had built a cult following for his tough-tackling style and no-nonsense defending, but on this day he was to become a goalscorer extraordinaire, bagging the first two goals of a remarkable first-half performance.

His first came as the Reds were awarded a free kick for a foul by Mertesacker wide on the Liverpool left, halfway into the Arsenal half. Gerrard sent in a perfect cross that was between the goalkeeper, Szczesny, and his defenders, and Skrtel ghosted in at the far post to volley past the keeper with his knee. He then set off to the crowd to celebrate a rare goal at the right end. Overall, he was to play over 300 matches for Liverpool, scoring 18 goals, but also had the bad habit of scoring at the wrong end, mainly due to his determination to get in the way of opponents' shots.

Three minutes later, Sturridge had a shot from distance saved by Szczesny as the Reds continued their positive start to the match. Then after nine minutes Skrtel was at it again. Liverpool won a corner after good work by Sturridge had played in the overlapping Flanagan, whose tight-angled shot was saved by Szczesny. Gerrard's outswinging corner was met by Skrtel's stooping header that looped over Oxlade-Chamberlain, who was protecting the far post, for 2-0. This time, off set Martin with his shirt pulled over his head as Anfield went wild.

Liverpool soon had the opportunity to go three up, when a ball forward to Suarez was brilliantly directed first time by the Uruguayan into the path of Sturridge. With just the keeper to beat and no defenders in sight, Sturridge somehow put the ball well wide of the gaping net, as Suarez looked on in disbelief (or was that disgust).

They had an even better chance two minutes later when Sterling ran into acres of space on Liverpool's left and put in a low cross that evaded Suarez and was put behind for a corner by Wilshere. Gerrard sent his corner kick low to the edge of the penalty area where Suarez was waiting. He controlled the ball before hitting a superb shot that beat Szczesny all ends up but cannoned against the post. The ball rebounded straight to Touré, who had an open goal but put his shot wide.

Just 12 minutes of the match had elapsed, and Liverpool could have had four goals. It was an amazing start to the match, which was about to get better on 16 minutes. Henderson won the ball on the halfway line and set off towards the Arsenal penalty area, playing in Suarez on the right wing. He sent in a first-time low cross to the far post where Sterling was racing in to slot the ball past Szczesny for number three, as Liverpool continued to run riot against a stunned Arsenal.

On 20 minutes it was 4-0, as Özil misplaced a pass in the Liverpool half and they broke quickly through Coutinho, who played a slide-rule pass through for Sturridge, who was racing down the middle. He outpaced the Arsenal defence and shot low past the keeper to cap an incredible 20-minute spell for the Reds against the league leaders.

Unsurprisingly, the tempo dropped after such a whirlwind start to the match, and Liverpool went into the break just the four goals to the good, with Arsenal only having had one serious attempt on goal. However, the Reds didn't exactly sit back at the start of the second half and soon added to their tally when Sterling got his second on 52 minutes. A superb long ball down Liverpool's left wing by Touré saw Sterling inexplicably all alone and through on goal, as Arsenal's defenders seemed to have gone AWOL. His first shot was straight at the keeper, but he knocked in the rebound to make it 5-0.

Sterling should have had a hat-trick when Gerrard sent in a free kick from the halfway line that eluded everyone and found Sterling creeping in at the far post. He slid in to try to divert the ball in but found the side-netting.

All five goals had been scored by players whose surnames began with S, and Suarez tried to add to that just after the hour mark when he decided to shoot from a 40-yard free kick when everyone was expecting a cross. He had Szczesny scrambling to tip the ball over the bar, as the Reds looked like scoring seven or eight against Arsenal's inadequate defending.

Coutinho was putting on a typical masterclass in midfield and set up another opportunity as he broke from just outside his own penalty area, showing great balance to shrug off challenges before sending a pass forward to Henderson, who was breaking on the right. He clipped a neat shot towards the far post, but it curled away to safety.

Although Liverpool looked like scoring at any time, it was in fact the Gunners who scored what was to be the final goal of the match in the 69th minute. In a rare attack, Oxlade-Chamberlain found Sagna wide on Arsenal's right wing, who played a return ball to Oxlade-Chamberlain just inside the penalty area. A rash challenge by Gerrard brought down the future Liverpool man for a penalty, which was converted down the centre of the goal by Arteta for 5-1.

Liverpool continued to search for goals though, and again Sterling had the chance for his hat-trick as he hit top gear down the left wing, leaving Arsenal defenders in his wake. As Szczesny came out, Sterling shot but only managed to hit the keeper's legs, and the ball trickled past the post, agonisingly close, but out for a corner.

The match may have ended 5-1 but it could easily have approached double figures, given Liverpool's dominance and missed opportunities, as they put a large dent in Arsenal's title challenge.

※ ※ ※

In fact, this was a season when Liverpool went on to score over 100 league goals, hitting five or more in a match on four occasions, but it wasn't to be quite enough. After beating Manchester City 3-2 on 13 April 2014, the Reds led the league title race by two points from Chelsea and seven points from City, who had two matches in hand.

It was now in Liverpool's hands, but their next match was at home to Chelsea, which turned out to be the match in which the title slipped away, literally, as Gerrard's slip allowed Chelsea to take the lead, to which they added a second goal in the 90th minute as Liverpool chased the equaliser.

Manchester City now had one match in hand and trailed Liverpool by three points but had a better goal difference. Next up for Liverpool was an away match at Crystal Palace, in which they showed a bit of naivety after leading 3-0 and cruising to victory. Rather than settle for the win, Liverpool went for broke and continued to attack in an attempt to improve their goal difference, but this backfired when Palace scored three times in the final 11 minutes to draw the match. This draw more or less sealed the title for Manchester City, who then won their match in hand and their final match of the season to take the title once again, leaving Reds fans wondering whether their team would ever get their hands on that coveted trophy.

44

Jürgen's Specs Go Walkabout

Norwich City 4 Liverpool 5
Premier League
23 January 2016
Carrow Road
Attendance: 27,108

Norwich City	Liverpool
Rudd	Mignolet
Pinto	Clyne
Martin	Touré
Bassong	Sakho
Brady	Moreno (Caulker 89)
Grabban	Milner
Howson	Henderson (Benteke 75)
Redmond (Jarvis 69)	Lucas
Naismith (Jerome 81)	Can
Hoolahan (Olsson 69)	Ibe (Lallana 58)
Mbokani	Firmino
Manager: Alex Neil	*Manager:* Jürgen Klopp

AFTER THE disappointment of losing the title race in 2013/14, hopes were high that the Reds would go one better in 2014/15 but, alas, it wasn't to be. They finished sixth in the league, 25 points adrift of champions Chelsea and again went out of the Champions

273

League at the group phase. There were two semi-final appearances in the domestic cups, but defeats meant that they finished the season empty-handed. There was even the embarrassment of a 6-1 defeat by Stoke City in the final match of the season, Liverpool's biggest defeat since 1963, when they lost 7-2 to Spurs.

The pressure was on Brendan Rodgers, and a poor start to 2014/15 meant that time was up for him, and he was replaced by Jürgen Klopp, who had been so successful at Borussia Dortmund. It was a difficult time to step into the hot seat, and three draws in Klopp's first three matches in charge gave no indication of what was to come. However, the results soon started to flow, as Liverpool progressed through to the League Cup semi-final and to the next stage of the Europa League. Things were looking up, although they were still only sixth in the league table, which was led by Manchester City, with Leicester City surprisingly giving them a run for their money.

Liverpool's league form didn't really improve over the remainder of the season, but one match epitomised the spirit that Klopp was beginning to instil in his team, which at that stage seemed to be something along the lines of however many you score, we'll score more.

Although Norwich had drawn 1-1 at Anfield earlier in the season, Liverpool had a good habit of scoring plenty of goals against the Canaries, beating them 3-2 and 5-1 in 2013/14, and 5-0 and 5-2 in 2012/13. This match was to be no exception.

※ ※ ※

It wasn't an explosive start to the match at Carrow Road, as Liverpool took 15 minutes to have their first attempt on goal, Firmino hitting his shot high and wide. Meanwhile, Norwich had created nothing, and there was no sign of the fireworks to come.

However, just three minutes after his miss, Firmino was on the mark to give Liverpool the lead. Ibe played the ball wide to Moreno on the Liverpool left, who slipped the ball inside to Milner on the edge of the penalty area. Milner's quick pass to the feet of Firmino took the Norwich defence by surprise as they raced out to try to catch the Brazilian offside. Firmino's low shot was possibly going wide but struck the feet of the Norwich keeper, Rudd, as he came out to block the attempt, and the ball was diverted towards the far post, struck the inside of the woodwork and went in.

It may have been a bit lucky, but Bobby Firmino didn't mind. It was only his second goal away from Anfield all season, his first season with Liverpool after signing for £29m from Hoffenheim, but after a slow start he was now starting to make a great impression with his hard work and creativity.

Despite the goal, the match still didn't spring into life, and the expected goal avalanche from Liverpool didn't arrive, Moreno being the only player to have an attempt on goal but putting his shot wide. Then on 29 minutes, after a bout of head tennis in and around the Liverpool penalty area following a Norwich corner, the ball eventually came to ground on the edge of the Liverpool goal area at the feet of Mbokani. He had his back to goal but decided to back-heel the ball, taking the defence and Mignolet completely by surprise for an excellent innovative goal to level the scores. Liverpool had been struggling to defend corners in recent matches and had now conceded another goal from a corner in this match.

Liverpool's performance didn't improve, having only Clyne's blocked shot to show for their efforts, and five minutes before half-time they found themselves behind. Hoolahan had the ball just inside the Liverpool penalty area on the Norwich right, and Naismith, making his debut, made a good run inside him and wasn't picked up by any player in a red shirt. He strolled on to the ball and drove an angled shot past Mignolet and inside the far post to the delight of the home fans. It was 2-1 to Norwich at half-time and Liverpool's defensive play had been pretty appalling.

Things needed to improve drastically in the second half, but they only got worse when Moreno conceded a penalty just seven minutes after the restart after fouling the lively Naismith. Hoolahan stepped up, and although Mignolet dived the right way, he didn't get a hand on the ball and it was 3-1, with the match rapidly slipping away from the Reds and Klopp looking on grim-faced.

Hope was restored within two minutes though, when Henderson scored a rare goal to reduce the deficit. Clyne played in a low cross from Liverpool's right towards Firmino, who helped it on its way to the onrushing Henderson, and he calmly stroked the ball past Rudd for an excellent finish. A dull match had suddenly sparked into life and the travelling fans had something to sing about at last.

After 58 minutes, Klopp brought on Lallana for Ibe, and what an inspired substitution it turned out to be, when just five minutes later Lallana set up Liverpool's equaliser. Firmino started the move on the halfway line, passing the ball wide to Milner, who helped it on to Lallana racing down the left wing. Firmino had immediately moved forward after his earlier pass, and Lallana's pinpoint low cross fell perfectly for the Brazilian to control and guide the ball over Rudd for 3-3. It was a devastating break and clinical finishing that epitomised Liverpool's attacking play, and there was still nearly half an hour to go.

Norwich must have been devastated at losing a two-goal lead, but their heads didn't drop, Mignolet being forced into a save by Bassong. Meanwhile, at the other end, Firmino set up Moreno but Rudd saved his shot, as both teams sought what could be the winning goal.

On 74 minutes it seemed as if Liverpool had finally broken Norwich's resolve when they completed a remarkable comeback to lead 4-3. After Can put in a meaty but clean challenge on the halfway line, the ball fell to Martin. He decided to play a back pass to his keeper and, despite facing his own goal, he hadn't seen Milner lurking. Milner raced on to the ball and was clean through on goal. As Rudd came out, Milner switched the ball to his right foot to open up the angle and slotted the ball into the net.

There were just 16 minutes remaining and it looked as if Liverpool had got out of jail and would go on to close the match out. However, that was then. They can do that now, but back then they didn't know how to defend a lead and I was never comfortable unless they were at least three goals ahead. You knew there was always a mistake coming or that they would invite too much pressure at the end of the match. And they didn't sit back and defend their lead here either, Firmino having a shot saved and Milner having his shot blocked, but as the clock ticked past 90 minutes, Norwich knew that they would probably still have one more opportunity.

That opportunity came two minutes into added time when they had a free kick halfway into their own half. Pinto pumped the ball up to the edge of the Liverpool penalty area where it was challenged for and broke to Bassong 30 yards out. The big defender just hit a low hard shot that flew past Mignolet and it was 4-4. Simple but effective, as Carrow Road went absolutely crazy, and Klopp argued with the fourth official about the added time.

It was already a remarkable match and a remarkable scoreline and I was watching in disbelief that the Reds had let this slip after such a great comeback, despite my misgivings about their ability to defend a lead. But this team was made of something much sterner when they faced a crisis, and they weren't done yet.

Klopp had earlier brought on Caulker to try to defend the inevitable late onslaught by Norwich, which he'd failed to do, but he at least played a part in Liverpool's winner. Rather than let their chins drop after throwing the match away, the Reds went straight back on the attack, throwing players forward from the restart. Can, on Liverpool's left wing, played in a deep cross that fell to Caulker, whose shot was blocked, but the ball fell to Lallana, who met it with a left-foot shot that bounced into the ground and up into the top corner of the net.

Norwich fans, who had still been celebrating their team's equaliser, couldn't believe what they were witnessing as Lallana set off on a celebratory run, shirtless, and Rudd sat in his goalmouth, distraught.

Klopp raced up the sideline and was caught up in a massive celebration of his own with Lallana and some of his players, then the rest of players and staff joined in and Klopp was somewhere in the middle of the melee.

Although the referee eventually managed to restart the match, that was it, and Liverpool had won 5-4 in a quite incredible climax to the match. In the after-match interviews it transpired that, in the celebrations, Jürgen Klopp had lost his famous spectacles. He had no idea what had happened to them but really didn't care after such a dramatic win. Slow-motion replays showed them flying into the air, broken, as he was swallowed up in the crazy scenes following Lallana's goal.

Despite Lallana's late heroics, Firmino was man of the match, having scored two and set up another, and has gone on to become a pivotal part of Klopp's team. He's now played over 200 matches, scored over 70 goals, and is one of the first names on the teamsheet. Let's hope we can hang on to him for a very long time.

※ ※ ※

Just to show the other side of their personality, Liverpool's next match was a 1-0 home defeat to Stoke City in the second leg of the League Cup semi-final, having won the first leg by the same scoreline at the Britannia Stadium. However, the Reds won the penalty shoot-out 6-5 to progress to their first cup final under Klopp in only his first season in charge.

The topsy-turvy form continued but, as the season progressed, the good started to outweigh the bad. Unfortunately, there was no League Cup trophy, although they matched Manchester City at Wembley, the match finishing 1-1.

This time the penalty shoot-out went the wrong way, as Willy Caballero became a hero in the City goal, saving three Liverpool penalties.

Progress continued in the Europa League, however, Liverpool beating Manchester United comfortably 3-1 on aggregate to set up a mouth-watering quarter-final against Borussia Dortmund, Klopp's old team.

The first leg in Dortmund was all going swimmingly when Origi put the Reds one up after 36 minutes but Hummels equalised 12 minutes later to earn Dortmund a 1-1 draw to take to Anfield, although Liverpool remained favourites to progress to the semi-final. And if you wanted another example of how the previous never-say-die attitude of Liverpool now fused with the *gegenpressing* style of Jürgen Klopp's new approach, the second leg had it all.

45

Another Stunning Comeback

Liverpool 4 Borussia Dortmund 3
Europa League Quarter-Final Second Leg
14 April 2016
Anfield
Attendance: 42,984

Liverpool	Borussia Dortmund
Mignolet	Weidenfeller
Clyne	Piszczek
Lovren	Sokratis
Sakho	Hummels
Moreno	Schmelzer
Milner	Gonzalo (Gündoğan 82)
Coutinho	Weigl
Lallana (Allen 62)	Mkhitaryan
Can (Lucas 80)	Kagawa (Ginter 77)
Firmino (Sturridge 62)	Reus (Ramos 83)
Origi	Aubameyang
Manager: Jürgen Klopp	*Manager:* Thomas Tuchel

GOING INTO this match, I felt extremely confident that Liverpool would progress, as Dortmund hadn't really shown anything in the first leg that worried me too much, although Aubameyang had a good reputation despite doing nothing of note in the first leg.

So, I settled down to enjoy the match on TV without the usual trepidation.

That feeling didn't last long. Within nine minutes, Dortmund were two up, the tie looked to be over already and Aubameyang had made his mark. He had one curling left-foot shot go wide after only three minutes, as Dortmund looked to attack from the start. Then on five minutes, Coutinho gave the ball away on the left, deep into Dortmund's half, and the German team broke quickly, with several Liverpool players out of position, having moved forward. Kagawa had acres of space to run into and played a ball towards the Liverpool penalty area, where it was lobbed over the Liverpool defence by Gonzalo to Aubameyang, onside and with only Mignolet to beat. Aubameyang volleyed, Mignolet pulled off a brilliant save but the ball fell to Mkhitaryan, who had the simple job of sliding it into the empty net.

Liverpool were opened up again just four minutes later when, for the second time, they lost the ball deep in the Dortmund half. Having pushed men forward again, they had left space for Reus to run into as the defenders back-pedalled. He played a beautiful curling pass that took out the defenders and left Aubameyang clear. He still had a lot to do, as the angle didn't really favour him, but he blasted a shot into the roof of the net, giving Mignolet no chance. Dortmund now led 3-1 on aggregate and had two away goals, so Liverpool needed to score three times to progress. Not impossible given the time left in the match but could they avoid conceding another goal?

Liverpool's first opportunity came on 16 minutes when Clyne found Milner on the right wing. He played the ball inside to Lallana, who played a clever first-time pass to Origi, who had found space inside the penalty area. Origi's shot was partially blocked by Sokratis but flew up and hit the post, going out for a corner.

It was all-out attack now for the Reds, Moreno blasting high and wide after good work by Origi, who looked to be the likely source of a goal if one was going to come. And he had his chance on 25 minutes when Milner took the ball to the byline on Liverpool's right and sent in a powerful low cross. Origi did well to get in front of his marker and flick the ball towards goal, but he got a bit too much on it and turned it beyond the far post.

It seemed as if it was going to be a frustrating night for the Reds, as they now began to get into the match but couldn't turn their possession into the all-important goals. However, Dortmund were still a threat on the break, and Aubameyang was clear again just one minute after Origi's miss, but Sakho managed to get a foot in just as Aubameyang shot, and the ball fell kindly for Mignolet. A minute later, Firmino went close with a header from a Coutinho cross, as the action swung from end to end.

After a brief lull, it was Aubameyang who was nearly played in again on 31 minutes after Piszczek's overlapping run down the Dortmund right had left Can in his wake. Piszczek reached the byline and pulled the ball back to the waiting Aubameyang but Mignolet got down low to his right and just got a fingertip to the ball to divert it away to safety.

Aubameyang could have already had a hat-trick, and perhaps his easiest chance was to come five minutes later when he played a one-two with Reus and found himself free in Liverpool's penalty area but he rushed his shot, putting it well wide of the gaping goal.

Meanwhile, as an exciting first half came to a close, Liverpool were still threatening to find a way back into the match, Coutinho and Origi both going close, but there was no change to the scoreline by the break, and Liverpool needed three goals in front of the Kop with only 45 minutes to play.

Hopes were raised of yet another famous European comeback when Origi finally got on the scoresheet three minutes after the restart. Good play by Can from the halfway line saw him play a couple of one-twos then slide a pass through to Origi, who controlled the ball before guiding it past the advancing keeper to reduce the deficit.

However, Liverpool's hopes appeared to have been dashed just nine minutes later when Dortmund stretched their lead, leaving Liverpool needing three goals with only 33 minutes remaining. Hummels strode forward from the Dortmund defence and slipped a perfectly weighted pass inside Clyne for Reus to run on to. He only had Mignolet to beat and slid the ball around the keeper, curling it inside the far post. Liverpool fans had gone crazy when Origi had scored, but they were now stunned, as Reus celebrated in front of the travelling fans at the Anfield Road end.

Liverpool needed to hit back quickly, and Klopp called upon reinforcements by bringing on Allen and Sturridge for Lallana and Firmino. Allen immediately got into the tempo of the match and started the move that led to Liverpool's second goal of the night. He played the ball wide to Moreno, who slid it forward to Coutinho. He played a slick one-two with Milner on the edge of the penalty area, then hit an arrow-like shot, low and hard into the corner of the net. It was now 3-4 on aggregate but Liverpool knew they needed to win the match to reach the semi-final.

Origi was having an excellent game, and the 20-year-old was doing everything he could to keep the Reds in the match, turning and shooting narrowly too high on 68 minutes. Meanwhile, Liverpool's defenders, while not performing well at one end of the pitch, were doing their part to try to get their team back in the match, Clyne having a shot blocked and Lovren putting a shot wide after a Milner corner.

It was to be another defender, Sakho, who was to really give the Reds hope with 12 minutes remaining. Coutinho's low corner was helped on its way by Sturridge at the near post, and Sakho was on hand to divert the ball in to send the Kop wild. They knew that 12 minutes was plenty of time for this Liverpool team to score the all-important fourth goal.

Dortmund now went completely into their shell and decided to sit back, bringing on the more defensive Gündoğan and Ginter for Gonzalo and Kagawa, and Liverpool were throwing everything and everybody forward in search of the killer goal. On 84 minutes, Milner sent in a deep free kick to the right of the Dortmund penalty area, where Lovren had peeled away into space. However, the big Croatian had a rush of blood and blasted a shot way over the bar, rather than controlling the ball and playing it across. We may be able to forgive him for that rush of blood now but, at the time, the fans behind the goal and me watching on TV thought that it may have been the one big chance that the Reds were going to get.

On 90 minutes, Liverpool had another free kick from the same spot, and Milner feigned to play it high into the penalty area, where there was the usual crowd scene. Instead he played it low to the right of the penalty area for Sturridge, but his control was poor and took him wide with his back to goal, the opportunity to create something seemingly gone. Milner had spotted Sturridge's problem and ran forward into the space, Sturridge cutting the ball inside for him to take to the byline. Milner crossed, and there was the head of Lovren to power the ball past the keeper to send the crowd wild, and I distinctly remember screaming, 'They've done it!' at the top of my voice.

Cue the mass pile-up of players in the corner at the Kop end and the now-famous fist-pumping action of Jürgen Klopp. There was, though, one further scare to come when Dortmund won a free kick just outside the Liverpool penalty area after a foul by Lucas as the clock ticked into the final minute of added time. Gündoğan lined up the free kick and all hearts were in mouths, but his shot was narrowly wide, and it proved to be the last kick of the match. Anfield erupted at yet another thrilling Liverpool comeback and another European glory night.

Dejan Lovren proved to be the hero of the night. The Croatian international had been at the club for two years after signing from

Southampton and it would be fair to say the jury is still out on him even now, as he can sometimes be a colossus at the back but then make a stupid mistake that leads to an opposition goal. He's only scored eight goals for the club in over 180 matches, which for a big centre-half who should get on the end of set pieces is not enough, but he will always be seen as a hero for his goal that sent Liverpool into the Europa League semi-final.

%% %% %%

In the semi-final, Liverpool faced Villarreal, losing 1-0 in the first leg in Spain, but comfortably progressing to the final with a 3-0 home win. In that final, it was to be Spanish opposition again, this time Sevilla, who had won the trophy for the past two seasons. The league season had finished with Leicester City beating all the odds to take the Premier League title by ten points, with Liverpool finishing a disappointing eighth, so winning this final was the only route to European football for the following season.

It looked as if the Reds were going to coast to victory after a superb first-half display, but they had only a solitary Sturridge goal to show for their efforts. When they talk about a game of two halves, sometimes that really is the case, as Sevilla looked like a different team in the second half, and so did Liverpool. The equaliser came in the very first minute of the restart and Liverpool suddenly looked very shaky, as Sevilla added a second on 64 minutes and a third on 70 minutes to seal their hat-trick of Europa League trophies in a well-deserved win.

Sadly for Liverpool, they had lost two finals in the season, but the future was still looking bright, and two cup finals in the first season of a new manager are not to be sniffed at. Certainly, the Liverpool fans were very optimistic going into 2016/17.

46

How to Beat Man City

Liverpool 3 Manchester City 0
Champions League Quarter-Final First Leg
4 April 2018
Anfield
Attendance: 50,685

Liverpool	Manchester City
Karius	Ederson
van Dijk	Walker
Lovren	Otamendi
Robertson	Kompany
Alexander-Arnold	Laporte
Milner	Fernandinho
Henderson	De Bruyne
Oxlade-Chamberlain (Moreno 85)	Silva
Firmino (Solanke 71)	Gündoğan (Sterling 57)
Salah (Wijnaldum 52)	Sané
Mané	Jesus
Manager: Jürgen Klopp	*Manager:* Pep Guardiola

THE INEVITABLE optimism for 2016/17 proved to be a bit premature, although Liverpool did improve their league finish to fourth, meaning that they were back in the Champions League for the following season. There were no trophies for the cabinet, the closest being a semi-final appearance in the League Cup that led to a disappointing two-leg defeat against Southampton during a dismal run at the start of 2017 when the Reds won just two of 12 matches to also slip out of contention for the league title and out of the FA Cup.

The following season saw Liverpool progress through the Champions League qualifying round with a comfortable 6-3 aggregate win over TSG 1899 Hoffenheim, and start their Premier League campaign well, including a 4-0 drubbing of Arsenal. However, following Mané's 37th-minute sending off at Manchester City in the next match, the Reds subsided to a 5-0 hammering.

The Champions League group stage was a topsy-turvy affair, Liverpool conceding leads both at home and away to draw twice with Sevilla, but then hitting seven goals past both NK Maribor and Spartak Moscow to progress through to the knockout rounds.

Goals were flowing in the league too, the Reds putting four past West Ham and Bournemouth, and five past Brighton and Swansea. There was also a memorable return match with Manchester City, in which Liverpool showed that attacking them was the only way to beat them, racing into a 4-1 lead, as the front three of Mané, Salah and Firmino showed what a force they were becoming. A late flurry from City led to them pulling two goals back as Liverpool's earlier hard work resulted in them tiring, but they were able to hang on to show that City were beatable.

At this stage Liverpool were third in the league and remained in the top four for the remainder of the season, finally finishing fourth, after some more big wins against West Ham, Watford and Brighton. However, despite hitting 84 league goals in the season, they lagged 25 points behind champions Manchester City, with both teams also having their eyes firmly fixed on Champions League success.

Liverpool's first knockout stage opponents were Porto, and again the goalscoring machine was in full flow, as the Reds stormed to a 5-0 victory in Portugal, with Mané hitting a hat-trick, and Salah and Firmino scoring the others. A dull goalless draw at Anfield was more than enough to see Liverpool through to the quarter-final, where they were to face the might of Pep Guardiola's Manchester City, the first leg being at Anfield.

I must admit that the prospect of facing City over two legs was pretty daunting, and although the Reds had shown that they could beat them in a one-off match, I didn't truly believe they could do it over the two legs. Liverpool needed a good result at home in the first leg to take to the Etihad to give them any chance but I'm sure even they couldn't have dreamed of just how good a result they were going to get.

%, %, %,

The atmosphere inside Anfield was, to put it mildly, hostile. European nights have always brought something extra, but this was akin to the atmosphere at the likes of Galatasaray – pretty scary if you were a City fan or player I imagine. There had also been some unsavoury scenes before the match as the City players' bus arrived, which were completely out of order but again must have played on the players' minds as they approached a crucial match.

However, City started the match on the front foot, forcing a corner from their first attack in the opening minutes, as Sané's shot from a tight angle was blocked by Lovren. In fact, for the opening ten minutes City looked to be in control, as Liverpool struggled to find a foothold in the match. But that was all to change on 12 minutes when Salah played in Firmino, who cut inside Otamendi, sending him to ground. Firmino's low shot was saved by Ederson, the ball falling to Walker, but he couldn't sort his feet out and Firmino nipped in to square the ball to Salah, who was completely free just seven yards out. Although Kompany had got back to guard the goal line, Salah simply passed the ball round him and into the net to give the Reds the lead, as Anfield erupted in jubilation, and the atmosphere stoked up to an even higher level.

Sané was perhaps City's main danger, using his speed to break just two minutes later as the Liverpool defenders backed off, allowing him to shoot from the edge of the penalty area, but he dragged his shot wide to the jeers of the crowd.

On 20 minutes, Oxlade-Chamberlain showed Sané just how it should be done. As the ball was played up to the feet of Firmino, he was crudely chopped down from behind but the referee allowed play to continue as Milner won the loose ball, which then fell to the Ox. He controlled the ball and moved it forward a yard before hitting an absolute screamer past Ederson from 25 yards to double the lead.

Liverpool were now rampant, and City clearly rattled by the two goals, which had lifted the whole stadium to even higher levels of fervour. The Reds continued to attack, knowing that sitting back against City is the worst thing you can do, and probably feeling that they needed to take advantage of their dominance while they had the chance.

Mané had been quiet so far but had a great chance to add to the lead on 25 minutes when Firmino's firm low cross found him in the six-yard box. Unfortunately, the cross was so firmly hit that Mané couldn't control it and the ball bounced away to safety. However, he soon made up for this when he added Liverpool's third on 31 minutes. After concerted pressure, Salah had the ball on Liverpool's right, just inside the penalty area. He sent a lovely curling cross in with his left boot, and the diminutive Mané rose above everyone to power a header into the ground and past Ederson.

I'm always amazed at how good Mané is in the air. He has a tremendous spring that gets him above taller players and scores many a headed goal. The Senegal international had been a thorn in Liverpool's side when at Southampton, scoring twice as the Saints came from two down to win 3-2, and Klopp had brought him to Anfield for £30m the season after that great performance. Since then he'd become one of a fearsome front three for the Reds and a regular goalscorer, often at crucial times when the Reds needed a goal. This goal may have been the third of the night, but it proved to be a killer blow to City, and even I now began to believe that Liverpool would get through to the semi-final.

Three minutes later, Liverpool were surging forward again through Robertson. For me, the rampaging left-back doesn't shoot often enough, preferring to cross the ball low and hard for others to benefit from, but this time the cross wasn't an option as Fernandinho was tracking his run. The Scot decided to shoot low and hard but Fernandinho stuck out his leg to block the shot and concede a corner.

City were creating nothing now and Liverpool were playing with supreme confidence, Firmino the next to go close five minutes before half-time but his shot from distance rose just above the bar. In fact, City hadn't had a shot on target yet, which is a rarity in itself, although Otamendi was only a yard wide with his optimistic shot from distance.

However, the same big defender was soon in trouble with the referee, receiving a yellow card for scything Firmino down from behind just before half-time. From the free kick, van Dijk rose to win the ball in the air but his header was just off target, and the half ended with the Reds 3-0 ahead, but it could easily have been more as they dominated City in a way that Guardiola had probably never seen before.

It would have been nice to have seen the Reds go on to score more and really settle the tie in the first leg but there was to be no addition to the scoreline after the break. Obviously, City couldn't be as poor as they had been in the first half, and they came out on the attack in the second, forcing a few corners but still not threatening to reduce the deficit.

Liverpool had no option but to sit back now, as City tried to force their way into the match, Sané again proving a danger as he found space on the City left but he couldn't wrap his foot around his shot, sending it wide of goal yet again. I imagine that Karius in the Liverpool goal couldn't believe that he was having such a quiet night against the usually free-scoring City team, but a mixture of poor finishing and excellent defending was making it a comfortable night for the keeper.

The Reds, who are usually so devastating on the break when other teams attack them, created nothing at the other end in the second half until 70 minutes, when substitute Solanke sent in a low cross towards Mané. Good defending prevented the striker from getting in a decent shot and the ball bounced up kindly for Ederson.

The pattern of the match continued until the referee's final whistle, City attempting to throw everything at Liverpool but players in red shirts putting their bodies on the line, tackling, blocking, cutting out passes and crosses in a superb performance that was as much a joy to watch as their usual attacking play. It was a sign that the Reds were learning how to defend a lead, which is something they had previously struggled with, but was something that we would soon become used to.

※ ※ ※

Despite having a 3-0 lead after the first leg, there was still an element of trepidation in the Butler household for the second leg, knowing just how devastating City could be on their day, which to be fair was most days.

That trepidation was increased when Jesus scored after just two minutes and City had a second goal controversially ruled out just before half-time, as they dominated the first half. However, Liverpool were magnificent after the break, and counter-attacked brilliantly, Salah and Firmino netting to secure a 2-1 win and a 5-1 aggregate victory that set up an equally thrilling semi-final tie against AS Roma, where the Reds showed that they still had a thing or two to learn about defending a lead.

47

Salah's Highs and Lows

Liverpool 5 AS Roma 2
Champions League Semi-Final First Leg
24 April 2018
Anfield
Attendance: 51,236

Liverpool	AS Roma
Karius	Alisson
van Dijk	Fazio
Lovren	Manolas
Robertson	Jesus (Perotti 67)
Alexander-Arnold	Florenzi
Milner	De Rossi (Gonalons 67)
Henderson	Strootman
Oxlade-Chamberlain (Wijnaldum 18)	Kolarov
	Ünder (Schick 46)
Firmino (Klavan 90)	Nainggolan
Salah (Ings 74)	Džeko
Mané	*Manager:* Eusebio Di Francesco
Manager: Jürgen Klopp	

MOHAMED SALAH had arrived at Liverpool from Roma just a few months previously for a fee of £43.9m. He was seen as a bit of a gamble, having failed to secure a place in the Chelsea team, and being loaned out to Fiorentina and Roma before the latter signed him in 2016. He'd done so well at Roma, scoring 29 goals in 65

292

league appearances that he attracted Liverpool's attention and they paid a club record fee for him.

He became an instant sensation at Liverpool and had set the Premier League alight with his goalscoring ability and his link-up play with Firmino and Mané to form a fearsome front three for the Reds. This was a night when the Egyptian king was to show Roma what they were missing.

Roma started the match on the front foot, clearly not intent to sit back and let Liverpool get their usual fast start. Within two minutes the Italian team had the first shot of the match, Strootman shooting from distance after tidy build-up work on the edge of the Liverpool penalty area, but Karius saved comfortably.

Three minutes later it was Liverpool's turn, Firmino put in on the right, inside the Roma penalty area. The angle was tight and there was no one to pull the ball back to, so Firmino attempted the shot, which skimmed across the goal to safety, with Alisson beaten. Next it was the turn of Oxlade-Chamberlain, who tried to repeat his goal from the quarter-final, but this time didn't get the power, and the save was easy for Alisson.

Sadly, the Ox was soon to play no further part in the match or the remainder of the season. After just 15 minutes, having made an excellent tackle, he remained on the ground clutching his knee. It transpired that he had multiple knee ligament damage that kept him out of football for nearly a year.

Roma came close to opening the scoring on 18 minutes when Kolarov, who carries a powerful left-foot shot, decided to try his luck from 30 yards. The shot was straight at Karius but, as he often did, he made a real hash of his save but at least managed to get enough of a touch on the ball to deflect it on to the bar and away to safety. However, the danger signs were there, and Roma looked like a good team going forward, although it was to be their defensive performance that was to let them down as the match went on.

It had been a pretty frenetic start to the match, and Roma were giving the Reds a stern test, but Liverpool really should have taken the lead just before the half hour when Mané was released on the halfway line by Firmino and outsprinted the Roma defence, bearing down on Alisson in the Roma goal. However, the Senegal striker, usually so deadly in a one-on-one situation, blasted his shot over the bar to the disbelief of the fans. Then only a minute later he missed again when Firmino bamboozled the Roma defence on Liverpool's right with a deft turn and played a pass to Mané, who was on the penalty spot. Again, Mané blasted his shot over, this time by about three yards, as it landed near the top row of the Anfield Road stand.

Next up it was Salah, who played a fortuitous one-two with a Roma defender before trying to curl a left-foot shot past Alisson, but the keeper pulled off a good save to deny him. Liverpool were now beginning to dominate, having weathered Roma's early pressure, and it seemed only a matter of time before the goals started to come. The fans thought the first goal had come on 34 minutes, when Robertson slid a cross in from the left, and this time Mané finished brilliantly, but he was rightly flagged offside. Firmino then tried his luck from distance, bending a right-foot shot, but again Alisson was equal to it and held on to the shot as Salah waited for any fumble.

However, there was nothing the keeper could do just two minutes later as Liverpool finally got the goal their dominance deserved, and it was that man Salah against his old club. It was a typical Salah goal, too, as he received the ball on the edge of the Roma penalty area, controlled, looked up, then sent a left-foot curler past the keeper and into the top corner. Trademark Salah, and the Anfield crowd erupted.

Lovren then came close to scoring his first European goal since that dramatic night against Dortmund, when he rose to head a Salah corner against the bar, as Liverpool ramped up the pressure, seeking the second goal. And it wasn't long before it came, on the stroke of half-time. After a quick break, Firmino played a short pass forward to Salah just outside the Roma penalty area, and Roma's defence was torn apart as Salah took the ball forward. Alisson raced out and spread himself, but Salah cheekily chipped the ball over him, and the ball rolled into the empty net. It was a killer blow for Roma but no more than the Reds deserved for their first-half performance.

In the second half, Roma's defence was in tatters on many occasions, as they couldn't find a way to deal with Liverpool's movement up front. Just 11 minutes after the restart Salah turned from goalscorer to provider when he broke down the Liverpool right and could have gone for goal. Instead, he cut the ball back for Mané, who made no mistake from six yards for 3-0.

Roma seemed to be completely shell-shocked and Liverpool players seemed to be able to find space all over the pitch, particularly in the middle, where the Roma midfield was offering no help to the team's beleaguered defence. And it got worse for the Italian team on 62 minutes when Salah again found himself free on the right, sliding the ball across to the far post where Firmino had the simple task of tapping the ball in from two yards. Salah had scored two and made two, but Firmino had also been excellent throughout, thoroughly deserving his goal.

He was soon to get his second, just seven minutes later, when Milner sent in a corner and Firmino headed in for 5-0 in what was becoming a rout. However, Roma didn't give up, and Karius soon had to make a smart save when Perotti's cross was met by the head of Schick. Again, Roma showed that they were dangerous going forward, but could their defence prevent Liverpool adding to their goal tally?

Jürgen Klopp clearly thought that five was enough, as he took off Salah on 74 minutes, perhaps thinking of the away match at Chelsea coming up just four days later. There was to be no hat-trick for Salah, who received a standing ovation from the Anfield faithful.

It looked as if the Reds would have a massive lead to take to the Stadio Olimpico, but with nine minutes remaining Roma scored what looked to be just a consolation goal, when Nainggolan's chip into the penalty area eluded Lovren's jump and fell to the deadly Džeko, who made no mistake from close range. The crowd went a bit quiet, but surely it was just a minor blip, even though it was an away goal. Roma would still need to win 4-0 at home, and what were the chances of them keeping a clean sheet in the second leg?

However, just four minutes later the tie changed again when Nainggolan's shot from distance was blocked by Milner but the ball had hit his arm and the referee awarded a penalty. Perotti put his penalty kick into the top corner for 5-2 to give Roma some hope for the second leg.

It had been a fantastic performance by Liverpool for 75 minutes but a disappointing climax, as they had sat back for the last 15 minutes and paid the price. Those two late Roma goals had put a different complexion on the tie, although they still needed to win 3-0 in the return match.

※ ※ ※

In the second leg it again looked comfortable for the Reds when Mané scored after only nine minutes. Despite Milner scoring an own goal six minutes later, Wijnaldum restored Liverpool's lead, which they kept until half-time, to lead 7-3 on aggregate. But, again, Roma showed great heart and hit back, scoring one on 52 minutes to make it 7-4, then scoring two very late goals to make the final aggregate score 7-6. However, their final goal came with virtually the last kick of the match, so it was made to look a lot closer than it actually was.

Unfortunately, the final will be remembered for being a disappointment, as Real Madrid showed all their experience to nullify Liverpool's main threats to win 3-1, particularly when Sergio Ramos manhandled Salah and put him out of the match after only 31 minutes with a serious shoulder injury that would also limit his participation in the upcoming World Cup. It will also be remembered for Loris Karius making a couple of serious blunders that led to two goals, although there are claims that he was suffering from concussion after an aerial challenge.

However, it had been another exciting season under Jürgen Klopp, and Liverpool were beginning to show that they could match the best in Europe. If Liverpool could just get themselves a decent goalkeeper now that they had Virgil van Dijk as the rock they had needed in the centre of defence.

Interestingly, it was the Roma goalkeeper Alisson Becker that they signed, having put seven goals past him just a few months before. Alisson was signed for £65m, a world record fee for a goalkeeper, but maybe they would now concede fewer goals and finally get their hands on the Premier League title or win a major cup competition in 2018/19. Guess what ... hopes were again very high going into the following season!

48

The Miracle of Anfield

Liverpool 4 Barcelona 0
Champions League Semi-Final Second Leg
7 May 2019
Anfield
Attendance: 52,212

Liverpool	Barcelona
Alisson	ter Stegen
van Dijk	Roberto
Robertson (Wijnaldum 46)	Piqué
Matip	Lenglet
Alexander-Arnold	Alba
Fabinho	Rakitic (Malcom 80)
Milner	Busquets
Henderson	Vidal (Melo 75)
Shaqiri (Sturridge 90)	Coutinho (Semedo 60)
Mané	Suarez
Origi (Gomez 85)	Messi
Manager: Jürgen Klopp	*Manager:* Ernesto Valverde

SEVEN STRAIGHT victories at the start of 2018/19 was a good sign of what was to be a great season for Liverpool and they also showed more resilience in defence as fewer goals were being conceded. This run included a memorable victory over one of the favourites for the Champions League, PSG, in the first group match. This was a team that included Mbappé, Neymar and Cavani, but

298

the Reds dominated large parts of the match and led 2-0 after 36 minutes. However, it seemed as if Liverpool would have to settle for a draw when PSG scored twice. It would have been a disappointing result after a great performance, but Firmino popped up with an excellent goal on 90 minutes to seal a great win and an excellent start to Liverpool's Champions League campaign.

It turned out to be a Jekyll and Hyde group phase, as Liverpool's away form was very poor, losing all three matches, but winning all three home matches was enough to see them through to the knockout stage.

In contrast, league form was good, both home and away, and the Reds headed the table for large parts of the season. There were some memorable wins, 3-1 against Manchester United, 5-1 against Arsenal and 5-0 against Watford, but Manchester City couldn't be shaken off and led the table by the time the Champions League knockout phase began in February 2019.

Liverpool faced Bayern Munich, with the first leg at Anfield. It was clear that Bayern feared the attacking power of the Reds, and I've never seen this mighty German team play so negatively, simply wanting to take a 0-0 draw back to the Allianz Arena. They got what they wanted, but even stranger was the fact that they played the same way at home, and got what they deserved, a 3-1 beating. The Reds performed with quality and experience, taking the lead through a brilliant Mané goal, then overcoming an unlucky own goal by Matip, before taking control in the second half with goals from van Dijk and a second for Mané to stroll to victory.

The team was playing confidently and were in the midst of a run of 19 matches unbeaten in the Premier League and Champions League that saw them leading Manchester City in the title race, although City had matches in hand. City had a tough run of matches coming up, including a Manchester derby, and I've never wanted United to win a match quite as much, but they failed me. To be fair, City went on a great run themselves and were to pip

Liverpool to the title by just one point, with Chelsea a full 25 points behind in third.

In the Champions League quarter-final, Liverpool again faced Porto, and again took them apart over two legs. It didn't look a forgone conclusion after the home leg, with Keita and Firmino scoring in a 2-0 win, which wasn't that convincing, but a 4-1 victory in Portugal, with goals from Mané, Salah, Firmino and van Dijk made everyone wonder why Liverpool's away form in the group phase had been so poor.

The semi-final was to turn out to be one of the greatest ties ever witnessed in the Champions League, as Liverpool faced favourites Barcelona, playing the first leg at the Camp Nou. This was another strange match, as the Reds played really well, creating several good chances but failing to score, only to be taken apart by Lionel Messi, who scored twice in a 3-0 win for the Spanish team.

I'd been offered the opportunity of going to see Harry Redknapp doing a show in Liverpool on 7 May, as it was the eve of my birthday, but fortunately Gwen did ask me whether there were any matches on, so didn't book tickets. After the 3-0 defeat in the first leg, I did wonder whether I'd done the right thing, but given the number of chances Liverpool had created in the first leg, I'd an inkling that the tie wasn't yet over. However, could the Reds keep Messi quiet? I wasn't to know just what a night it would turn out to be … quite a birthday present.

%% %% %%

Liverpool were forced into some changes from the first leg, with Salah and Firmino ruled out, which meant rare starts for Shaqiri and Origi up front. But how would they fare without two of their much-feared front three when they needed at least three goals to reach the final?

Both replacements were to be involved in the action soon after the kick-off. It was Shaqiri who had the first chance in the very first minute, when Milner sent Mané away down the Liverpool left. He played a short ball inside to Shaqiri, who had moved into the penalty area, and he sent a low shot towards the far post, which was deflected away for a corner just before Henderson could divert it towards the goal. It was a typical fast start to a European tie that the Reds had become famous for.

Then the Reds got the early goal that they desperately needed. After just seven minutes, Matip played a long ball forward, which was poorly defended by Alba, heading it straight to Mané, who was this time on the right. He controlled the ball and slipped it inside for Henderson, who was able to continue his forward run into the penalty area. Two touches and Henderson was facing ter Stegen in the Barcelona goal, who managed to save his shot but only parried it straight to Origi, who put it into the open goal.

The Belgian international has been with Liverpool since 2014, and it's easy to forget that he's just 24 years old. At the time of writing, he'd only played 126 matches for the Reds after lengthy loan spells at Lille and Wolfsburg but he's now starting to make an impact. He's also in danger of taking on the David Fairclough mantle of supersub, such is his reputation for coming on and snatching late winners in dramatic circumstances, but tonight he was on from the start and was to star throughout the match.

Liverpool fans' hopes were raised, but this was still Barcelona, with the likes of Messi, Suarez and Coutinho, who could rustle up some magic out of nothing, so the Reds couldn't afford to be gung-ho in their search for more goals.

On 13 minutes, such a moment nearly arrived when Barcelona attacked down Liverpool's right through Alba and Coutinho. Messi had pulled back to the edge of the penalty box, where he received the ball and sent a dangerous shot towards the top corner of the goal, but Alisson was equal to it. However, it showed just how quickly the match could turn if Messi was allowed too much time and space.

Just four minutes later, Alisson was called into action again when Messi broke quickly down the centre, and Barça had a three-on-two situation. Messi played Coutinho in on their left, but Alisson was able to push his low shot away. The follow-up led to a corner, which Liverpool failed to deal with, and Messi went close again with a powerful drive that had Alisson sprawling across his goal. It looked only a matter of time before Barcelona got that all-important away goal, and perhaps more, as Liverpool's defence struggled to cope with their speed and movement.

It had certainly been a lively start to the match, and Henderson was soon on the end of a Robertson pullback, but Piqué was in the way to block his driven shot. Then Robertson was having a go himself after Mané's cross was blocked and fell invitingly for the Scot to send in a powerful left-foot shot that ter Stegen palmed away.

Suarez was up to his usual tricks, making contact with players, falling over, then waving the imaginary card at the referee, but whereas Liverpool fans had loved all this a few years earlier, they now gave him the whistle every time he tried it on.

Following the frantic start, things calmed down and the rest of the first half passed without major incident until added time when Barcelona broke quickly after a Liverpool corner gave possession away. Coutinho moved the ball forward quickly to Messi, who played a slide-rule pass to Alba, charging up from defence. He was through on goal, but again Alisson denied Barça as he charged out of his goal to block. It was 1-0 at half-time but Liverpool still had an awful lot of work to do if they were going to progress.

The Reds were forced into a change at half-time, Robertson being replaced by Wijnaldum, after having to give way to injury following a sly Suarez kick, but the substitute was to play a major role in the night's proceedings. Just nine minutes into the second half, Alexander-Arnold won the ball on Liverpool's right in an advanced position and sent in a low cross to the penalty area. Wijnaldum was surging forward and he met the ball perfectly to smash a low shot past the keeper to send Anfield wild, sensing that something special might be about to happen.

Just one more goal was needed to level things up, and it wasn't long in coming. Just two minutes after his first, Wijnaldum was on hand again. Shaqiri sent in a pinpoint cross from Liverpool's left and Wijnaldum had made another great run forward, this time meeting it with his head to send the ball into the top corner to make it 3-0. Two goals in two minutes and Barcelona players' heads were down. To quote the great Corporal Jones from *Dad's Army*, 'They don't like it up 'em'.

Now level on aggregate, the last thing needed was for the Reds to concede a goal, which would mean they needed two more. But Barcelona looked shell-shocked, unable to cope with the ferocity of the comeback and the noise emanating from around the stadium. In fact, they didn't muster anything in the next 23 minutes, at which point we witnessed an extraordinary goal that made it 4-0 and summed up Barcelona's disarray.

Alexander-Arnold won a corner on Liverpool's right and, as is usual, the centre-backs started to make their way forward as Barcelona started to sort out who was marking who and waiting for the big defenders to arrive in the box. The young right-back was by the corner flag, having placed the ball, but started to walk away from it, as if leaving the corner for someone else to take. However, this young superstar looked up, quickly returned to the ball and sent in a low corner kick to Origi, who had seen what was going on and had found space. The ball arrived perfectly for Origi's right boot to smash it into the net to the amazement of everyone in the ground.

Barcelona defenders just stood there dumbfounded. I fully expected them to complain and for the goal to be disallowed because the whistle hadn't been blown or for some other daft reason. But no, they knew they had simply been daydreaming, and that this semi-final was now turning into their worst nightmare. It was a stunning goal ... simple, but such quick thinking, and something I've never seen before.

The Reds, now ahead 4-3 on aggregate, had to hold on for just over ten minutes to seal a memorable win and yet another miraculous comeback. They actually came close to adding a fifth on 85 minutes when Milner sent in a cross that Shaqiri rose to head, but he directed his header over. Meanwhile, Barcelona never came close and Liverpool played out the remaining minutes cleverly, particularly the final throes when Milner was holding the ball up by the corner flag, surrounded by Barça players desperate to gain possession. But this Liverpool team was learning how to manage matches now and wasn't about to give anything away in the closing minutes.

At the referee's final whistle the scenes at Anfield were amazing, as the team and management celebrated with the fans in singing 'You'll Never Walk Alone', including Mo Salah in a black hoodie sporting the slogan 'Never Give Up'. How appropriate.

49

Ol' Big Ears Is Back

Liverpool 2 Tottenham Hotspur 0
Champions League Final
1 June 2019
Metropolitano Stadium, Madrid
Attendance: 63,272

Liverpool	**Tottenham Hotspur**
Alisson	Lloris
van Dijk	Trippier
Robertson	Alderweireld
Matip	Vertonghen
Alexander-Arnold	Rose
Fabinho	Sissoko (Dier 74)
Wijnaldum (Milner 62)	Winks (Moura 66)
Henderson	Eriksen
Firmino (Origi 58)	Alli (Llorente 72)
Mané (Gomez 90)	Son
Salah	Kane
Manager: Jürgen Klopp	*Manager:* Mauricio Pochettino

IT HAD been a two-horse race for the Premier League title for virtually the entire season, and for Liverpool to secure 97 points and still not win the league was gutting.

Spurs, as usual, had promised to compete for the title but again fell away when the going got tough, but they had come through a difficult Champions League group that included Barcelona, Inter

Milan and PSV Eindhoven, then defeated Borussia Dortmund in the first knockout round.

Their quarter-final tie against Manchester City was a classic, with the first leg ending 1-0 to Spurs. The second leg at the Etihad started with a flurry of goals and City leading 3-2 after 11 remarkable opening minutes. Both teams scored again to make the score 4-3 on the night before VAR intervened to disallow a City goal in time added on that would have sent them through. The change from ecstasy to agony in the demeanour of Pep Guardiola was a joy to behold.

Spurs even had the cheek to claim that their semi-final comeback against Ajax was the greatest of all time, but it was only a young Ajax team, not the might of Barcelona, that they beat. Spurs trailed 1-0 after the first leg at home, then went 2-0 down in the second leg, but a second-half Lucas Moura hat-trick, the winning goal in added time, sealed a remarkable comeback for an all-English final.

※ ※ ※

Given the goalscoring feats of both Liverpool and Spurs, and the fact that they are both attacking teams that play great football, it was an eagerly awaited final, but one that once again failed to ignite and provide the entertainment anticipated. In fact, all the best action was crammed into the first few and last few minutes. However, when your team wins, the entertainment value is secondary.

Spurs welcomed back Harry Kane, who hadn't played due to injury since the first leg of the quarter-final, which meant that semi-final hat-trick hero Lucas Moura was unfortunate to be left on the substitutes' bench. I for one was relieved, as Kane looked completely out of sorts, while Moura would have been much more of a threat. Meanwhile, Liverpool were at full strength, and also had the luxury of having a strong bench to call on if needed.

Liverpool kicked off the final, and within the first 30 seconds they were attacking through Mané on their left, on the edge of the Spurs penalty area. Spurs were pulling players back to try to block Mané's cross, one being Sissoko, who was waving his right arm about to direct other players as he entered the penalty area. It almost looked as if Mané had spotted this as he crossed with his right foot and the ball struck Sissoko on the arm. The referee had no doubt in awarding the penalty, as Spurs players and fans looked on in utter disbelief.

Even Spurs fans that I've spoken to since agree that it was a penalty, and that Sissoko was foolish in waving his arms in the penalty area. In fact, the only person who thought it wasn't a penalty was Glenn Hoddle in the TV studio, who sulked his way through the half-time and full-time analysis like a little child who couldn't get his own way, and refused to engage with those who were clearly more objective and agreed with the referee's decision.

As Liverpool's main penalty taker, Milner, was on the bench, Salah was given the penalty-kick duties. He actually has a good record from the spot, but I'm never that confident when he steps up, unlike when Millie is taking a penalty. Salah took a long run-up in a strange arc, as Lloris waved his arms about in the Spurs goal, and everyone held their breath. Lloris went the right way, but Salah struck the ball firmly and it beat the keeper's outstretched arm to find the back of the net. A superb penalty and a fantastic start for Liverpool after the disappointment of the previous year's final.

The early drama had a strange effect on the match, as everyone expected a fast start by both teams but with the Reds a goal ahead, they seemed to be caught in two minds as to whether to continue with their fast start or to sit back and defend the early lead, and draw Spurs on to them and perhaps counter-attack when they had the chance.

Sissoko did try to make amends at the other end after ten minutes but hit his shot high and wide. Then, two minutes later, Liverpool came close to a second when Alexander-Arnold picked up the ball 25 yards out and drove in a low and powerful shot that was just a yard wide of Lloris's right-hand post.

As both defences coped easily with any attacks, chances were rare, and it was Liverpool's other full-back Robertson who took matters into his own hands when he picked the ball up inside the Spurs half and drove forward before sending in a curving and dipping left-foot piledriver that Lloris did well to tip over the bar.

At the other end, I think Alisson was smoking a cigar, as he was having such a quiet night so far, with Spurs' shooting, when they did manage to create an opportunity, being way off target, as they grew ever more anxious as the first half came to a close.

The second half was a bit more exciting than the first, although neither team created much to start with. Fabinho tried his luck from distance early on, but his shot was half blocked, taking the sting out of it so that Lloris gathered comfortably. The Spurs keeper had to then be sharp when Robertson put in a dangerous low cross that was just falling nicely for Mané before Lloris got down to smother the ball. Meanwhile, Spurs were creating nothing and Kane was nowhere to be seen, as Liverpool's defence dealt with anything that the North London team had to offer.

On 58 minutes, one of Liverpool's semi-final heroes, Origi, entered the fray, replacing Firmino, then four minutes later another hero from the Barça match, Wijnaldum, made way for Milner. Four minutes after that, Moura finally got his chance for Spurs, as they opted for a more attacking formation, taking off the defensive midfielder Winks, who had surprisingly failed to influence the match.

Just seven minutes after coming on, it was Milner who gave us the first real spark of the second half, when he skimmed in a low shot from the edge of the penalty area that left Lloris rooted to the spot, but the ball went just the wrong side of the post.

There were just 20 minutes left, and surely the match would soon start to open up a bit as legs began to tire and Spurs started to push forward in search of the equaliser. Well not exactly, although Spurs did manage to get their first shot on target after 73 minutes when Dele Alli attempted to curl a shot past Alisson but didn't get it right and the ball went straight to the keeper. At least it gave Alisson something to do.

Spurs had built a habit of coming on strong late in matches and scoring very late goals, and they did start to pose a threat in the final 15 minutes, Alli again getting into a good position but his header from Kane's cross was off target. With ten minutes remaining the usually dangerous Son had his first attempt at goal, driving in a low shot, forcing Alisson to get down smartly to push the ball to safety. As Rose picked up the loose ball, he passed it to Moura, who was free in the penalty area. He shot, but didn't get enough power on it, leaving Alisson with an easy save. Then a minute later it was Son again, who had obviously found his shooting boots now, sending in his second shot within a minute, that forced Alisson into a good save. Spurs were now piling on some pressure at last, and nerves started to jangle in the Butler household, as the equaliser seemed inevitable.

Spurs sent on yet another forward, Llorente, in place of Alli, as they now went for it with four forwards on the pitch. I was screaming for Klopp to bring on another centre-back to deal with the inevitable high balls that would be sent into the box now that Llorente was on.

Hearts were in mouths for a moment in the 83rd minute when Milner dangled out a leg and caught Rose just on the edge of the penalty area, but the referee rightly adjudged that it was outside the box, despite Rose's histrionics. However, with the normally deadly Eriksen lining up the free kick, Liverpool fans looked on in trepidation. Would he cross or shoot? Eriksen sent in a curling shot to Alisson's left-hand side but the keeper had anticipated well and got across to palm the ball away for a corner.

Then on 89 minutes the victory was sealed by Liverpool's talismanic Origi. Spurs failed to clear a high ball in their penalty area and Matip prodded the ball left to Origi. He had a lot to do, given the angle and distance from goal, but he drove in a powerful, angled low shot to Lloris's far post that gave the keeper no chance.

Klopp finally brought on that third centre-back, Gomez, as Liverpool decided to shut up shop for the added time that was left, but they weren't going to let anything slip away now. Rose had a tame shot from distance and Son sent in another dangerous low shot that Alisson palmed for a corner but that was all they had to offer before the referee brought the match to a close, and Liverpool were European champions for the sixth time.

The scenes after the match were amazing as Liverpool players celebrated with each other, their manager and staff, as well as with the crowd. In particular, one scene brought a tear to my eye as captain Jordan Henderson celebrated with his father. Henderson is such an influential player for Liverpool but often doesn't receive the credit he deserves. I've read so much drivel about him on social media as so-called fans complain that he's in the team. I sometimes can't resist replying, telling them that they obviously know nothing about football or they would appreciate his worth. I suggest they watch him for the whole match as he breaks down the opposition's attacks and very often originates Liverpool's best moments.

Henderson so deserved this victory and all the plaudits that went with it, and it was a pleasure to see him lift the trophy in his eighth season at the club, to go with a League Cup from 2012. He was appointed captain of the Reds in 2015 and should, in my unbiased opinion, be captain of England too, as he has the uncanny knack of being able to raise his team when they most need it. This victory couldn't happen to a nicer bloke.

※ ※ ※

Liverpool were once again champions of Europe and they had a rapturous homecoming in Liverpool as they paraded the trophy on an open-topped bus through the city. The Champions League Final was to be the last featured match of this book; however, one more iconic match was to occur late in 2019. As European champions,

Liverpool were invited to take part in the FIFA Club World Cup in Qatar, a competition they could perhaps have done without, given the fixture chaos around Christmas and New Year, but a trophy that the club had never won.

50

World Champions

Liverpool 1 Flamengo 0 (aet)
FIFA Club World Cup Final
21 December 2019
Khalifa International Stadium, Doha
Attendance: 45,416

Liverpool	Flamengo
Alisson	Alves
van Dijk	Rafinha
Gomez	Caio
Robertson	Mari
Alexander-Arnold	Luis
Keita	Gerson (Lincoln 102)
Henderson	Arão (Berrío 120)
Oxlade-Chamberlain	De Arrascaeta (Vitinho 77)
Firmino	Ribeiro (Ribas 82)
Mané	Henrique
Salah	Barbosa
Manager: Jürgen Klopp	*Manager:* Jorge Jesus

DECEMBER 2019 was a hectic one for Liverpool, a month which many people said would prove to be too much for a squad that also had a few players missing with injury. They faced the prospect of nine matches, five in the Premier League, one in the Champions League (which they couldn't afford to lose to progress to the knockout phase), one in the League Cup quarter-final, and the possibility of two matches in the FIFA Club World Cup, assuming they reached the final. At the start of the month, the Reds led the league by 11 points following a nervy 2-1 victory over Brighton at Anfield, in which Alisson was sent off, so would be banned for the following league match against Everton. By the end of the month, having beaten Everton, Bournemouth, Watford, Leicester and Wolves, they had extended the lead to 16 points, as Manchester City's form failed to match that of the previous season, while Liverpool were unbeaten in the league for 40 matches, having won 35 of them.

Champions League progress was also assured with a 2-0 victory in Salzburg against Red Bull, so the only blot on a perfect record was the defeat to Aston Villa in the League Cup quarter-final. However, this match was the night before the semi-final of the Club World Cup, so Liverpool were forced to play an incredibly young team with an average age of 19.5 years, only 16 first-team appearances between them and with eight players making their debut. They actually performed well against a team that included eight internationals, but experience won the day and Villa ran out 5-0 victors.

The next day, the semi-final of the Club World Cup pitched the Reds against Mexican team Club de Fútbol Monterrey in Qatar. Liverpool started excellently, scoring after only 12 minutes through Keita but were pegged back by a goal only two minutes later, as Monterrey came to terms with Liverpool's speed and passing and were the better team for much of the rest of the match. Klopp had opted to rest a few key players, including Alexander-Arnold, Mané and Firmino, all of whom were called into action as the match headed towards extra time. Firmino, who hadn't been in great goalscoring form leading into the match, entered the fray in the 85th minute and was the hero, scoring in the 91st minute to send Liverpool to the final and avoiding the dreaded extra 30 minutes.

※ ※ ※

Liverpool started the final in the usual attacking manner, and Firmino, Liverpool's hero of the semi-final with his last-minute goal, should have scored in the first minute after being put clear by Alexander-Arnold. However, he somehow managed to hit his shot from seven yards over the bar. It was an incredible miss for a player with such ability, and I for one was hoping that Liverpool wouldn't come to rue missing such an early chance.

The feeling of missed opportunity increased just four minutes later when Salah teed up Keita just inside the penalty area but he also hit his shot over. It wasn't as easy a chance as Firmino's but anything on target would probably have been a goal.

Liverpool got closer two minutes later, as their frantic start to the match continued. This time it was Alexander-Arnold who surged forward to shoot from 30 yards, but his low shot just passed the keeper's right-hand post.

It took Flamengo 15 minutes to get to grips with Liverpool's passing and movement, but they gradually found a way into the match, Henrique heading wide and Barbosa having a shot blocked as the Brazilian team's confidence grew. Then on 24 minutes, only the speed of Gomez prevented Henrique getting a shot on target as the centre-back stretched to get a toe in and send the ball for a corner.

Those were the best chances of a first half that ended goalless and pretty even in terms of possession and territory. Liverpool realised that they were in a match and needed to improve in the second half, and again Firmino should have scored at the start of the half when he brilliantly flicked the ball over a defender's head in the penalty area and shot, the ball bouncing into the turf and against the post, before virtually rolling along the goal line and away to safety as Salah closed in for the rebound. It was incredibly unlucky but again was a missed chance.

A few minutes later, Alexander-Arnold sent in a dangerous cross, which Salah hit first time on the turn but shot a yard wide of the goal. Then Flamengo had their first serious attempt of the second half when Barbosa shot just over the bar. The same player was then unlucky not to score on 53 minutes when Alisson pulled off a great save low down to push his driven shot for a corner.

It was certainly turning out to be a more eventful second half, and Salah was next to try his luck but his left-foot shot was a bit rash and flew over the bar, but at least both teams were now carving out some shooting opportunities and goals seemed more likely to come than they did in the first half.

Barbosa was the main danger in the Flamengo attack, and he next tried an acrobatic overhead shot, but he didn't get a perfect connection, and Alisson had plenty of time to move to his left to save by his left-hand post. However, as in the first half, chances dried up and the match moved to the 80th minute before the next shot on goal, provided by Alexander-Arnold, but it was straight at Alves in the Flamengo goal.

It was Liverpool who had the better of the final ten minutes, Salah having a shot blocked, then Henderson sending a long-range curling effort towards the top corner, only for Alves to pull off an acrobatic save with only four minutes of normal time remaining. Henderson's head was in his hands, as he thought he'd won the match with an absolute screamer.

In the final minute we then had one of those VAR moments, which have come to blight football. Mané was racing through on goal but was brought down from behind on the edge of the penalty area. The referee awarded a penalty, and a red card should have been shown as Mané was through on goal, but the referee waved a yellow. Obviously Flamengo protested vehemently, even though it would have to go to VAR to confirm the decision (or not). The contact was on the line of the penalty area, so the referee's decision was correct – penalty; however, for some strange reason, the decision was overturned completely. Not only was it not a penalty but VAR and the referee decided it wasn't even a foul. What they saw, or didn't see, I'll never know. If they deemed the defender to have played the ball, then at the very least it was a corner to Liverpool but the decision was a drop-ball for Flamengo. Who knows? The match went to extra time.

The last thing Liverpool wanted was extra time, given their schedule, but at least a goal soon arrived when Firmino scored on 99 minutes to make amends for his dreadful misses at the start of each half. Liverpool broke quickly and Mané fed the ball to Firmino in the centre of the Flamengo penalty area in acres of space. Bobby certainly took his time ... in fact, I thought he would never get his shot away, as he feinted to shoot, took the ball past one defender, took another touch, then shot past the keeper and a covering defender to give the Reds the lead at last. Cue Firmino ripping off his shirt and parading around in celebration.

Liverpool never looked in danger of conceding the equaliser, and should perhaps have added to their tally, as Salah, Milner, van Dijk and Firmino all had efforts saved or blocked in the first period of extra time.

In the second period, Flamengo improved, with Barbosa again the main danger, sending one shot just wide, but that's as close as they came and Liverpool were crowned world club champions for the very first time in their history to add to their European title.

※ ※ ※

Since arriving at the club in October 2015, Jürgen Klopp has overseen a renaissance that has seen Liverpool climb to the top of the domestic league in 2019/20, become European champions and now world champions. Earlier in the season they also won the European Super Cup, defeating Chelsea in a penalty shoot-out, to show that they are now developing a winning mentality.

Simply the Best

HAVING COVERED 50 iconic matches over the last 60 years, I was wondering how to bring the book to a close. A colleague and I were chatting about my book idea over a coffee and he suggested that Arsenal must be the best English team over the 60 years. While they did have a successful period, I thought that only Manchester United could challenge Liverpool for that accolade, so we discussed how I could work out which was the most successful team.

We agreed on a formula that gave the league champions ten points, runners-up nine points, third place eight points, etc. down to tenth position getting one point. I then awarded points for trophies, both domestic and European, to arrive at a score for each team. I know it's not scientific and I've not shared the complete formula here because many people won't agree with it, but it's just a bit of fun and a way to finish off the story of Liverpool during my lifetime. So, here's how it turned out:

1	Liverpool	627 pts
2	Manchester United	535 pts
3	Arsenal	463 pts
4	Chelsea	372 pts
5	Tottenham Hotspur	317 pts
6	Everton	258 pts
7	Leeds United	219 pts
8	Manchester City	203 pts
9	Aston Villa	161 pts
10	Nottingham Forest	145 pts

Quite how far Liverpool are ahead of the others is surprising, but when you consider their dominance in the 1970s and 1980s, perhaps we shouldn't be too surprised. Manchester City still have a lot of catching up to do.

It's also unlikely that any team will dominate English football in the way that Liverpool did during those two decades or that any Liverpool manager will exceed the trophy haul of Bob Paisley. However, at least my book has ended on a positive, with Liverpool on top of the world.

I hope you enjoyed this trip down memory lane.